Beyond the State

To Fred and Frieda
and to young people everywhere –
you all deserve a future

Beyond the State

An Introductory Critique

John Hoffman

Polity Press

First published in 1995 by Polity Press
in association with Blackwell Publishers.

Editorial office:
Polity Press
65 Bridge Street
Cambridge CB2 1UR, UK

Marketing and production:
Blackwell Publishers Ltd
108 Cowley Road
Oxford OX4 1JF, UK

Blackwell Publishers Inc.
238 Main Street
Cambridge, MA 02142, USA

ISBN 0 7456 1180 X
ISBN 0 7456 1181 8 (pbk)

A CIP catalogue record for this book is available from
the British Library and the Library of Congress.

Typeset in 10½ on 12 pt Times by Pure Tech Corporation, India
Printed in Great Britain by T. J. Press Ltd, Padstow, Cornwall

This book is printed on acid-free paper.

Contents

Preface and Acknowledgements

This book builds on the themes of earlier writings, and develops for the first time what I am tempted to call a radical view of the state which goes 'beyond' Marxism. I have greatly benefited from discussion on earlier papers presented to the Political Studies Annual Conference in 1991 and 1993, the PSA's Marxism Group (particularly in 1991) and the European Consortium on Political Research in Limerick in 1992.

Bhikhu Parekh encouraged me with this project and David McLellan has been highly supportive over the years. Mike Gane responded conscientiously to one of my conference papers and Alexander Chryssis and Pavel Barsã have shown a stimulating interest in my work. I am also grateful to Ian Harris and Norman Geras for bibliographical help.

Writing this book was made possible by a sabbatical term from the University of Leicester and the head of the Department of Politics, Bob Borthwick, has assisted greatly in freeing me from normal burdens. My thanks are also due to James Hamill, Stephen Hopkins, Phil Lynch and Wyn Rees, who shouldered teaching commitments in my absence. The university library provided me with invaluable support, and Andrew Winnard of Polity has been an exemplary editor.

My chapter on Marxism draws heavily upon my article 'The state: has the "withering away" thesis finally withered away?', *The Journal of Communist Studies*, 8 (1992), pp. 84–106 which appeared as part of a special issue on *Beyond Stalinism: Communist Political Evolution* edited by Ron Hill. I am grateful to the publishers

Frank Cass for allowing me to reproduce parts of the article in this work.

A particular debt is owed to Andrew Vincent, Andrew Mason and James Meadowcroft who all kindly took time out of busy schedules to read and comment on particular chapters. They have proved sympathetic but trenchant critics and this book owes a good deal to them.

Finally, special thanks are due to Rowan Roenisch, who has been very supportive in my search for a radical position which goes 'beyond' Marxism and showed a particular interest in the chapters on postmodernism and feminism.

1

Overview

There exist today over 180 entities calling themselves states. They are recognized in international law, and to most people it seems inconceivable that there could be a world without them. It might appear therefore that looking beyond the state as this work proposes to do is a futile and irrelevant task.[1]

Yet it is over twenty years ago that an influential analysis of the 'Western system of power' warned that if a large part of the planet should be laid waste in a nuclear war, this will have been because 'men, acting in the name of their state and invested with its power, will have so decided, or miscalculated.'[2] It is a point worth taking seriously. A major work on the state in the mid-1980s emphasizes the extent to which war itself has become industrialized, and proceeds to pose a pertinent if disquieting question: what do we mean by 'a good society in a world of nation states' when states literally have the capability to destroy the whole of humanity?[3]

This capacity for destruction is growing inexorably and underpins the basic argument of this book. If we are to secure a future for humanity, then we should think about looking beyond the state.

The need to define the state

In the brave new world which followed the collapse of communism, we have not only witnessed the proliferation of new states; we have seen the proliferation of new levels of conflict and violence as well. If we are (as some suggest) confronting a turning point in human affairs, it is a watershed which places the state itself on trial, for it seems difficult to deny a link between the birth of new states on the one hand and an accelerating fragmentation and divisiveness on the other.

It is this sense of a watershed which makes Fukuyama's recent 'end of history' thesis provocative. Fukuyama's contention is that with the collapse of left-wing Communist Party states and right-wing authoritarian regimes, liberal democracy now constitutes the terminal point of humanity's ideological evolution.[4] He is fascinated by Nietzsche's characterization of the state as the 'coldest of all cold monsters' – the institution which 'tells lies in all the languages of good and evil'. Yet Fukuyama still depicts liberal democracy as a 'universal and homogenous state' which grants rights to citizens who in turn abide by its laws. The state, in other words, remains central to the liberal democratic ideal.[5]

On the one hand, Fukuyama argues that humans can really be satisfied only by a recognition of their status and dignity – the part of the soul which (following Plato) he calls *thymos*. Liberal democracies alone (he tells us) enable each citizen to recognize the dignity and humanity of every other citizen – to meet this deeply rooted *thymotic* propensity for self-esteem. On the other hand, Fukuyama clearly accepts that states are monsters which lie, divide and use force. It is the coexistence of these two points which brings us face to face with the problem which is central to this book. How can we reconcile freedom, dignity and autonomy (inherent in the notion of *thymos*) with the activity and character of the state?

It is not difficult to see why one writer has declared the state to be the most problematic concept in politics.[6] Recognition of this has given rise to an argument which I shall examine in chapter 2, namely that the state is *so* problematic it simply cannot be defined. I characterize this argument as an 'indefinability' thesis since it contends not merely that the state is an arbitrary and elusive institution but that its ambiguities are such that it should not be part of our theoretical discourse. The most persistent and vigorous advocate of this position has been the behavioural political theorist David Easton who has singlemindedly sought (in virtually all his published work) to discredit the state as a viable political concept and to find a suitable alternative.

Supporters of the indefinability thesis raise a number of important points which are crucial to a critique of the state. The state as a concept (they contend) is mystical, vague, elusive and contradictory. This is certainly true but the problem remains: does the state (for all its conceptual obscurities) still continue to *exist*? This 'existential' difficulty bothers Easton a good deal, and to get round it he substitutes a notion of the 'political system' for the state. The political system, Easton argues, enjoys an empirical status and conceptual clarity which the state lacks.

However the ambiguities and contradictions of the state do not disappear simply because a conceptual alternative is put in its place. Easton's critics have found it relatively easy to demonstrate that his notion of the *political system* displays the same kind of mystification which he ascribes to the state. Hence the problem: if the state continues to exist with absurdities, dichotomies and mysteries integral to its institutional reality, then whatever substitute we propose will still suffer this conceptual blight. Proponents of the indefinability thesis are right to emphasize that the state is contradictory and mystifying, but it is not possible to get to grips with its problematic character unless we begin by *defining* it.

The centrality of force

In chapter 3 I argue that the definition which best enables us to tackle the elusive and ambiguous character of the state is that formulated by Max Weber: the state is an institution claiming to exercise a monopoly of legitimate force within a particular territory.

Weber's definition commands a wide degree of scholarly consensus, and it is particularly useful for the critique which I seek to make. In the first place the definition helps us to go beyond what might be called the 'curate's egg' approach to the state – that the state is good in some parts and bad in others. Weber's definition makes it both possible (and necessary) to assess the state *as a whole* since his celebrated formula identifies the state in terms of four interrelated elements – monopoly, territory, legitimacy and force.

Each of these elements is interrelated in such a way that it is not possible for one to exist without the others. Unless its 'claim' is monopolistic, territorially focused *and* underpinned by a force which is legitimate, the state cannot function in Weberian fashion. The definition is not merely coherent, however, it is also *structured* since one of the elements within the interrelated whole forms the basis for the others. Weber argues (rightly in my view) that it is force which constitutes the primary (although not the sole) attribute which makes the state a state.

In emphasizing the centrality of force (albeit a force which is monopolized, legitimate and territorially focused), Weber makes it possible to sustain a distinction (although he himself failed to do so) which is crucial to my overall critique – the distinction between the state on the one hand and *government* on the other. Postwar anthropologists in particular have pointed out that government can exist without the state. The 'anthropological argument' (as I call it) enables us to identify government as a process which resolves disputes through a range of sanctions all of which fall short of the use of organized force.

This distinction between state and government is not merely important in helping us to understand stateless societies of a tribal or indeed international kind. It also enables us to identify *within state-centred societies* activities which do not, in and of themselves, have to be underpinned by a monopoly of legitimate force. It becomes conceptually possible to ask whether *governmental* institutions involved with law- making, adjudication and administration might not exist in domestic societies (as they do in international societies) without the support of inherently statist agencies (like the army and the police) – agencies empowered to use physical force. It is of course true that, empirically speaking, government and state inextricably intertwine in the political processes of the modern world. Nevertheless it remains crucial to distinguish them in analytical terms.

But what implications does Weber's definition have for locating the origins and development of the state? In chapter 4 I explore what I call the 'limitation argument' which accepts that the state *can* be defined – but only a *modern* phenomenon. Only the modern state (i.e. the state itself) exercises a monopoly of legitimate force since earlier polities do not conform to the Weberian definition. Thus 'limitationists' argue that pre-modern polities lacked a sharply differentiated public/private divide; they did not possess supreme or sovereign power; these polities were unable to provide uniform protection for all their subjects; they were organized on a personalized 'patrimonial' basis with offices dispensed as favours, and, lacking bureaucracies organized according to impersonal rules, they had limited capacity to administer their subjects and extract revenues.

There can be no doubt that there *are* significant discontinuities between the modern state and its predecessors. The problem with the limitationist case however is that it stresses these discontinuities in a way which downgrades the fact which is central to *all* domestic polities (since the demise of tribal societies) – the presence of rulers who seek to secure order through force. Government by way of contrast (and as the anthropological argument asserts) resolves disputes through sanctions which, though often punitive and painful, are essentially *non-violent* in character.

It is only by stressing the centrality of force that we can evaluate the real drama of the state's origins. Indeed such an emphasis also makes it possible to see why the *other* elements of the Weberian definition emerge (embryonically and incoherently it is true) in pre-modern systems. Organized force itself requires powerful rulers to focus their laws *territorially* – on one group of people rather another – and these forceful acts can be exercised by particular rulers only if this activity is (in some sense) absolute and (at least implicitly) monopolistic in scope and character. The modern state is intelligible, in other words, only as an institution which builds upon the intrinsically statist attributes of its less coherent predecessors.

Contradiction and the legitimacy problem

Weber argues that states merely 'claim' to exercise a monopoly of legitimate force for a particular territory. It is true that traditional states were manifestly unable to assert this monopoly in a coherent and convincing manner, but should we assume that modern states have succeeded where earlier states failed?

There can be little doubt that modern states are able to secure a monopoly of legitimate force rather more comprehensively and efficiently than traditional post-tribal polities. But the point is that the more the state 'approximates' to the Weberian definition, the more problematic its identity becomes. The very need to exercise a monopoly of legitimate force arises only because states are challenged by rebels and criminals who themselves resort to force, and who (either implicitly or explicitly) *contest* the legitimacy of the laws they break. The most universal of monopolists is (of necessity) beset with unruly competitors! The state which actually *succeeds* in imposing a monopoly of legitimate force thereby makes itself redundant since a gulf between ideals and reality is essential to the state's very *raison d'être*.

The state, in other words, has a contradictory identity. It asserts a monopoly of legitimate force which it does not (and cannot) have, and this is a contradiction which blights all its other attributes as well. The state focuses its activities within a given territory and upon the members of a particular nation because (and only because) its boundaries are challenged and its national identity is contested. Once we emphasize the contradictory character of the state, we can show that the state's success in claiming its monopoly of legitimate force is even more tentative than Weber himself assumed. For the same reason we can demonstrate that Weber's attempt to define the state solely in terms of its means rather than ends also fails.

Weber (and his supporters) contend that the state is best understood 'structurally' in terms of what it *is* rather than 'functionally' in terms of what it *does*. It is certainly true that many bodies seek order (the state's function or end), but it is equally true (as Weber himself acknowledged) that other bodies use force (the state's means or structure). Once we grasp the contradictory character of the state, it is becomes clear that any attempt to define the state one-sidedly – in terms of *either* its structure *or* its functions – is unsatisfactory, since the state pursues order through force in a way which makes *both* its structure *and* its functions peculiar and distinctive.

The more the state seeks to differentiate itself from society as a *sovereign* body, the more problematic its identity appears. On the one hand it is autonomous and separate, public rather than private; on the other hand the universality of its compulsory jurisdiction means that it permeates and structures the *whole* of society (including the most intimate and private realms of its subjects). A coherent critique of the state needs therefore to draw upon (and at the same time to go beyond) *both* the limitation thesis – that the modern state is distinct and different – *and* the argument of the indefinability thesis – that the state is a mystifying and problematic institution.

Of all the attributes which constitute the Weberian definition of the state, the question of legitimacy is certainly the most controversial. Weber's argument is that all states *by definition* claim legitimacy but in my view legitimacy (as with the other attributes) can exist only in a contradictory form. States claim a monopoly of legitimacy only because this legitimacy is contested, and as a result some 'Weberians' support what I call a 'differential' argument: that what is legitimate for the powerful is illegitimate for their victims. This is a tempting position but it fails to get to grips with the problem of legitimacy as a *relationship* in which the subordinate accept (as natural and normal) the paternalism of the powerful.

The emphasis upon legitimacy as a relationship confronts us with a fresh dilemma. If the differential argument unduly narrows the state's claim to legitimacy, the 'relational' position appears to broaden it to such an extent that legitimacy becomes compatible with force, slavery and despotism. As long as a relationship is stable, it is legitimate! Yet the problematic character of the state is rooted in the fact that it is an institution which resorts to force to settle differences. This problem is brought sharply to the fore by the modern *liberal* state which asserts that free and equal individuals must consent to the laws they obey. Legitimacy excludes the use of force. But if this is so (and I believe it is), how can legitimacy exist as a relationship between rulers and ruled?

To resolve this difficulty, we must make a distinction between force on the one hand and *coercion* on the other. Classical liberalism confuses the two since it postulates freedom as a property which individuals somehow enjoy and possess outside of society. Once we accept that this asocial 'state of nature' is a myth, we can conceptualize social relationships themselves as coercive (as Mill himself at least implicitly did) while distinguishing this coercion from force.

Coercion in other words arises from constraints which individuals have take account of in realizing their goals. Coercion does not prevent people from making choices although in its more direct forms (where people act under 'duress'), it may severely limit these choices. Force by contrast prevents people *from exercising a choice at all* since the victim of force (or violence) ceases to be an agent and becomes an object or thing. Although direct forms of coercion may threaten force, it is force and not coercion which (strictly speaking) undermines our freedom.

This distinction enables us to assert that force is incompatible with legitimacy (as indeed classical liberals rightly argued) whereas coercion is not. Where the state actually uses force, it undermines its legitimacy: where it merely coerces (in more or less punitive ways) it acts 'governmentally' since stateless societies themselves rely upon various forms of social coercion (ostracism, moralism, economic pressures, etc.) to secure order. As a consequence the state has a built-in legitimacy problem since it does not merely threaten force. It actually uses it.

It is at this point that we need to bring together the insights of both the differential and the relational arguments. Clearly legitimacy is a particular problem for those who are the direct recipients of force – hence the existence of a 'differential'. But force is also *mutually* degrading in character. When one individual or a group treats another as a thing (i.e. uses force), they 'relate' in a way which is mutually dehumanizing. Moreover this is a moral 'contamination' which blights the society as a whole since the sovereign state imposes its claim to monopolize force upon *all* who live within a particular territory. Legitimacy therefore becomes a problem for all individuals who obey the law in the knowledge that, if they do not, then force itself will be used against them. How many

of us in state-centred societies comply with laws for moral reasons
alone?

It is true that official force may be the only way to hold in check
the unofficial force of the criminal or the terrorist. But the point
remains nevertheless that the state cannot avoid undermining its
own legitimacy since it necessarily compromises the freedom of all
who live within the shadow of its force.

Abstract individualism in liberalism and anarchism

Part I of the book seeks to define the state, focus it historically,
explore its contradictions and analyse its contentious claim to
legitimacy. Part II examines alternative critiques against the background of the conceptual spade-work already undertaken.

We begin with liberalism as a theory which simultaneously
supports and opposes the state. It sees the state as unnatural and
'conventional' and seeks on the basis of this assumption to resolve
the problem of order and obligation. It is an assumption which
brings us face to face with the 'schizoid malady' (as it has been
called) which characterizes liberal theory as a whole. On the one
hand individuals are free: on the other hand they are subject to
force. In the case of Hobbes as the 'illiberal' founder of liberalism,
this leads to the paradoxical juxtaposition of an abstract concept
of freedom (which people possess outside of society) and an
abstract or one-sided case for the use of force (or terror as
Hobbes bluntly calls it) which is necessary to secure compliance to
the state.

Although subsequent liberals like Locke seek to soften the
paradox by stressing the sociable character of humans, the 'schizoid malady' does not disappear since, the further we move from
the idea that individuals freely authorize the law (as we see with the
utilitarians), the more we depart from the liberal tradition. Without
a concept of natural rights, liberalism becomes indistinguishable
from conservatism and authoritarianism. This indeed is the problem with the recent revival of a rights-based liberalism (deriving
from Kant) which postulates justice and rationality as ethical
'ideas' rather than 'natural' rights so that the use of force by the
state ceases to pose a problem for freedom. Hence modern theorists
like Rawls or Hayek (despite the significant differences between
them) espouse a form of liberalism which has lost its anti-statist
(and thus arguably its inherently liberal) character.

If liberals equivocate over the state, anarchists explicitly reject it, but their problem is this. The anarchist critique rests upon the same abstract individualism which bedevils classical liberalism so that philosophical anarchists (like Godwin, Stirner and Wolff) are unable to explain how individuals can *co-operate* to secure their freedom. Individualist (as opposed to philosophical) anarchists actually postulate stateless scenarios which they contend are practical, arguing that the free market can provide the social cohesion which makes the state redundant. But it is far from clear how this might work, since the problem of disparities in wealth and power, of crime and unintended (but damaging) 'spill-overs' like pollution, can be tackled by 'individualists' only if they assume that stateless actors are roughly equal members of the same community – precisely the assumption they are anxious to avoid!

It is true that 'communitarian' anarchists do stress that humans are naturally co-operative but this sociability is seen to be instinctive in character. Spontaneous self-activity does not express itself through social relationships since relationships (as anarchists rightly note) restrict as well as empower, and anarchists are opposed to hierarchical dependencies of every kind! As a result even the 'communitarians' oppose coercion as well as force, and are as hostile to the notion of government as they are to the state. A painful irony ensues. Since all forms of political organisation are equally unacceptable, anarchists often resort in practice to authoritarian methods of energizing the (inexplicably) sceptical masses and may even be tempted to express their opposition to the state through acts of outrageous violence. A collision between emancipatory ends and repressive means is inherent in an abstract individualism which ultimately derives from the liberal tradition.

Marxists, feminists and postmodernists against the state

Marxism accepts the need for political organization and acknowledges the governmental character of social relationships. On the face of it therefore the Marxist critique of the state appears more promising than the anarchist.

However, Marxists stand accused of a 'despotism thesis' which points to the repressive Communist Party states of Eastern Europe as the *practical* (and inevitable) consequence of Marxist *theory*. It is true that Marx and Engels sought to go beyond (rather than simply reject) liberalism by insisting that abstract rights must become concrete realities. The free development of each is the condition for the free development of all. Only the intervention of unfortunate 'circumstances' (subsequent Marxists argue) have prevented these emancipatory ideals from being realized.

But resorting to a 'circumstances argument' to account for the gulf between a 'post-liberal' theory and an illiberal practice creates fresh difficulties, since Marxists also contend that it is precisely the respect for historical 'circumstances' which makes Marxism a materialist and scientific form of socialism. Thus what happens if – as with the Paris Commune of 1871 or indeed the Russian Revolution of 1917 – 'circumstances' demand solidarity with political events that can succeed only if their participants resort to authoritarian forms of rule? We cannot avoid asking whether there is something within the theory itself which causes Marxists to frustrate their own 'post-liberal' concepts.

Three 'deficits' deserve attention. An absolutist view of history suggests that communism is the only (thinkable) outcome which can flow from events; a monopolistic view of class implies that the proletariat is a privileged historical actor in relation to which all other emancipatory struggles are subordinate and derivative, while the notion of a preordained class with a predetermined end encourages a dismissive attitude towards morality. Taken as a whole these 'deficits' account for the inherent tendency of an anti-statist theory to generate forms of the state which militantly refuse to 'wither away'.

Like anarchism and Marxism, feminism derives its conceptual arguments from the 'schizoid malady' of classical liberalism. Feminists rightly protest that although liberals hold the state to be 'conventional' and artificial, they also see it as underpinned by a hierarchical relationship between men and women which is deemed natural in character. Liberalism accepts a sexual division of labour which assumes that women care for the family while men are the 'abstract individuals' who authorize and control the state. Hence even those feminists who ostensibly accept liberal principles find themselves (at least implicitly) challenging this division of labour by arguing that the 'public' attributes of citizenship should be extended to supposedly 'private' women.

'Naturalism' is not merely a patriarchal ideology which afflicts liberalism. Although Marxists link patriarchy to private property and the state, they embrace a notion of production which downgrades the importance of women's work and depicts 'nature' in masculinist terms. Yet the link (which Marxists assert but cannot coherently sustain) between patriarchy and the state is a potent one. Men (some feminists argue) are able to dominate women only when they live in a society in which slavery and private property exist. It is true that a sexual division of labour has already begun to develop in tribal society, but this provides the basis for patriarchal oppression only when the development of the state itself enables men to use violence against women.

The violence which is central to the state is ultimately the violence of men who predominately enforce (as well as break) statist laws. Male supremacy rests upon force so that the violence of rape (for example) can be understood only as an extension of the violence of 'normal' sexual relationships and the pornographic portrayal of women as things.

However, the impact which feminism can make upon a critique of the state is blunted by the argument that because male domination pervades social relationships as a whole, the state itself has no particular significance for feminist theory. Yet (as we have seen) the violence of the sovereign state is itself universal in scope so that the public/private divide (which feminists necessarily challenge) is a statist principle for organizing society in general. No critique of patriarchy can be credible unless it at least implicitly confronts the repressive and divisive character of the state.

Postmodernists pose a different problem for a critique of the state since they appear to reject the very idea of 'critique' itself. Yet the postmodernist attack on what it calls 'logocentric' discourse has important implications for a critique of the state since logocentrism implies that the world is divided into rival concepts at war with one another. It is not difficult to see that just such a logocentrism lies at the heart of the state which stands or falls as an institution seeking to to impose monopolistic conformity upon a world of pluralistic diversity. What else is *force* – the attribute central to the identity of the state – but an absolutist attempt to obliterate difference and deconstitute the 'other'? The postmodernist concept of 'deconstruction' – i.e. exposing contradictions and paradoxes – is crucial to a critique of the state.

However, it is at this point that postmodernists encounter a problem. Can a (well merited) attack upon logocentrism generate an argument which looks *beyond* the state? Postmodernists require the kind of historical analysis which feminists (for example) employ when they note the way in which liberal patriarchy has progressed beyond classic patriarchy. In the case of the latter, men openly dominate women; in the case of the former, domination is masked by the abstraction of the individual. This historical argument is crucial therefore to a coherent post-statism.

Unfortunately postmodernists frequently embrace a relativist position which equates all 'discourses' as equally arbitrary, and identifies logic itself as logocentric in character. Down with rationality; long live nihilism! But a nihilist stance not only makes a serious critique of the state impossible, it also contradicts postmodernist support for pluralism and self-activity. A (postmodern) world in which diverse differences are all equally respected has to be a world in which the modernist (i.e. liberal) ideals of freedom and equality have become a reality. Unless the modern world is conceptually 'privileged', it is impossible to look beyond it.

Democracy and international society as an order beyond the state

If Part I of this book sets out the conceptual problems afflicting the state and Part II assesses the strengths and weaknesses of contemporary challenges and alternative critiques, Part III seeks to explore the practical possibilities for realizing a stateless world.

Here the concept of an international society is particularly helpful. International society (as Hedley Bull conceptualizes it) exists as a form of anarchy and yet at the same time works to secure order. Bull conceives of international society as an order in which common interests embody notions of justice that conflict with the partisan interests of the state. However, he also argues that international society is nothing other than a system of states – no more than the sum of its parts. The state in other words is here to stay. Bull derives his uncritical view of the state from his uncritical analysis of sovereignty. In order to defend sovereignty, he divides it into two apparently contrasting forms. *External* sovereignty simply denotes the independence of states (although they share power), while *internally* sovereignty means that states reign supreme. But this argument fails to engage the way in which 'foreign' constraints necessarily curb domestic power. It also frustrates the critical potential of Bull's own concepts.

What makes international society an 'anarchical order' is the fact (as Bull himself points out) that international law is a body of rules which secures the compliance of states without the existence of a 'higher' body claiming a monopoly of legitimate force. This must imply that international society is a 'governmental' order which transcends the state, and respects the autonomy of participants in a way in which statist order does not. Bull speaks of a 'new medievalism' with its overlapping authorities and criss-crossing loyalties as a possible (though unrealistic) alternative to the contemporary world. In fact his own analysis of (an increasingly comprehensive) international law, the growth of regional associations with a continental focus, and the rise of transnational organizations of every kind all suggest that a 'new medievalism' is *already* emerging as a political (and post-statal) reality.

But what is to prevent this 'new medievalism' from plunging world society into the kind of chaos reminiscent of the medievalism of old? The post-statal order must be premissed on a recognition that liberal states (with their formal opposition to violence) are preferable to authoritarian states, and that these liberal states must themselves be willing to acknowledge the case for looking beyond the state. Here the concept of common interests which Bull himself invokes in his analyis of order is highly significant. For what makes this concept central to the post-statist argument is the fact that it is the existence of common interests which enables states themselves (like the individuals within domestic societies) to settle their differences without force.

The concept of common interests must however be conceived dynamically rather than statically if it is to assist in charting a world beyond the state. The point is that technological and social changes mean that we now have common interests where none existed before. With the development of nuclear weaponry, new levels of environmental pollution and the outbreak of regional conflicts capable of generating tidal waves of refugees, we all have a common interest in settling *more and more* of our differences (in an increasingly interdependent world) through institutions which negotiate, arbitrate and forge consensus. International society demonstrates how the necessity and rationale of the state is indeed 'withering away'.

This is why the wellnigh universal acclamation for democracy in the postwar world works to strengthen the case for looking beyond the state. The problem is that democracy is often presented as nothing more than a form of the state itself. If however we are to understand the historic tension which existed between democracy and liberalism, we have to engage the anti-statist character of a concept which concerns itself after all with empowering the mass of the population. The idea that democracy might promote 'a tyranny of the majority' demonstrates the problem which democracy's critics have in conceptualizing a world in which freedom can exist only in mutual terms. If democracy involves the right of *all* individuals to govern their lives (as it surely must), then this implies not merely the absence of a 'tyrannical' state but the absence of the proceduralized violence of the liberal political order as well.

Those who attack democracy for generating an oppressive 'wel-

fare state' invariably fail to distinguish between policies which
provide resources which empower individuals, and policies which
subject individuals to the arbitrary whim of patriarchal-minded
bureaucrats. The welfare state encapsulates the contradictory mix
of divisive and emancipatory measures inherent in the democratic
state itself. The fact is that statism (in whatever form) necessarily
reflects and entrenches radical conflicts of interest so that the
provision of welfare is democratic only when it works to strengthen
community and autonomy.

This point is crucial in linking democracy with participation.
Participation deepens democracy only when it enables real people
with different resources and interests to acquire greater power over
their lives. Democracy in other words presupposes both representation and participation: the two must be mutually reinforcing if
the 'gulf' between society and the state is to be increasingly
reduced. Democracy involves recognizing *both* 'difference' *and* the
existence of common interests which enables people with different
identities to 'change places'. To emphasize one at the expense of
the other takes us back to the monopolistic and divisive practices
of the state.

Because democracy is about individuals, it embraces localities,
nations and regions *and* an increasingly interdependent global
order in which the freedom of one individual can be sustained only
by the freedom of all others. Hence democracy is international as
well as national. On the one hand a cosmopolitan democracy
requires international courts and assemblies underpinned by an
international law enshrining human rights; on the other hand it
would also need states to provide organized force as long as
differences between and within nations cannot be resolved in a
non-violent manner. Democracy (that is to say) involves a 'utopianism' embedded in the world of reality.

Forging and consolidating cohesive common interests takes time;
it requires the kind of order and stability which violent individuals,
like violent states, prevent. There is therefore a role for violence in
creating a stateless democratic order but the point is that it is a role
which is residual and transitional. Violence can never eliminate the
need for the state since it is intrinsic to statism. But in so far as it
makes it possible to pursue *positive* policies which provide resources which empower individuals and strengthen communities, it has
a role which can be conceptualized as self-dissolving in character.

As subjects have become citizens and society more integrated and
complex, so states have become less and less able to promote
civilized life. With the industrialization of war and the increasingly

destructive capacity of armaments, states are now capable of destroying humanity itself. Looking beyond the state is integral to the concept of democracy. It is a 'utopian' process which derives (and can only derive) from our realistic desire to survive. Increasingly we all have an interest in avoiding the resolution of disputes through force since force itself is rapidly and inexorably becoming more and more suicidal in character.

The post-statal order, painfully struggling to emerge in our midst, deserves to be taken seriously only if it can be shown that, without it, our reality as a self-governing species is put at risk. This in a nutshell is the argument of the book.

Part I

Identifying the Problem

2

Can the State be Defined?

I want to begin by arguing that while the state is certainly a complex and elusive institution, it can and must be defined. Those who contend that the state *cannot* be defined inevitably come up against the problem that the state (whether we like it or not) actually exists. Its absurdity constitutes a practical as well a theoretical difficulty so that it is hardly surprising that, when another term is substituted, this alternative suffers from the same conceptual dilemmas which afflict the state.

The German romantic Adam Müller once declared that the state defies definition because its complexity places it beyond the grasp of finite minds.[1] Over fifty years ago the *Encyclopedia of the Social Sciences* declared that the word 'commonly describes no class of objects that can be identified exactly'. It bears no list of attributes that has the sanction of common usage and hence must be defined 'more or less arbitrarily'.[2] It is however one thing to argue that the state is difficult to pin down, but what I shall call the indefinability thesis goes further. It contends that the state should not form part of our theoretical discourse on politics. The ambiguities of the state are so disabling that the term itself is conceptually unusable.

Clearly the indefinability thesis poses a serious problem for our critique, since, if we are to establish the problematic character of the state, we must be able to define the state in a way which demonstrates just how problematic the state really is. It is not a question of denying that the state is a curious and elusive institution. Rather it is a question of arguing that these problematic features cannot be critically grasped unless they are incorporated into a definition which is sufficiently open-textured to acknowledge the elusiveness and ambiguity of the state.

Müller's contention that the state defies definition stems from a romantic conservatism which sees the state as a 'body' that cannot be understood through the abstract reason of the Enlightenment. The indefinability thesis that I wish to tackle here however derives from very different conceptual sources, and can be identified with three distinct bodies of argument. The most sustained is that of behavioural political scientists who not only query the utility of the concept but seek to employ alternative conceptions. Less vigorous versions of the thesis can be found in linguistic analytical contentions that the state is too vague and woolly to be philosophically interesting, while a third argument derives from the radical view (which itself takes various forms) that the concept of the state implies a concentration and focus for politics which is misleading and unhelpful.

The Eastonian attack on the state

If the indefinability thesis is presented in its most sustained form by the behaviouralists, the political theorist who has been most tenacious in advancing it is David Easton. A critique of his particular position is useful for the way it demonstrates the dilemmas of the argument as a whole. What is distinctive about Easton's position is the fact that he explicitly rejects the state's theoretical credentials and explicitly argues that a conceptual alternative must be found. Easton devotes a central chapter of his early but seminal work *The Political System* (1953) to arguing this case.

In essence his position is this. Such is the ambiguity of the concept, it is impossible for political scientists to agree upon what the state is. Theorists are unable to decide when states first arose or what states are. Some define the state in terms of its morality, others see it as an instrument of exploitation. Some regard it simply as an aspect of society, others as a synonym for government, while still others identify it as a unique and separate association which stands apart from social institutions like churches and trade unions. Some point to the sovereignty of the state, others to the limited character of its power. What makes the state so contentious, Easton argues, is the fact that the term is imbued with strong mythical qualities, serving historically as an ideological vehicle for propagating national sovereignty against cosmopolitian and local powers. Given the disagreement and contention the state inevitably provokes, it seems pointless (Easton suggests) 'to add a favoured definition of my own'. Scientific political theory requires clarity and clarity requires us to abstain from using the term altogether. The state defies definition.[3]

This attack on the state by Easton in particular (and by behaviouralists and radical and linguistic analysts in general) seems initially to have met with a good deal of success. For around three decades after the Second World War, the state (conceptually at any rate) appeared to have 'withered away'.[4] But in 1981 Easton could comment that 'a concept that many of us thought had been polished off a quarter of a century ago, has now risen from the grave to haunt us once again'.[5] Seemingly crucified by its opponents, the state was determined to return! Why? Easton noted at least four factors: a 'third coming' of Marxism in the USA emphasized the importance of developing a coherent theory of politics around the state. A conservative yearning for stability and authority focused nostalgic aspirations through the state while those who rediscovered the importance of the market also rediscovered the state as their conceptual *bête noir*. Finally, students of policy studies found in the state a convenient tool of analysis.[6]

Despite these developments, however, Easton remains unrepentant. He recalls the numerous definitions of the state which he had noted in 1953 and suggests that inherent and 'irresolvable ambiguities' have only proliferated since then. Much of his analysis in 1981 is taken up with a witty and hard-hitting critique of the Althusserian Marxist Nicos Poulantzas whose 'astonishing discovery' that the state is an 'indecipherable mystery' Easton is delighted to endorse. As Poulantzas sees it, the state is not a 'Thing' – a piece of machinery over which classes fight for control – nor is it a 'Subject' or collective actor endowed with a rationalistic will. Although Poulantzas argues that the state seeks to maintain the cohesion of a class-divided society, he does not tell us what the state actually is. The definition of the state as 'institutionalized political power' is circular since what is 'political' is never indentified independently of the state. Nor (according to Easton) is Poulantzas able to make up his mind as to whether the state is ideological (embracing socially sanctioned rules) or simply material – a mere apparatus. He refers to the state as a 'material condensation' of a relationship between classes but insists that it is not reducible to these relationships.

Even those, it seems, who have sought 'to bring the state back in' have had to yield to the iron logic of the indefinability thesis. The state 'is the eternally elusive Pimpernel of Poulantzas's theory'.[7] It is either 'some kind of undefined and undefinable essence' – a vacuous term referring to an emergent, ineffable phenomenon which reveals itself only in the garb of apparatuses – or it is simply the totality of its apparatuses. If it is the former, then Poulantzas himself has conceded the indefinability thesis. If it is the latter, it is no more than a substitute term for 'government' and its associated private institutions.[8] Poulantzas's problems merely confirm the obscurity, vacuity and ambiguity of the concept. Its interment is well overdue.

Do states exist?

Easton's attack has three distinct (although related) elements. Firstly, the state is highly disputed and no one seems able to agree on a definition. Secondly, it is a thoroughly ambiguous concept which clearly lends itself to endless and irresolvable contention. And thirdly, it is a mystical and abstract notion which cannot be pinned down and rendered operational. Taken together these elements account for the state's inherent indefinability and underline the need to get rid of it.

There is however a nice irony here which is conceptually crucial to resisting the indefinability thesis. Proponents of the indefinability thesis sound almost like anarchists or Marxists in their anxiety to dispose of the state and encourage its withering away. Indeed the critique which we wish to develop here is not unsympathetic to these anti-statist aspirations. But in order to dispose of the state, we need first to decide whether in fact it exists, or whether it is merely a tiresome and misleading *word* unrelated to an external social or institutional reality.

The point is posed sharply in a comment in the *International Encyclopedia of the Social Sciences* (written in 1968) where we are told that 'political scientists generally prefer to use other terms in describing the phenomena that were once subsumed under the concept "State" '.[9] For this raises the question: do these 'phenomena' once described as states continue to exist? Or have they changed sufficiently so it is not merely the term but the reality itself which has 'withered away'? An analogy might be drawn with an argument about centaurs, unicorns or spiritual creators like gods or God. As far as the atheist is concerned, an argument about the idea of God turns upon the question of existence. Clearly God exists in people's minds as an idea in the same way as numerous and fantasical notions about goblins and centaurs and unicorns exist. But, for the atheist, God is not real because logically and empirically it is impossible to imagine a material world produced by a spiritual creator. God is a myth. The idea of God exists, but not God himself. Is this also true of the state? Is the state a fantasical notion which has no institutional or material reality? Is the state merely a 'divine idea' which *pace* Hegel does *not* exist on earth but only in people's imagination?

Some have argued that the state is too diverse, divided and contradictory 'to evoke as an entity'. Indeed it is even argued that to refer to the state as 'contradictory' is misleading since the discourse of contradiction implies a unity of state form which then surprises us when the state appears to act in unexpected ways. Better to see the state as 'erratic and disconnected rather than contradictory'.[10] This argument still takes it for granted that the state – entity or no – is 'something' which exists. Perhaps we should not think of it as a coherent institution but as a fluid and disconnected set of arenas. A definition of some kind is nevertheless possible.

It is only really plausible to argue that the state cannot be defined if the state does not exist. The proponents of the indefinability thesis must argue that, like centaurs and unicorns or the atheist's view of God, the state itself is a fiction. Many commentators from Hobbes to Marx have stressed the metaphysical and quasi-religious identity of the state but they have still accepted that the Leviathan is perfectly real and, like the Sphinx in Carlyle's *Past and Present*, it is 'a thing of teeth and claws' which we ignore at our peril. It might be objected however that centaurs and unicorns *can* be defined although they do not exist, and a Wittgensteinian might suggest that games which do exist cannot be defined.[11] But the point that is relevant here is that definitions of unicorns, centaurs or anything else are not open to serious challenge if there are no existential realities to which they refer. Likewise games cannot be verbally identified at all if they lack common characteristics which make them (at least in some very general sense) definable. Thus the radicals who criticize the centrality of the state in political theory still accept that the state exists and therefore can and must be defined.[12]

The figure who is generally regarded as the founding father of modern behaviouralism is Arthur Bentley, whose pioneering work *The Process of Government* (1908) pronounces the state to be infected with the 'soul stuff' of an abstract holism. But even Bentley does not meet the existential point raised above. He insists that there is nothing special about the state that makes it qualitatively different from any other 'government', but at the same time he does not deny that states exist. The state is just another form of government whose penalties are simply 'special forms' of a great class of penalties imposed by all social organisations. In order to strip it of its unique and metaphysical characteristics, the state has to be defined.[13]

A similar point emerges in T. D. Weldon's classic of Oxford language philosophy, *The Vocabulary of Politics*. Weldon protests (like Easton and Bentley) that the concept of the state is frequently invested with dangerously misleading mystical overtones which lead to its deification. It may be that only unphilosophical 'first order' definitions of the state (imported from the confusing world of practice) are possible, but we all know (Weldon insists) that the USA and Switzerland are states whereas Surrey and the United Nations are not.[14] Whatever we think of the practical merits of this quest for conceptual purity, there is no suggestion by linguistic analysts that states do not exist.

Easton's equivocations

In *The Political System* Easton raises a number of objections to the concept of the state, none of which appear to meet the requirements of the indefinability thesis as set out above. He complains (rightly) about the way in which states are surrounded by myths of national sovereignty,[15] and he argues that no state exists before the seventeenth century. He cites MacIver's definition of the state as an association which embraces the whole of the people of a specific territory and which promulgates its coercive laws through government. But this definition is problematic, not because territorial states do not exist but rather because they should not be seen as the be-all and end-all of politics.[16]

A third objection develops this point by insisting that at most the 'state concept' merely illustrates one kind of political phenomenon: there are historical periods in which the state did not exist and the same may be true in the unknown future.[17] But this view merely asserts that the state is a more limited phenomenon than many have assumed: it does not deny that, at least within certain periods of history, the state exsts. Yet Easton wants to go further. His argument is not simply that the state is a limiting concept but that it is a highly dubious one. Hence he refers at times to the 'state concept' rather than the state in order to suggest that state itself is impossibly elusive. He tells us that the *concept* has served as an instrument for achieving national cohesion, but is this also true of the state as an institutional reality? Easton equivocates. On some occasions Easton refers to political science studying an institution 'often called the state'. But on others he suggests that the state does indeed exist but only as 'a single, even if important, instance' of a wider whole.[18]

The equivocation is also manifest in Easton's foray into political anthropology. In *The Political System* he speaks of societies 'in which the so-called state institution is non-existent'.[19] In 1959, however, he refers simply to the fact that tribal societies are 'stateless'. His critique of Radcliffe-Brown turns on the fact that the latter has identified politics as organized force, and this is not a definition which is appropriate to understanding the politics of stateless societies. The point is that states and stateless societies are meaningful categories of analysis. Easton complains that the anthropologist Smith has failed to realize that substantial and important differences 'do seem to exist' between these two types of politics.[20] Clearly states can hardly be differentiated from stateless societies unless they have a reality of their own. Yet Easton never retreats from his earlier argument that states are so ambiguous and elusive that it is pointless to try and define them.

It might however be argued that it is unfair to confront Easton with his equivocations over whether the state exists since he is a sceptic rather than a realist who holds that concepts are neither true nor false. They are only more or less useful. Political life, he argues, does not have to have a 'natural' coherence so that logically there is nothing to prevent us from considering a duckbilled platypus and the ace of spades as our political system.[21] But Easton concedes that a platypus/spades construct of the political system would be 'conceptually pointless', and later comments that, although a definition might be arbitrary, it should not be 'whimsical' or 'capricious'. What makes a concept useful or interesting? Useful concepts, it appears, are those which have what Easton calls an 'empirical status': they must in principle at least be empirically observable and testable.[22] But this suggests that it must be possible to assess concepts 'existentially' since an entity which does not exist (or correspond in some way to a realm of existence) can hardly be said to have empirical status. Indeed in his more recent work Easton in fact argues that even high-order structures of a particularly abstract kind nevertheless 'exist out there', independent of the individual will.[23]

Whether the concepts analysing them are simply useful rather than true, in practice institutions do exist. Indeed Easton even argues in his more recent writing that politics can be defined in terms of both social interactions and institutions, whereas earlier he had insisted that the behavioural approach deals with activities and behaviour *rather than* institutions 'such as government and the state'.[24] The shift is a significant one for, if the political system can now be analysed in institutional terms, might not one of these institutions be the state?

Substituting the political system

As long as Easton considered that statist concepts had been all but abandoned, his energies were basically taken up with the case for the political system rather than the case against the state. By the 1980s however the vanquished ghosts have returned and Easton finds himself preoccupied with the work of 'neo-statists' (as he calls them) who not only accept the legitimacy of the term but are positively celebrating its conceptual revival. A more explicit and vigorous rebuttal of the state now seems necessary.

Whenever the term is used, it is invariably placed in inverted commas and accompanied by conceptual protest. In analysing the work of Poulantzas, Easton tells us that he is obliged to proceed on the unwarranted assumption that we clearly understand what is meant by the state when in fact 'our point of reference remains an object clouded in conceptual ambiguity'.[25] A more militant anti-statism is required given the fact that use of the term has become increasingly difficult to ignore. At one point he uses the term state 'loosely' to refer to what he calls the 'whole political system', at other times the state merely embraces the political regime (i.e. part of the overall political system), while on a third occasion the term best translates into what Easton calls 'political authorities'. Sometimes these are combined as when Easton writes that 'instead of the state, I prefer to speak about the political system and its authorities'.[26] The implication of this argument would seem to be that the state *qua* state does not exist (or at least not in a way which is 'empirically observable' and conceptually useful). On the other hand the state *qua* political system, political regime and political authorities *does* exist or has 'empirical status', since these terms have a conceptual clarity which the state manifestly lacks.

If Easton's version of the indefinability thesis is to hold, then we must accept that states do not exist at least in the sense that political systems do, or, to put the matter somewhat more 'analytically', political systems are not themselves bedevilled by the ambiguity, obscurity and metaphysics that afflict the idea of the state. There is no need therefore to try to define the state because in the conception of a political system we have an analytically superior definition which accounts coherently for the same phenomena which the state-concept seeks to define in a muddled and unsuccessful manner. Easton's critics are rightly sceptical. They point in particular (as I have argued elsewhere[27]) to the problem Easton has in defining politics in relationship to 'society'. His argument in essence is that, while values may be 'authoritatively allocated' in all kinds of social organisations like churches and trade unions, they become authentically 'political' in character only when institutions within society are unable to settle their differences in private, and an agency whose scope covers all of society's activities has to intervene.[28]

But what constitutes a society? Easton is open to the objection that his reference to 'society as a whole' has 'empirical status' and is conceptually meaningful only if it denotes a society demarcated by the legal framework of the state. The political system can be coherently delimited only if it is another term for the state. To get round this problem Easton argues that in fact political systems can exist in societies without states and between societies with states. Moreover the mechanisms which authoritatively allocate values may be violent as well as peaceful so that war and secession can also be said to characterize the political process. But, if this is so, in what sense can we speak of values being authoritatively allocated for society as a whole? On the one hand Easton defines society as a 'special kind of human grouping' in which people develop 'a sense of belonging together'. On the other hand he argues that international and tribal orders are themselves 'genuine societies' even if they are less 'integrated' and 'rationalized' than national ones.[29]

But all this makes the notion of society, so crucial to his definition of the political system, extremely problematic. If (as Easton allows) war, violence and secession operate as mechanisms to allocate values authoritatively, then in what sense can it be said that a society is 'genuine' when dissatisfied clans may leave or nations destroy one another? The same problem affects Easton's analysis of the political system in relationship to the problem of change. In seeking to show that the political system is something other than a state, Easton argues that a political system can 'persist' even though its authorities and regime dramatically change. One overarching political system can embrace multiple lower-level political systems just as society persists analytically while warring parties go their own way. The political system, as one reviewer rightly complains, becomes a shadowy abstraction which could only perish if all its popular participants were physically obliterated.[30]

In other words, Easton's concept of the political system is subject to a criticism which is disquietingly similar to the one which he himself levels against Poulantzas. Poulantzas, we recall, either has to accept that the state consists merely of its repressive and ideological apparatuses or it is a mysterious essence which no one can pin down. Easton's dilemma is the same. Either the political system refers to an observable territorial entity which in reality is nothing other than the state (hence notions of change and of society as a whole can be given some empirical purchase) or the political system becomes an 'undecipherable mystery', an undefinable essence which lurks beyond empirical reality, as indestructible and empirically elusive as any Platonic truth. Substituting the political system for the state has not removed any of the 'irresolvable ambiguities' about which Easton protests.

The dichotomous definition and its disadvantages

In an early review of *The Political System* Dahl takes issue with what he sees as the metaphysics, essentialism and holism of Easton's text. Particularly relevant here is his objection to Easton's conception of the authoritative allocation of values for society as a whole. What makes an allocation authoritative? asks Dahl. The fact that it must be obeyed. But obeyed by whom? By how many? Does society as a whole mean every last man, woman and child? Criminals evidently do not believe that criminal statutes must be obeyed.[31]

The point is a good one. Easton does not exclude the use of force in authoritatively allocating values within his political system. Are we to assume therefore that even those who break coercive laws (and are punished as a consequence if they are caught) can still be said to find them binding or authoritative? It is true (and revealing) that in his later definitions Easton does not actually refer to politics as the authoritative allocations of values for a society – this is the classic definition for which he is so well known – but speaks instead of politics as decisions 'considered binding by most members of society, most of the time'.[32] But the reformulation hardly rescues his concept from the kind of ambiguity and obscurity for which he was earlier criticized by Dahl. For what are we to understand by the phrase 'most of the members, most of the time'? How many is most? The crime rate in Britain is reckoned to have doubled since

1979. What effect does this fact have on the proposition central to Easton's definition of the political system that most people accept decisions as binding most of the time? In South Africa hundred of thousands of Africans were prosecuted in the 1950s and 1960s for breaking the pass laws. Given the fact that South Africa remained a political system during that period, must we assume therefore that most members of society accepted political decisions as binding most of the time?

The problem which confronts us is not simply one which affects Easton's definition of the political system. It extends to the state itself and it is one which will preoccupy us a good deal throughout this book. It is the problem of ordering divided societies. Substituting the phrase 'most of the members, most of the time' for the earlier reference to 'society' no more resolves this problem than substituting an Eastonian political system for the state. This point is made very clearly by Dahl who accepts that in seeking to define something he calls 'the Government' he is basically referring to what others have called the state. The state therefore can be defined but (Dahl protests) this is a 'dichotomous definition' which suffers from a number of disadvantages. The 'disadvantages' which arise when defining Government (or the state) uncannily echo the problems which Dahl had already raised with Easton's definition of the political system. If, as Dahl comments, the state has the right to the exclusive regulation of force, how do we explain that other individuals also use force? How can this force be seen as legitimate when criminals clearly flout coercive laws?[33]

These 'disadvantages' will be examined in detail later but they are raised here to indicate only that ambiguities and obscurities do not disappear by substituting an Eastonian political system for a supposedly indefinable state. Putting Dahl's critique of Easton alongside his own definition of 'Government' makes it very clear that, if metaphysical difficulties arise with Easton's 'political system', they do so precisely because his political system is simply a behaviouralist version of the state.

This point is borne out even more brutally by Almond and Powell's argument that the definitions advanced both by Dahl and Easton necessarily associate the political system with the use of legitimate physical coercion in societies.[34] For, as Easton makes clear in his own critique of Radcliffe Brown noted above, to speak of legitimate physical coercion is to speak of the state. Almond and Powell take it for granted that political systems make sense only as state-like institutions, and they therefore reinforce the argument of Easton's critics that he is unable to give 'empirical purchase' to his definition of politics without implicitly referring to the state.

Has the state ever been left out?

Easton's later writings are haunted by those who argue that the state must be brought back into political theory. At one point in *The Analysis of Political Structure* he declares with some irritation that in fact the state has never been left out: political scientists have simply referred to 'the influence of government (the state?) on politics and society'.[35]

It is an expression of exasperation which finally seals the fate of the indefinability thesis. His argument that the state has never been left out gives the concept an academic legitimacy which he has spent most of his academic life trying to deny. For this suggests not that the state is a conceptual absurdity which political scientists are right to push aside but rather that the political system, like the term government, is simply another way of speaking of the state. Like Dahl who 'prefers' to call the state 'the Government', this position accepts that states exist in both their domestic as well as their external roles, and that ultimately there is no reason why they should not be defined.

Easton therefore identifies with the argument pursued by Almond and other political scientists in an important discussion on the 'Return to the State' in 1988. In essence the contention here is that, while the state may have been put to one side in favour of a wider conceptual framework, it does not need to brought back into political science because it never really disappeared. Almond argues in considerable detail that the pluralists, for example, did not ignore the state (as their statist critics allege) but made use of a two-directional approach with the state influencing society and society influencing the state. Those who rather stridently claimed that they are bringing the state back in, define the state (Almond argues) in ways which are quite similar to mainstream definitions of government and the political system.[36] While Almond's debate with some of the other contributors to the 1988 discussion shows differences over just how much state autonomy the behaviouralists in practice allowed, there is complete agreement over the proposition, as Lowi phrases it, that 'the state was never really out'.[37] Nor are there any methodological obstacles to translating legal-institutional definitions of the state into concepts of the political system.[38] If Easton is now associating himself (as he appears to be) with this body of argument, then indeed he is all but conceding that the political system, like the term government, is just another term for the state.

We conclude therefore that, to pursue the indefinability thesis successfully, it would have to be argued not merely that the state is conceptually problematic or even it is more historically and geographically limited than many political scientists have supposed. Those claiming that no definition of the state is actually possible would have to contend that states themselves do not exist but that, like centaurs, goblins and the atheist's view of God, they are fictional constructs with no 'empirical status'. This is not the position of most who appear sympathetic to the indefinability thesis. Easton's position is exceptional. For as one militantly committed to a general theory of political life, Easton has sought to replace the state with the political system, and thus he comes closer (despite equivocation and obscurity) than any other theorist to supporting the indefinability thesis.

Nevertheless the venture fails. We accept the criticism by Easton and others that the state is an institution which is arbitrary, metaphysical, abstract and elusive. But what are we to say of the concept which supposedly replaces it? Easton's political system – so abstract and general that it is 'everything and nothing'[39] – is either a mysterious and transcendental entity which lurks outside of historical reality or it is merely another word for the state, no less prone to the soul stuff, metaphysics and ambiguity that characterize that latter concept.

SUMMARY

- Proponents of the indefinability thesis argue that because the state is a problematic institution it cannot be defined.

- This argument has to face the fact that states continue to exist in the real world. They may be mysterious and elusive, but no supporter of the indefinability thesis has ever denied unequivocally that states are institutional realities.

- David Easton seeks to get around this difficulty by substituting the concept of a political system but it is not difficult to demonstrate that this concept suffers from the same kind of mystification and ambiguity which afficts the state.

- This state is certainly a problematic institution. The point is that, since the state exists in the real world, it is only by *defining* the state that we can begin to get grips with its problematic character.

3

Force, State and Government

Here I want to define the state in a way which is both coherent and structured and identifies force as the key (though not the only) attribute of the state. This will make it possible to distinguish between the state on the one hand and government on the other – a distinction which is central to the argument of this book.

The state, we accept, is a problematic institution, but since it exists it needs to be defined. Hence we would endorse Nettl's comment that, even if the state has a 'skeletal and ghostly existence', the thing exists and no amount of conceptual restructuring can dissolve it away.[1] We live in a society in which people who break (or who are thought to have broken) laws are sent to prison; in which armed bodies (mostly of men) invade and defend territories in the name of sovereignty and self-determination, and in which the pursuit of order is intertwined (some think inextricably) with officially justified acts of force.

If the state is a reality – however problematic and ambiguous – then it requires a definition. Such a definition will inevitably embody a certain irony since the importance of defining the state arises from the fact that this is the only way to highlight, in an intelligible and critical fashion, its problematic and ambiguous character.

The Weberian definition

We have already noted that one of the reasons which Easton advances in support of the indefinability thesis is that political scientists find it impossible to reach an agreed definition of the state.[2] Yet despite the disagreement and diversity which arises when attempts are made to define the state, in fact there is a surprising degree of consensus around. Dahl, as we observed in our previous chapter, identifies the Government (capital G) with the state, and defines it as any government (small g) which successfully upholds a claim to the exclusive regulation of legitimate physical force in enforcing its rules within a given territorial area. We will later challenge this view of government but Dahl's notion of state is one which commands wide assent, and it is one which (he tells us) he has adapted from Max Weber.[3]

When Almond and Powell identify concepts of the political system with the use of legitimate physical coercion, they also express their agreement with Max Weber.[4] In criticizing Radcliffe-Brown for focusing on organized force as the distinguishing quality of political systems, Easton identifies this emphasis on force with a position laid down by Thomas Hobbes and reinforced by Max Weber.[5] In 1968 Watkins suggested that if there *is* any point in using the concept of the state, then it is in the Weberian sense, while those who proclaim the need to bring the state back in, explicitly highlight the importance of looking again at the definition of Weber.[6]

Hall and Ikenberry reinforce this point when they comment on the substantial agreement which exists among social scientists as to how the state should be defined. They stress three elements within their 'composite definition'. Firstly, the state is a set of institutions, the most important of which is that of the means of violence and coercion; secondly, its institutions lie at the centre of a geographically bounded territory usually referred to as a society, and thirdly, the state monopolizes rule-making within its territory. This is not only a definition which commands wide agreement: it is one which has been explicitly influenced by the work of Weber.[7] Political theorists may disagree about the merits of the state in general or about the merits of states in particular. They may even disagree as to whether 'normative' questions like these can be meaningfully evaluated in theoretical discourse. But they all define the state in a way which embraces at least some of the attributes – monopoly, territory, legitimacy and force – drawn from Weber's seminal definition.[8]

In 1918 Weber declared that the state is a human community that (successfully) claims the monopoly of the legitimate use of physical force within a given territory.[9] Subscribing broadly to Weber's definition of the state does not mean however that we have to support the conceptual implications which Weber himself believed flowed from adopting such a definition. Weber for example thought that he was defining the state purely in terms of its means rather than its ends.[10] He assumed that he was constructing a definition which was 'realist' in the sense of being ethically neutral, although it was also his personal conviction that the state is 'the highest and ultimate thing in the world'.[11] Moreover, as we shall also see, Weber tends to identify force not merely with the state but with politics in general.

We will challenge these and other arguments in our own critique of the state while broadly subscribing to Weber's definition. It is therefore possible (and necessary) to interpret the Weberian definition in a non-Weberian manner. Indeed Weber is said to have taken his own definition of the state from Leon Trotsky. He quotes Trotsky as saying at Brest-Litovsk that 'every state is founded on force' and comments: 'That indeed is right.'[12] But clearly such an endorsement hardly committed Weber to accepting the particular Marxist argumentation upon which Trotsky's view of the state rested. The definition is one thing; its wider conceptual and ideological implications are quite another.

But why should the Weberian definition provides a useful starting point for a critical analysis of the state?

Coherence and structure

A critical challenge to the state requires a definition which is logically coherent. Unless we can conceptualize the state 'as a whole', we cannot move beyond the curate's egg analysis in which bits of the state are good and bits are bad. If we are to criticize the state as such – i.e. in its totality – this is possible only if we have a definition of the state which is both coherent and structured. It is because Weber's definition has these features that it constitutes a useful point from which to begin.

The celebrated definition contains four interrelated elements: monopoly, territory, legitimacy and force. Although some supporters of Weber's definition tend to leave out 'legitimacy' (for reasons we shall deal with in detail in chapter 6), in my view all four elements need to be included. What makes this definition coherent is that each of the attributes forms an interrelated totality so that it is impossible for a state to exist which has some of the attributes but not the others. The inherent logic of the definition can be demonstrated if we conduct a simple identity test. This cannot of course establish the historical plausibility of the definition (a point

I shall tackle in my next chapter) but it is helpful in suggesting that the definition is coherent one.

Think of a 'state' which does not even try or claim to exercise a monopoly of legitimate force but, on the contrary, is willing to share power with rival bodies. Immediately its territorial focus must fragment since a non-monopolistic 'state' must allow other bodies to exercise power and claim allegiances within the same territory. Membership ceases to be exclusive. Force and legitimacy also crumble as distinguishing attributes. In the absence of the state's monopoly, rival bodies can exercise force so that it becomes difficult to see why the force exercised by the state should prevail, and, if it does not prevail, it is not clear why it should be obeyed. No monopoly, and the other three attributes of the Weberian state – territory, legitimacy and force – disintegrate.

Think of a state which *does* exercise a monopoly of force within a given territory, but exercises a force which has no claim to legitimacy. How would such a state distinguish itself from a band of robbers?[13] Take away territorial focus from the definition of the state, and the notion of monopoly becomes problematic; try to picture a state exercising a monopoly of legitimacy in a given territory but *without* having the capacity to employ physical force, and the most bizarre absurdity results. People with plural identities – gender, religious, class – would be expected to give exclusive allegiance to only one state (monopoly and legitimacy) and obey the laws of only one 'country' (territory): yet there would be no force on hand to compel them to do so!

The question of force as one of the state's distinctive attributes deserves particular attention, for so far I have spoken of a coherent definition as one which presents interrelated elements as a totality. Force is however not only an attribute which contributes to a coherent definition. It is the dimension which gives the Weberian definition its *structure*. A coherent definition must be a structured definition since the interrelationships which constitute it need to be linked together in a way which is not indeterminate. A definition can avoid arbitrariness only if the elements which constitute it do not simply interrelate but do so in a way in which one element provides a conceptual underpinning to all the others. It is this element which constitutes the 'basis' or foundation for the structure. In Weber's definition the central attribute which provides cohesion to the others is *force*.

The state is not simply a set of free-floating attributes. The definition has a structure since one of the attributes – in this case 'force' – provides the basis. A structured definition is not

reductionist because a reductionist definition only has *one* identifying attribute, and all the rest are of no consequence. Weber's
definition by contrast embraces the state as a whole. To locate a
decisive element is not therefore to locate an element which exists
apart from or outside of the structure as a whole but (as Easton
puts it) the structure *is* its parts 'in systematic interconnections'.[14]
The view that will, not force, is the basis of the state has been
ascribed to T. H. Green. Yet Green makes it clear that the state
does not consist *only* of will and morality, and he argues (somewhat theologically) that, without force, 'the wild beast in man will
not otherwise yield obedience to the rational will'.[15] This definition
is structured rather than reductionist since idealists accept that
force is also a characteristic of the state, but they see it as an
attribute which is secondary rather than primary, formal rather
than substantial, relevant rather than basic.

For Weber on the other hand force is central. The decisive means
for the state is violence. Without the use of force, the concept of
the state would disappear. But just as idealists do not 'reduce' the
state to will, so Weber does not 'reduce' the state to force since, as
we have noted above, force constitutes the state only when such
force is also legitimated, monopolized and focused territorially.
Hence Weber also insists: 'force is certainly not the normal or the
only means of the state – nobody says that'. Territory is also a
characteristic, so is monopoly ('the state is considered the sole
source of the right to use violence') and (as we have seen)
domination cannot be effective without legitimacy.

Nevertheless – to reiterate the point – force within Weber's
definition is conceptually privileged as 'a means specific to the
state'[16] even though force cannot take a statist form unless it exists
alongside the other attributes with which it interrelates. In Easton's
terms, the elements within the definition are not asymmetrically
causal in the sense that one precedes the other in time and space,
but rather they form a 'nesting hierarchy'.[17] They co-exist, are
mutually determinant but nevertheless are structured in a hierarchical
way. Force (it might be said) provides the conceptual 'glue' which
renders the interrelated attributes coherent and thus constitutes the
basic element of a structured and thus coherent definition of the state.

The anthropological argument

We have already seen that one of the reasons for the deep
dissatisfaction with the notion of the state in the postwar period is

the argument that the state should not be deemed central to a definition of politics. The problem is however that, as long as states exist, they need to be defined, but the fact that the state needs to be defined does not mean that it cannot be differentiated from politics in general. In fact Weber's definition, I shall argue, allows us to do just this even if Weber himself declined to do so.

Politics in our view arises from conflicts of interest which exist in all societies. Government is the process which enables individuals to resolve these differences. 'Politics' and 'government' are therefore closely linked since politics raises the problems for which government has to find a solution. The idea however that government necessarily involves force is, as Easton himself has pointed out, an ethnocentric one.[18] It assumes that, because societies have governments, they must have states – an assumption which rests upon the Hobbesian argument that without the state order is impossible. The Weberian definition focuses our attention on the particular character of the state as an institution which claims a monopoly of legitimate force, and this definition enables us to differentiate between the state on the one hand and government on the other. After all, it is a fact that humankind has survived for most of its existence without the state[19] – that is to say, it has conducted its affairs without the presence of an institution claiming a monopoly of legitimate force. If we assume, as I believe we must, that throughout these hundreds of thousands of years people have nevertheless had some kind of orderly existence, it becomes possible on the basis of Weber's definition to conceptualize government without the state.

It is significant that Easton's critique of ethnocentrism arises out of his assessment of the importance of political anthropology for political theory, for it is precisely anthropological evidence which makes it possible to understand how (non-statal) governmental activities can exist. In gathering data about processes for settling disputes in ways which do not rest upon physical force, anthropologists compel us to acknowledge 'in any reasonable connotation of the term' that stateless societies possess government.[20] While earlier investigators sometimes supposed that it was only because tribal peoples were 'instinctively' conformist that they could order their affairs without states, the anthropologist Malinowski is generally credited with debunking this argument. Malinowski demonstrated that in all societies rules not only exist but are continuously challenged and broken. Disputes and quarrels are inevitable – indeed they are part of the social condition – so that, if society is to survive, mechanisms must be found to resolve conflicts, reconcile differences and generally carry out the activity which we can identify broadly as *government*.

It is unfortunate (as already hinted) that Weber himself is unwilling to accept the implication of his own definition. Although he rightly insists that the state seeks to monopolize legitimate force, he argues that all political groups exercise force on a territorial basis. Politics can exist outside the state and political institutions preceded the state: both however involve a 'relation of men dominating men'. Government for Weber is constituted by the 'directing authorities' of political corporate groups, but, like the state, they too involve legitimate violence.[21] He does not accept that political groups can be concerned with government without relying ultimately upon physical force for their authority. He therefore ignores a crucial distinction which his own definition nevertheless facilitates. In so far as Weber drew upon social anthropology for his view of politics and government, he was (it would seem) influenced by earlier anthropologists who still tended to speak of tribal governments in a state-like way.

Thus as late as 1940 Radcliffe-Brown (whom Easton criticizes) could define all government – even the government of a stateless society – as 'the organized exercise of coercion through the use, or the possibility of use, of physical force'.[22] With rather less historical justification, writers like Poggi follow Weber in distinguishing between state and politics but at the same time continue to identify politics with force.[23] The problem is that, if we identify politics in general with force, then the specificity of Weber's definition of the state is frustrated and what I have called the anthropological argument is simply brushed aside. In more recent anthopological literature on 'Governments without the State' (as Mair entitles Part One of her *Primitive Government*), it becomes clear why the Weberian identification of politics with force is misleading. It may be that even the smallest and simplest political communities have their own territory[24] and it is certainly true that the chiefs enjoy legitimacy and prestige. It can even be argued that in certain contexts – when warriors embark on war – authority is (at least) momentarily monopolized. But these attributes have none of the significance they have in the context of the state and for one basic reason. The force which is decisive in Weber's definition of the state is merely incidental when we take account of the idea of government as presented in the anthropological argument.

We shall see in chapter 10 how feminist anthropologists have linked organized force with statist patriarchy, and the point is that, while force may exist in *some* though by no means all tribal societies, it is not central to government in the way that it is central to the state. Clastres's Amerindian chiefs may enjoy prestige and legitimacy but this does not enable them to exercise coercive power. On the contrary, the chief who sought to give an order – a command backed by penal sanctions – would be met by certain refusal and a denial of further recognition. The chief's prestige as one who seeks to persuade people to co-operate and to stop insulting or fighting each other stems from his (the male identity is alas not incidental) skills as a persuasive and entertaining orator. In what Clastres calls 'society against the state', it is the community rather than the individual leader who remains the locus of power.[25]

Identifying government and order

In many stateless societies government is characterized by what has been called 'settlement-directed talking'. In this situation the political leader is a mediator rather than a 'judge' in a statist sense since he has no force at his disposal to secure compliance. Even the notion of an 'arbitrator' or 'mediator' can be misleading since third parties seeking to settle disputes may adopt diversionary strategies which involve pouring scorn on the disputants, organizing festivals and hunting expeditions or defusing tension by blaming themselves for the trouble which has arisen.[26]

What is decisive to governmental activities as evidenced here is not force but discussion, persuasion and negotiation with a view to reconciliation. Unlike the judicial processes which take place in state-centred societies, here there are no winners or losers: all feel that they have gained something and customary rules are loosely and flexibly interpreted. Force is not the ultimate incentive towards compliance with socially accepted rules, and, while there are sanctions which 'enforce' rules, these are 'quite the opposite' of what we normally understand as force.[27] The most dreaded and effective of these sanctions in the face of sustained anti-social behaviour is probably ostracism i.e. the withdrawal by other members from social contact and the withholding of essential forms of economic co-operation. Shaming, public ridicule, sorcery and the resort to supernatural agencies are related sanctions which may also be extremely unpleasant but they do not involve physical force. At the most, as Easton comments, the coercion of the group is psychological or moral in character, but to equate moral coercion with physical force would be to divest the idea of physical force of all its meaning.[28] When other governmental mechanisms fail, dispersal and fission may occur and indeed are relatively commonplace among hunters and gatherers where there are no crops to be harvested or more or less permanent dwellings to worry about. But again the resort to fission and dispersal as ways of resolving disputes is 'quite the opposite' of a resort to physical force.

It is in this context that we need to understand the use of physical force which does exist in some though not all stateless societies. Mair acknowledges that Hobbes's view of 'savage people' in America existing in a state of nature characterized by a war of all against all is not wholly without foundation. People in stateless societies are hardly the competitive and atomistic individuals that Hobbes imagined them to be, but it is true all the same that, in a number of instances, fighting is recognized as a legitimate means of obtaining redress. This does not however vindicate the notion that government necessarily involves force. Even if we grant the Hobbesian appearances of say feuding among the Nuer people in the Sudan, the use of force in cases like these is not 'a means of dominating others'.[29] Order is not secured *through* violence but comes about when the feuding lineages exhaust themselves and a third party successfully intervenes.

Even when the use of force occurs in stateless societies, it is not therefore prosecuted in a statist manner. The ordinary members of society are involved either as avenging lineage groups or volunteer warriors. Force, in other words, is not concentrated into specialized agencies which stand permanently 'above' and 'outside' society, and among the New Jale of Guinea, for example, fighting is highly formalized and carefully contained so as to minimize disruption to the life of the community. Peaceful relations are regarded as normal and the purpose of rules is to limit force. When the warriors return from a military expedition among Clastres's native American tribes, the war chief loses all his power and the group returns to its normal life.[30]

Force, in other words, is seen as threatening to governmental processes. Even in societies where violence is common, it is limited, ritualized and perceived as potentially harmful. Among some peoples like the !Kung of southern Africa the outbreak of interpersonal violence would lead to the fatal disruption of essential food-gathering tasks, and, in the case of the native American tribes whom Clastres studied, the outbreak of violence represents a *failure* of government undermining the prestige of the chief.[31] Thus we can certainly accept that government (however fluid and microcosmic its form) is endemic in human relationships since it is hard to see how people can live together in a society without a degree of predictability, stability and regularity. But force, as Schapera notes, is 'only one of the mechanisms making for orderly life' and it may or may not exist in political communities.[32]

This is why it is crucial in distinguishing government from the state to challenge the idea that the state is indispensable to securing order. Radically different 'principles' are at stake. If force is decisive in defining the state, order, community and co-operation are central to identifying government. What is decisive and essential in the case of the one is incidental and contingent in the case of the other. Government therefore is a process of regulating social behaviour. This is its 'essence' and therefore force, like the war chief's temporary 'monopoly' of power, is at best incidental to this process.

Government as part of the state

If the anthropological argument is correct, then government needs to be sharply differentiated from the state. Yet in much of the literature the two are treated either as synonyms or at least as indissolubly connected. Thus Laver for example accepts Weber's definition of the state but insists on describing the agency controlling a monopoly of legitimate force as *government*. Dahl, as we have seen, similarly identifies what he calls 'the Government' in explicitly Weberian terms.[33]

The anthropological argument conceptualizes government as a process predating the formation of the state. But what of government or governments which exist within the context of the state? It might be argued that while historically (or pre-historically) government existed outside of the state, in state-centred societies the two are inextricably linked. The way in which Miliband handles this distinction provides us with a useful insight into the problem. Miliband argues that when we are referring to national institutions in Britain, the USA, France, etc., it is easy to confuse the government with the state. Government, he argues, is *the political executive* of the nation which speaks on behalf of the state, which is invested with its power, and which has to take ultimate responsibility for its actions. If the functionaries of the state are acting improperly, it is the government which is expected to put the matter right.[34]

In Miliband's view government represents only *one* element within the state, the others being the administration, the judiciary, the military and the police, local and regional government and parliamentary assemblies. Taken together these six components constitute the *state system*. But while this is a distinction which is widely echoed elsewhere,[35] it is one which fails to harness fully the critical potential of Weber's definition. The anthropological argument suggests not only that government is distinct from the state but that government seeks to secure order and co-operation, whereas the state rests on force. The two operate according to a logic which is mutually exclusive.

Yet it might well be objected that Miliband's state system is (like Weber's own definition) a coherent and structured whole. Government is integrated into the wider system and does not function in a way which is antithetical to the state. Not only do laws have to be passed before they can be interpreted and administered, but these laws also have to be implemented through force. The six components of Miliband's state system broadly correspond to the four attributes of the Weberian definition. Each national institution claims a monopoly for its activity. This monopoly is defined in terms of a specific territory; legal and judical procedures secure legitimacy for the laws, while the police and army ensure that they are effectively carried out.

As in Weber's definition, the elements interrelate but they are not all of equal importance. Just as the basic element within Weber's definition is force so by analogy the basic elements within Miliband's state system are the army and the police. They provide the coercive muscle which, in Weberian terms, underpins the system as a whole. Just as legitimacy, territory and monopoly are relevant to Weber's definition but not 'basic', so likewise parliament, the judiciary, regional and national executives and the administration are relevant to the state system but it is the police and army which constitute its core.

It seems difficult to see how on this argument government is anything other than an integral part of an interrelated whole. It works not against the state but as an agent acting on its behalf. Miliband after all argues that Western governments at any rate support the interests of organized capital – an economically based ruling class – and the other elements of the system, the civil servants, judges, police and army officers, local and regional elites reflect this conflict of class interests. It would be difficult to see how in this situation legislatures could continue to function, or judges operate, or administrators implement the law without the existence of coercive mechanisms to enforce legal, judicial and administrative procedures. If the state system operates in the interests of a capitalist minority, then a good deal of force, deception and manipulation is required to ensure its cohesion and stability.

But the analysis raises an intriguing question. Although the non-coercive elements of the state system work to provide legitimacy, monopoly and territorial focus for the state, they are, in terms of Weber's definition (which Miliband himself endorses)[36] the formal, contingent and non-essential aspects of the system. Emphatically this does not mean that they are not important nor that the coercive agencies can exist without law-making, adjudicating and adminstering institutions. But if we accept the anthropological argument that the process of governing is not inherently statist in character, then a highly subversive question arises: does it follow that parliamentary assemblies, courts, administrations etc. have to be underpinned by coercive agencies or could we imagine them existing without an army and police force?

The anthropological argument suggests that, while the analogy between the Weberian definition and the state system is empirically persuasive, it is not logically conclusive. In practice it is hard to see how in the context of radical disparities of power, legislating, adjudicating and administering could take place without armies and the police to underpin them, particularly when these 'governmental' activities are monopolistic and territorially focused activities seeking to generate legitimacy of an exclusive kind. But if the analogy between Weber's definition and Miliband's state system is empirically persuasive, logically nevertheless it falters. For why should law-making, judging and administering have (*a*) to be accompanied by coercive agencies and (*b*) operate in a monopolistic and territorially exclusive way which makes this coercion necessary?

In other words if we expand Miliband's notion of government not only to embrace a national political executive but to conceive of government as making as well as executing, administering and adjudicating laws, it becomes possible in the light of the anthropological argument to ask the following question. Is it at all conceivable that government in this broad sense might take place in a way which is *not* monopolistic and territorially exclusive and therefore which does not require underpinning from coercive agencies like the army and the police?

Disentangling government from the state

Support for the anthropological argument can be found if we examine instances where government appears not as a formal part of the state system but as a social component with an identity and cohesion of its own. Whereas Laver (like many political scientists) treats government as a synonym for the state, Dahl for example, employs the term government as part of his 'ubiquitous' view of politics which he defines as any persistent pattern of human relationships that involves to a significant extent control, influence, power, or authority.[37] Governments are conceived as existing in families, trade unions, schools, businesses, etc.

The problem however with this argument is that governments of a social kind are not seen as qualitatively different from 'the Government' (i.e. state). All are political systems of varying shapes and sizes involving power, influence, control and authority. Although Laver does not acknowledge a concept of government outside the state, what is significant about his argument is that he does at least explore the mechanisms by which people can regulate their lives without relying upon physical force as an ultimate sanction. In that sense he endorses implicitly the relevance of anthropological evidence which has, as Roberts rightly comments, 'prompted acceptance of the idea that a large burden of social control must be borne in all societies by extra-legal mechanisms'.[38] Even in societies with states, Laver argues, individuals and voluntary bodies can order behaviour in a non-statist manner although he insists on characterizing (erroneously in my view) these examples of the 'anarchy of everyday life' as non-governmental in character.

Driving on the same side of the road, queuing in an orderly fashion, abiding by rules of etiquette – these and similar activities do not in Laver's view depend on the state for their efficacy. If we link Laver's 'anarchy of everyday life' argument with Dahl's concept of ubiquitous governments, it then becomes quite possible to speak of churches and universities, families, businesses and a host of voluntary organizations having governments while not existing as states. The anthropological argument can, it would seem, be extended from stateless societies to an analysis of what might be characterized as stateless moments within a state-centred system. As in stateless societies of a tribal kind, moral and psychological pressures are doubtless at work, but physical force does not provide, as it does for the state, an institutional underpinning. On this argument therefore government is not simply different from the state in the sense that it occurs within the state or as part of the state: it functions along different principles and with a different logic.

This argument receives support in Foucault's intriguing analysis of 'governmentality' in which he argues that historically the question of how to govern oneself, how to be governed, how to govern others, etc. is quite different to the question which Machiavelli posed – of how to rule the state. The notion of government stresses the continuity between self-government, morality, organizing family life and managing the economy. It is concerned with disposing of things with a plurality of specific aims. The governor 'does not have to have a sting, that is to say a weapon of killing, a sword, in order to exercise his power'. He requires patience rather than wrath since 'it is not the right to kill, to employ force, that marks the essence of the person of the governor'. Foucault's argument is that as the state becomes 'governmentalized', so the art of government loses these pluralistic and consensual features and the result is 'a singularly paradoxical phenomenon'.[39]

It is true that universities, families or cricket clubs (for example) apply rules which at the end of the day have 'ultimate' backing from the state both in the form of enabling statutes which confirm their status as private bodies and through the existence of coercive agencies able to intervene when informal procedures fail. In the same way it might be insisted that the individual is able to 'govern' his or her life in a Millian fashion only because the state itself provides a wider framework of law and order. Government (that is to say) even in its most fluid and embryonic form cannot be extricated from the all-pervasive reality of the state itself. Thus, to echo a comment of Hobhouse, the self-governing individual cannot be envisaged outside the confines of what he called 'the self-governing State'.[40]

But this objection is less damaging to the anthropological argument than it sounds. For while empirically it may be difficult to disentangle social government from the framework of the state, a distinction is still logically possible. The anthropological argument cannot be taken to mean that *existing* governments, as presently constituted in divided, hierarchical and state-centred societies, could continue to function unaltered in a stateless world. The point is rather that the Weberian definition (interpreted in a non-Weberian manner) makes it logically possible to separate government from state. The two operate according to different principles. Whereas the state claims a monopoly of legitimate force within a particular territory, government pertains to the pursuit of order within a community. Disentangling the two is crucial if a serious critique of the state is to be sustained.

SUMMARY

- The state can and must be defined. The definition which best serves the purposes of my critique here is Weber's formula that the state is an institution which claims a monopoly of legitimate force for a given territory.

- This is a coherent definition because it links inextricably together four attributes – monopoly, legitimacy, territory and force – thereby making it possible for us to to assess the state as a whole. It is also a structured definition which emphasizes the centrality of force.

- Weber's definition enables us to distinguish between the state and government – the latter being a process which resolves differences through sanctions which fall short of the use of physical force.

- Although it is true that in modern state-centred societies, state and government intertwine, it is important to separate them so that we can argue that a society without a state is nevertheless a society which has a government.

4

When Does the State Become the State?

In this chapter we will explore the contention that the state itself is only a modern institution since (it is argued) earlier polities lacked the kind of features which enable us to identify them as institutions claiming a monopoly of legitimate force for a particular territory. It is certainly true that the modern state differs significantly from its predecessors. However, once we emphasize the centrality of force, it becomes possible to see that pre-modern (but post-tribal) polities were states as well since they were governed by rulers who sought order through violent means.

We have argued so far that Weber's definition of the state provides a good starting point for our critique because it makes it possible to distinguish state from government. But this raises an important historical issue which we must now tackle – namely the question of when the state itself arises. Is the state as Weber defines it a purely *modern* phenomenon or can we speak of the state existing in ancient, medieval and 'pre-modern' times? This is an historical question which has important implications for the way we construe the Weberian definition.

Weber and the limitation argument

In resisting the indefinability thesis, I have defended a Weberian definition of the state (though not in a Weberian way) but this raises the question of where this definition stands in relation to what I now want to call the limitation argument. This accepts that states can be defined, but it contends that they are much more limited historically and geographically than is generally supposed.

It is argued that even if we accept that the state is an institution claiming a monopoly of legitimate force for a given territory, the modern (i.e. post-Renaissance) state is *the* state. The Greek polis, the Roman city state, empires, medieval principalities and kingdoms, Chinese, Indian and Islamic polities are not states at all. This limitation thesis can be given a geographical as well as an historical twist by arguing that, even within the modern period, some nations have governments rather than states since the state itself is a 'conceptual variable'. Societies (like Britain and the USA for example) which lack the historical, cultural and intellectual traditions of continental Europe remain stateless in character.[1]

The argument is an important one for my critique, for it is the centrality of force in Weber's definition which makes it possible and necessary to distinguish between states on the one hand and the notion of government on the other. If it can be shown however that organized force was used before the sixteenth century in governments which were not states or is utilized in contemporary societies which are themselves stateless, then the Weberian definition itself becomes somewhat problematic – at least in the way in which I have construed it.

Where does Weber stand in relation to the limitation thesis? His position is not entirely clear. On the one hand he appears to be arguing that the very definition of the state as an institution claiming a monopoly of legitimate force applies only to the state in modern times. On the other hand it seems that he accepts that his definition applies more generally while reaching its fullest development with the modern state.[2] Some 'Weberians' have argued that the modern state is merely a 'pleonasm' (the term 'modern' being superfluous).[3] What certainly complicates Weber's own position is the fact that, since he identifies politics in general with force, he tends to describe all political groups as having state-like features. Indeed at one point he suggests that there might even be a case for identifying the government of a tribal society as a state, but he adds that 'for our purposes it will be expedient to continue delimiting the "state" far more narrowly'.[4]

But how narrowly? If tribal societies do not have states, what about traditional feudal societies and empires? Weber argues that 'all states' may be classified according to whether their staff own the administrative means or are 'separated' from them. This suggests support for a broad rather than a 'limited' view of the state

since Weber himself identifies the process of 'separating' administrators from the means of administration with capitalism and
modernity.[5] Indeed Giddens criticizes Weber for 'generalizing back-
wards' by ascribing to all states features which only really pertain
to the modern[6] and, whatever the merits of the criticism, this again
suggests that despite some ambiguity in his statements Weber was
not a proponent of the limitation thesis. But should he have been?

The case for discontinuity

I shall concede right away that modern states are different from
earlier states and these differences are of the utmost significance in
making a critique of the state itself. If the indefinability thesis is
useful in the way it emphasizes the problematic features of the state,
the limitation thesis is valuable for the stress it places upon what is
new and different about the state in the modern period. Moreover
(as Weber himself suggests) it is possible to define the state in
general only when we have an understanding of the state as it exists
in modernity. This fact gives the limitation argument a good deal of
plausibility so that it is not surprising that some who broadly
subscribe to the Weberian definition argue at the same time that
the state is of relatively recent historical origin.

   Dunleavy and O'Leary are a case in point. They explicitly
identify themselves with those political theorists (among whom
they apparently number both Weber and Easton!) who regard the
state 'as an ineluctable feature of modernity'. Polities based upon
either kinship or feudal patronage are best categorised as 'pre-
modern governing systems'.[7] The modern state (or state per se) is
a special type of government with five characteristics and
these characteristics all appear to derive from the Weberian definition.

   We will comment on each in turn. The first is that the state is a
recognizably separate institution or set of institutions, so differentiated from the rest of society as to create 'identifiably public and
private spheres'.[8] In earlier polities this public/private divide is
blurred. The Greek polis lacked a conception of the individual as
a private person distinct and separate from the state. Even though
Roman law *is* celebrated for its distinction between public and
private law, this distinction was still partially overlaid by the fact
that laws derived in some unspecified way from the people. This is
even a problem with the notion of 'civil government' in Locke.
Individuals have yet to be 'abstracted' from 'government' as

'private' citizens in a quintessentially 'statist' way. Under feudal-ism, bonds of loyalty between king and vassals were direct and political – public and private at the same time. Assemblies sought to defend and maintain privileges and immunities of specific sections of the population so that a sharp separation between society and the state was nowhere drawn.[9]

Proponents of the limitation thesis lay particular stress in this context on the etymological argument about the 'state'. When the term 'state' itself was used with reference to earlier polities, it merely denoted, as Skinner points out, a quality, a high condition, a majesty which 'belonged' to kings and therefore treated public power in personal and charismatic terms. Even Machiavelli's use of the term *lo stato* implies the standing of the prince rather than the modern notion of a public power which acts apart from ruler and ruled and is thus separated from society and government.[10]

The second characteristic which Dunleavy and O'Leary identify with the state as a modern institution also appears to derive from the Weberian definition: the state as sovereign or supreme power within a given territory. Under the feudal system of rule, fragmen-tation and criss-crossing powers and claims made it impossible for any single ruler to claim a monopoly of legitimate force. The system has often for this reason been referred to as a form of anarchy – a state only in inverted commas.[11] No unitary sovereign was possible in a world of multiple associations, many of which – clergy, guilds, nobility, estates – had their own rules and courts. The only loyalty which transcended local attachments was allegi-ance to the universal Church and even at this level power was divided between Pope and Emperor. The presence of a clearly demarcated public power exercising sovereignty ties in with the concept of the state as the ultimate authority for all laws. By contrast, the assemblies of the Greek polis (for example) were more concerned with debating issues according to the values of the society than with making specific, uniform and general rules. Indeed throughout the Middle Ages law was conceived as merely one aspect of collective life – a set of practices, habits or customs. Making law was not a manifestation of *will* – a universal capacity to legislate – but merely a recognition of what already existed as a body of accepted rules in a society.[12]

The third characteristic constituting the state for Dunleavy and O'Leary relates to the fact that the state's sovereignty extends equally to all who hold formal positions of government or rule-making. Sovereignty is an abstract quality distinct from the person-nel who occupy particular offices, and applies to all who reside within a given territorial area. In the case of the Greek polis, however, protection was a political privilege really extending only to citizens. Slaves were excluded and even a stranger required the patronage of a citizen in order to claim this protection. Under feudalism, protection from attack depended upon fealty to a particular lord. Loyalties were not territorially demarcated but derived from particular dependencies and duties. The modern concept of territoriality implies demarcating *borders*, but pre-modern polities generally had frontiers where the physical environment – deserts, mountains, swamps, rivers, forests – was pre-eminently important in determining boundaries. Under feudalism, polities were often, as Hall and Anderson put it, 'territorially discontinuous'.[13]

Asserting sovereignty over a given territory implies that the state has the capacity to govern its subjects. Yet, as Giddens has noted, in traditional societies the general lack of capacity to penetrate the societies controlled makes it questionable whether we can actually speak of these polities exercising a regularized administration over the territory which they claim. This is why Held prefers to speak of subjects in pre-modern systems being ruled rather than governed.[14]

A fourth characteristic stressed by Dunleavy and O'Leary relates to the fact that the (modern) state's personnel are mostly recruited and trained for management in a bureaucratic manner. Earlier polities were run along what have been called 'patrimonial' lines in which offices were seen as the property of particular individuals and could be bequeathed and inherited as such. A bureaucratic system by contrast emphasizes the impersonality and rationality of rules which apply to all regardless. Even in absolutist systems in the sixteenth century when a centralized bureaucracy had emerged, positions were still sold to individuals in order to raise revenue for the monarchy – a practice which clearly works against the notion of the state as a form of impersonal and bureaucratically organized rule.[15]

Linked to this bureaucratic characteristic is the final item of Dunleavy and O'Leary's check list – the capacity of the state to extract monetary revenues (taxation) from its subject population. In pre-modern systems this capacity was limited. Military force had to be employed to exact tribute as an extraordinary and emergency measure, and in general rural communities were left to conduct their own affairs. Hall and Ikenberry have demonstrated vividly how deficiencies in transportation and communication were linked to a scarcity of resources which in turn reflected the absence of a social infrastructure capable of raising revenue or mobilizing the people.[16]

On the face of it, therefore, it would seem that there is a substantial discontinuity between the state as defined in Weberian terms and pre-modern but post-tribal polities. The evidence as presented above suggests that the state is an institution peculiar to the modern period, so that what Dunleavy and O'Leary call 'pre-modern governing systems' should not be called states at all.

The problem of force

The limitation thesis appears to derive logically from the Weberian definition, but, despite its apparent attractiveness, it has one overwhelming drawback. For we have argued that what gives Weber's definition its coherence and structure is the fact that it identifies force as the central feature of the state. In emphasizing the importance of the public/private divide, law, sovereignty, territory, bureaucracy and impersonal rule as the defining features of the state, the limitation thesis downgrades the centrality of force in Weber's definition. It is certainly true that the modern state asserts a claim to a monopoly of legitimate force in a manner which distinguishes it sharply from its predecessors, but the point is that the modern state is not the first political institution in history to have imposed force upon its subjects.

Hence D'Entreves is right to insist that the substantial differences between the political structures of the past and those of our own time can best be understood if we use the term 'state' to signify what is 'common to these different experiences'. The differences between say the Greek polis and the modern state may be legal, ethical and philosophical, but the first step in political theory requires the recognition that for any state to achieve its ends and set up its structures, 'force has to be resorted to' and 'force has to be effective'.[17] If we assume therefore that the state itself emerges only in the sixteenth century, what are we to say about these earlier polities? Are we to suppose that rulers before this time did not employ physical force in a concentrated and 'statist' manner when punishing, suspending, expelling or eliminating law breakers and dissidents?[18]

It is significant that when Giddens defines the state as a political organization able to mobilize the means of violence to sustain its rule, he includes the polities of empires and traditional societies within this definition.[19] For Roberts, what is crucial to the state is the 'presence of a supreme authority' with the power of life and death over his subjects. Since violence is an 'essential ingredient' to the state, he makes it clear that post-tribal polities deserve to be called states as well.[20] It is true (as we have noted above) that Greek political institutions (for example) did not embody concepts of sovereignty and the public/private divide in the way that these manifest themselves in the modern state. But Greek thinkers certainly provided important insights into the problem of ruling through force. The question of how to impose order through organized violence lies at the heart of those hierarchical ontological dualisms which Hannah Arendt complains are inherent in traditional political philosophy.[21] Of course Plato rejects the stark 'realism' of Thrasymachus who sees the ruler simply as a wild beast battening on its prey, and insists that rulers need wisdom, philosophical training and the access to 'noble lies'. But the fundamental problem of the state – how to create order through organized force, how to bring community to a divided society – is already apparent.

Take D'Entreves's analysis of St Augustine and Luther who see princes as the 'executioners' or 'scourges' of God, tackling evil with terror to bring order and peace to 'a world peopled by corrupt men'. Surely both can be said to exemplify the basic problem of the state. Machiavelli's use of the term 'state' may be neither consistent nor wholly modern but the question of exercising force to maintain order is central to his writings.[22] It is true that the patrimonial power which characterizes traditional states is very different from the impersonal and bureaucratized power of the modern state, but it still presupposes and precipitates the kind of conflicts which require organized force to resolve them. Studies of dynasties suggest that periods of stable individual rule are usually quite short and broken by forcible overthrow, but the relatively unsuccessful and incoherent character of this organized coercion does not detract from its repressive reality.[23] Traditional Islamic, Hindu and Chinese societies may sit on top of social relations which they can do little to alter, but their relatively insignificant infrastructural capacities are matched by high levels of formal despotism.[24] It is the organized violence of these despotic systems which make it entirely proper for Hall and Ikenberry to identify them as *states*.

The problem then is this. By driving a sharp conceptual wedge between modern states and post-tribal polities, we are in danger of downgrading what in Weber's view is the central feature of the state itself – its violence. Although the differences between ancient and modern states are significant, the limitation thesis is liable to distract us from what is a feature common to all forms of the state.

The anthropological argument and the limitation thesis

It is the great merit of the anthropological argument that it enables us to distinguish between state and government: the state is based upon force, while government involves conciliation, negotiation and persuasion in pursuit of order. If we argue, however, that only the modern state is the state, then the dramatic birth of an institution rooted in concentrated force is ignored, and the importance of the anthropological argument is lost.

Traditional political theory in general and social contract theory in particular saw the emergence of the state as a development of great significance. Those who expressed an interest in the birth of the state identified the state with organized force, and this identification is possible only when we embrace a broad rather than a 'limited' view of the state. The stateless society is not one in which despots blur the distinction between the public and the private by ruling along patrimonial rather than bureaucratic lines, articulating particularistic customs rather than making general laws. On the contrary, the stateless world is one which is relatively egalitarian and unhierarchical and where (even in the Hobbesian account) there is an absence of rulers able to utilize concentrated force. If the state is defined simply in terms of the institutions which characterize the modern state, this point is lost. By emphasizing (indeed absolutizing) secondary discontinuities which distinguish one form of the state from another, proponents of the limitation thesis miss the most important discontinuity of all: the gulf which separates co-operative government where sanctions are informal and diffuse from the coercive state based on the use of force.

Southall has argued that, although the stateless societies of the past were less developed than the state-centred societies which succeeded them, they contain nevertheless a number of positive and instructive features. They were societies in which the responsibility for maintaining social cohesion is much more widely dispersed throughout the adult population than is the case in state-centred societies. Indeed what we witness is 'the remarkable spectacle of societies positively maintaining themselves at a high level of integration without any obvious specialized means of enforcement' and this has undoubtedly led to new insights into politics in general.[25] But how is it possible for societies to be governed by leaders who have to persuade, negotiate, display generosity and mediate but who have, as we have seen, no organized force at their disposal to ensure compliance with rules?

In contrast to the stark inequalities and hierarchies which characterize states, the anthropological argument emphasizes the fact that, in what we can loosely call tribal societies, all enjoy much the same levels of material income and political influence (although as we shall see later males are becoming privileged), and all typically share the same culture, language and religion. Tribes have a vested interest in minimizing social differentiation, and hence (as Crone puts it rather dramatically), they have to be destroyed in order to make way for states.[26] Unless we emphasize the continuity (as well as the discontinuity) which exists between post-tribal polities and modern states, then the remarkable character of the stateless society is ignored. I have elsewhere briefly commented on the problem of origins in relation to the state,[27] but here it is worth noting how Hall and Ikenberry introduce a fascinating element of 'voluntarism' into this question when they suggest that, even where tribal peoples were able to create the material conditions and political institutions appropriate for a state, they frequently declined to do so. A cyclical pattern can be detected. A movement towards a state in the form of more centralized chiefdoms is followed remorselessly by repeated retreats once the implications of permanent rule are realized. Human beings, so good at evasion hitherto, suddenly became caught inside permanent organizations of coercion.[28]

De Jasay has suggested that a first step to an adequate understanding of the state is to think about an environment without one.[29] But if the state itself is defined as the modern state, then no real insight into the nature of how order can be secured without organized coercion is possible. The point is – and the classical political texts of the pre-modern period eloquently bear this out – that post-tribal polities are already locked into the problem of trying to impose order upon radically divided societies in a relatively specialized and explicitly coercive fashion.

Force, territory and law

We have already conceded that there is significant discontinuity between pre-modern and modern states. Clearly, developed notions of the public/private divide, sovereignty, law-making, territoriality, administrative and bureaucratic organization are characteristic only of the modern state. However once the centrality of force is emphasized and full weight is given to the drama of the state's origins, then the discontinuity between the modern state and its predecessors can be properly evaluated.

The Dunleavy/O'Leary check list examined earlier essentially elaborates the three attributes of the Weberian definition which I have identified as formal in character – territory, monopoly and legitimacy (although Dunleavy and O'Leary are, for reasons we will examine later, reluctant to use this latter term). If we start with territory, it is worth noting that even a 'limitationist' like Parekh has argued that post-tribal polities (as opposed to modern states) occupied 'specific and easily identifiable territorial areas'.[30] It is perfectly true that territorial boundaries here are not as sharply focused as they are in modern states, but once we emphasize the centrality of force it becomes easier to understand why some notion of territorial boundary is inherent in the state itself.

If force is to be applied by particular rulers who have the power of life and death over their subjects, this force must be contained and bounded in some way. Those who embrace a 'broad' definition of the state have no difficulty in suggesting that rule takes place over a specific population and territory. It may well be that not all inhabitants who are subject to force are entitled to protection but, if rulers expect compliance to their acts of force, this rule must have some kind of territorial focus. The very notion of organized violence implies a 'test' of within what boundaries and over which peoples the state can enforce its will.[31]

The point about territory applies also to the question of law. Although the character of law in the modern state clearly differs from traditional notions of law, organized force itself requires a degree of explicitness that entitles us to identify the decrees of traditional states as legal in character. If organized violence operates within territorial boundaries (as it must), it also has to be focused as a specific act of will since it is targeted against specific subjects. Force involves concentrating power, and therefore diffuse customs have to be articulated increasingly as particular laws – as a 'legal' will (as Hall calls it). State power is 'formalized' power, and Held, in his broad definition, identifies the state as 'a legal system, backed by a capacity to use force'.[32]

All this makes it possible to understand why the basis for the modern state is founded in both the theory and the practice of post-tribal polities or, as Giddens calls them, traditional states. Aristotle, for example, had begun to develop the notion of the state as a legal concept even though his classificatory systems mixes a 'government of laws' in with moral pursuits and has a place for 'exceptional men' who can ignore these laws. Roman writers placed great emphasis upon the legal character of political structures. Since rulers occupy offices which are created by law, state power emerges as something which is impersonal, thus making it necessary to distinguish between what is public and what is private.[33]

Making force the central attribute of the state implies therefore a dimension of territoriality; the presence of a legal will and institutions; and an embryonic public/private divide. After all no ruler can exercise concentrated power without possessing some kind of specialized administration. It is true that this administration is run, as we have seen, along patrimonial rather than bureaucratic lines, but traditional states still have what Giddens calls a 'hierarchy of officials who specialize in administrative tasks' even if tension exists between centralized control over the means of violence and the decentralized military power wielded by local warlords.[34] As a 'means of domination', the traditional state like the modern state exists as a differentiated, specialized and permanent organ of political and administrative action, which however imperfectly 'is applied to a territory'.[35]

We argued in chapter 3 that the Weberian definition emphasizes force as the central but not the exclusive characteristic of the state. Territory, law, and administration as a public and relatively specialized activity are also involved. As formal attributes of the state, these aspects can be understood only in relationship to the force which underpins them, and by stressing the centrality of force it becomes possible to identify these characteristics in earlier forms of the state where they are less explicitly and coherently developed. The limitation thesis therefore not only tends to distract us from what might be called the 'content' of the state but it fails to see just how 'state-like' these formal attributes are when confronted in a less advanced stage of their development.

Sovereignty and the continuity problem

If some of the 'formal' attributes of the state can be found in earlier states, where does this leave the crucial question of monopoly or sovereignty? It may be that the post-tribal polity involves coercive rule through a legal administration operating within a territorial framework, but unless it can be said to possess a monopoly of legitimate force it does not really conform to the Weberian definition. Surely the concept of sovereignty (which I link here to monopoly) is a modern concept which applies only to the modern state? D'Entreves, for example, has argued that the problem of the birth of the modern state is nothing other than the rise and final acceptance of the concept of sovereignty while Forsyth, who is also sympathetic to a broad view of the state, insists nevertheless that post-tribal polities were too divided and compartmentalized to be considered sovereign.[36]

This position is, it seems, advanced also by Giddens, who at one point limits his definition of the state to the presence of a political organization which is territorially ordered and able to mobilize the means of violence to sustain its rule. He deliberately declines to 'accentuate' the monopolistic (and legitimate) character of this force on the grounds that the latter are key elements of the modern state and 'help to constitute its distinctiveness as compared with traditional states'. If some of the attributes of Weber's definition apply to all states, others, it appears, extend only to the modern state.

I shall deal later with the problem of legitimacy, but it is revealing that on the question of monopoly Giddens equivocates. At a later point in his argument he accepts that traditional as well as modern states lay claim to 'the formalized monopoly over the means of violence within their territories'.[37] The point is that the very notion of force as a method of rule is tied not merely to territoriality, public administration and law: it also connects with the idea of monopoly. To use force is to concentrate power, and this is why Nicholson, in an interesting analysis of the problem, distinguishes between force and conflict. Conflict, he argues, captures the notion of an activity dispersed among multiple actors: force on the other hand suggests concentration and unity. 'By the very nature of force, only one body is able successfully to back its decisions by force.' Hence the use of force in society must form a 'unitary system'.[38] As a mode of rule force implies domination, and domination implies monopoly.

The notion of monopoly may be problematic and contested, but this is true also (as we shall see) of all the attributes of the state. The point however is that even where a number of rulers in different spheres make chaotic and conflicting claims upon their subjects, all necessarily seek to impose an administration which is exclusive, and laws which are monopolistic. This absolutism is inherent in the very idea of rule by force. Nor are we denying that sovereignty (which we link here to Weber's notion of monopoly) is embryonic only within pre-modern polities. Traditional empires like the Roman confined universalizing concepts within their own territories, and it was only the medieval theorists who sought to construct a much more universal notion of law and sovereignty by identifying the impersonal rule of law with the power of God. Modern statecraft employs a notion which is both universal and secular: it recognizes the sovereignty of all other states and does not treat its own institutions as in principle generalizable across the rest of the world.[39] If the notion of an absolute power expressed through impersonal and rational rule is new, the idea is nevertheless rooted in earlier concepts.

The Romans had already developed the notion that there resides in a community a 'supreme power' from which the law emanates. If traditional rulers did not explicitly claim to be sovereigns in the modern sense, they did seek to impose decisions by force in a way which *implicitly* denied the right to use force by their rivals. Prior to Bodin a sixteenth-century champion of absolute monarchy, traditional rulers had always been 'sovereigns' in the sense that they were acknowledged at least by those lower in the state apparatus to be the 'supreme authority' in the political order.[40] True, they were not particularly effective and they sat astride societies they could not really control. But the modern concept of sovereignty can be understood only if we trace its roots back to more chaotic and diffuse notions of sovereignty in post-tribal polities.

We have already argued that all states imply a concept of territory, but territory for its part implies a notion of concentration which links it to sovereignty. A law-making power within a territorially demarcated state must be exclusive and thus in some sense 'sovereign'. When Poggi comments that 'rule always involves a more or less exclusive disposition over the means of coercion', this captures precisely the linkage between territory, law, monopoly and sovereignty. To say, as he does, that the great bulk of the population under feudalism were looked upon essentially as 'the objects of rule' is to recognize that they were subject to a force which was (implicitly at least) exclusive and supreme, monopolistic and sovereign in character.[41]

None of this denies the undeveloped, inchoate character of earlier states. The point is however that to understand the modern state we need to grasp the real continuity which exists with its predecessors. Any individual of rank could be a 'sovereign' in the fifteenth and sixteenth century, whereas for Bodin there can only be one. But this highly concentrated view of power presupposes the existence of earlier notions of sovereignty and political supremacy. Even the idea of the impersonality has its roots in earlier periods. Although hereditary kingship in its original form vested sovereignty in an individual, it is the position itself, Poggi argues, rather than the individual which was 'the pivot of the system'. Absolutism – generally seen as laying the basis for a modern statecraft – built upon older notions of despotic rule by incorporating the state itself in the person of the monarch. Once power was concentrated in this extraordinary way, the ground had been prepared for the idea that the supreme authority of an individual should be tied to a more generalized interpretation of state power.[42]

We shall deal later in more detail with the particular problem of legitimacy, but there is – to reiterate – nothing in my critique of the limitation thesis which would deny that, in pre-modern states, sovereignty is conceptually inchaote, monopoly imperfect, administration patrimionial and laws largely customary. But the point is that what might be called the 'formal' attributes of the state as presented in Weber's definition are tied to the 'substantive' exercise of rule by force. Once we place force at the centre of our understanding of the state, as Weber himself did, it becomes possible to see how the modern state can be grasped only as a developed form of the state itself.

SUMMARY

- The supporters of what I call the 'limitation argument' contend that Weber's definition really applies only to the modern state.

- Ancient, medieval and imperial polities should not be called 'states' (it is argued) on the grounds that they lack the distinct and differentiated features and the bureaucratic and organizational character of the modern state.

- While it is true that the modern state is significantly different from its predecessors, the limitation argument fails to emphasize the central part which force plays in identifying the state. As a result 'limitationists' overlook the fact that, wherever rulers secure order through force, a polity necessarily exhibits a statist character.

- An emphasis upon force also makes it possible to locate the (admittedly) embryonic development of the other attributes of Weber's definition – monopoly, territory and legitimacy – within traditional or pre-modern states.

5

The State as Contradiction

I shall now argue that whilst traditional states were unable to impose a monopoly of legitimate force upon a given territory in a coherent and convincing manner, this is true also of modern states. *All* states assert a monopoly which they do not and cannot possess, and this contradictory identity manifests itself in all the attributes enumerated in the Weberian definition. It explains why states must be defined both 'structurally' as well as 'functionally', and why it is that the more modern the state is, the more problematic it becomes.

We have seen that, while the limitation thesis highlights the distinct features of the modern state, it erroneously supposes that earlier polities do not also display statist elements of territoriality, monopoly, sovereignty and law. The great merit of the Weberian definition is not only that it makes it possible to assert a substantial continuity between earlier and modern states but that, in identifying the state in terms of its claim to assert a monopoly of legitimate force for a given territory, it enables us to demonstrate just what a curious and contradictory institution the state really is.

Logic and the problem of success

Giddens has argued for a modified version of the limitation thesis. Traditional polities are indeed states but Weber's definition really 'fits' only the modern state. In essence his argument centres on the question of success and draws our attention to what is one of the most contestable features of the Weberian definition. Weber, it will be recalled, refers to the state as an institution which successfully claims a monopoly of legitimate force within a given territory, although in one of his definitions 'successfully' is placed in parenthesis. Giddens's argument is basically that while traditional states assert territorial force (and at times he accepts that they do so monopolistically), he insists nevertheless that only with the modern state is this assertion of force *successful*.[1]

Our analysis of pre-modern polities or traditional states certainly points to the tentative and incomplete way in which legitimate force is exercised. Here the state lacks a distinct public identity. Its force is openly challenged and rival bodies co-exist which also claim sovereignty. Law-making does not exist as a pure act of public will, but articulates custom and practice in a way which is clearly intertwined with the values of the community. The problems of coherence are real enough in traditional states but the question we need to pose is this. Are we entitled to assume that with the modern state these problems vanish? Must we suppose that, with the modern state, the exercise of a monopoly of legitimate force meets with success where previously it was dogged with failure and contradiction?

The anthropological argument which I have presented in chapters 3 and 4 rests upon the proposition that the state comes into existence because people cannot settle their conflicts of interest through negotiation and persuasion. Organized, centralized and concentrated force has to be employed – a physical force which is central and distinctive to the state. The force is necessary because people will not comply with rules in a voluntary manner. They resist, they rebel, they dissent. The origins of the state are complex and multicausal but there can be no doubting, as Hall and Ikenberry have stressed, the distinctively coercive character of the organisation which emerged as the state.[2] This coercion merits emphasis because it lies at the heart of what I shall call 'the problem of success'.

To exercise force, I have argued, is to seek a power which is monopolistic in character. But force is not exercised by the state simply once and then never again. It is exercised continuously. Its continuous exercise necessarily presupposes the existence of competitive acts of force which for their part continuously challenge the state's own pursuit of order. Weber is certainly conscious of this as a problem. Hence his definition of the state has a tentative quality. The state, he says, is an institution which merely 'claims' a monopoly of legitimate force. Taylor highlights Weber's problem when he protests that to claim a monopoly is not good enough: the state must actually exercise it. But to insist that the state actually should exercise a monopoly of legitimate force then makes the test too stringent. As Nozick comments, within the boundaries of the state there may exist groups such as the Mafia, the KKK, White Citizens Councils, striking unionists and the Weathermen that also use force.[3]

Weber seeks to resolve the dilemma by suggesting that, if the state does not actually exercise a monopoly of legitimate force, it does at least 'successfully claim' one. But this of course merely expresses the same problem in different terms since the question now focuses on what constitutes success. After all, as Giddens himself concedes, the success which the modern state supposedly enjoys in asserting a monopoly of legitimate force is far from self-evident. Its claim to exercise this monopoly, he asserts cautiously, is 'more or less successful'. But how successful is this? There are (Giddens notes) very many instances even in current times of states whose monopoly of violence is chronically threatened by armed groups or insurgent movements, and there are diffuse levels of violence in minor contexts in even the most politically quiescent societies.[4] This is a point which has of course become painfully apparent with the turbulent upheavals accompanying the birth of the 'new world order'. It may be that modern states are rather *more* successful in asserting a monopoly of legitimate force than traditional states – a point to which we will return – but Giddens's own qualifications indicate clearly that this success is only relative.

The 'relativity' of the state's success raises a problem of logic with the Weberian definition of the state. On the one hand we have already argued that the definition is coherent and structured since its four attributes – territory, monopoly, legitimacy and force – are logically interrelated and structurally differentiated. Force constitutes the 'essence' or 'basis' of the state: monopoly, territory and legitimacy its formal and secondary features. Hence we accept that the state has what Parekh has called 'an inherent logic'[5] and this inherent logic makes it imperative to move beyond the curate's egg approach by assessing the state as a whole.

On the other hand, if the state has an inherent logic, it has a logic which is deeply troubled. This is a problem at which Giddens hints but does not directly address or resolve. The fact is that, in claiming to exercise its monopoly of legitimate force, the state is never wholly successful nor is it wholly unsuccessful. It is of necessity only *partially* successful. Hence, as Hall and Ikenberry argue, 'the word "tends" . . . could be appended to virtually every statement in the definition'.[6] The state claims a monopoly but does not have one. The claim has to have some credibility, but at the same time this credibility is never more than partial and problematic.

Take the question of force in a situation in which a state wholly fails to assert the monopoly of violence it claims. In these circumstances its coercive organisations disintegrate (as when a state loses a civil war or yields to foreign conquest and rival claimants take its place). The argument is straightforward and uncontroversial. But the converse is also true. The state which *succeeds* – absolutely rather than relatively, completely rather than partially – in asserting a monopoly of force also loses its identity. Imagine a state which actually exercises an uncontested monopoly of force in the sense that no other body or persons in the society exercise any force at all. No rebels, no outlaws, no criminals. Lacking rivals, what would be the point of such a state having a monopoly of force at all? Under these (admittedly rather extraordinary) circumstances the coercive organizations would also disintegrate (however gradually), not because they have been overthrown by a rival force but simply because they have become redundant.

It is true that Weber argues that the state does not claim to exercise a monopoly of force per se, but a monopoly of force which is *legitimate*. This point is often contested even by those who generally endorse a Weberian view of the state, and we will deal with this question in detail in chapter 6. But here it is worth noting that the legitimate character of the state's force serves to heighten the illogicality of its identity and the problematic character of its success. Imagine a state which successfully monopolizes all legitimacy within a given territory. Under these circumstances none of its subjects have cause to dissent from the moral justifications the state invokes in passing laws. No dissent, no subversion, no law-breaking, no criminals. As a result there would be no need for force. Government, as we have defined it, would exist but the state disappears.

If the state is to be a state, it must of necessity assert a legitimacy which is contested and challenged. In the case of rebels and 'dissidents', the contestation of legitimacy is explicit. In the case of criminals, it is implicit but it is real all the same. It is true that this is a contentious point but it must be remembered that the state's laws are intended apply to *all* without exception. Crucial to their legitimacy is their purported impersonality and universality. To break these laws is (however implicitly) to contest their impersonality and universality and therefore to challenge attributes which are crucial to the law's legitimacy.

The tentativeness of the Weberian definition is thus all-revealing. To say that the state merely 'seeks' legitimacy, 'claims' a monopoly and is only 'more or less' successful is to acknowledge that the state's identity is troubled. The problem is a logical one, for it is not simply a question of suggesting that the state does not quite succeed in living up to its ideals. Complete success would mean ultimate oblivion. A conflict exists between the assertion and the reality, the theory and practice of an institution which has of necessity to strive towards a goal which it cannot possibly realize. Force has to be asserted monopolistically because it is continuously challenged, while the state would have no reason to declare itself the sole legitimate representative of all its subjects if all its subjects saw it that way.

Our argument then is basically this. What is obvious in the case of traditional states is also true of modern states. All states, traditional or modern, assert a monopoly of legitimate force which they do not and cannot have. Logically, as we have argued, the state *must* assert this monopoly in order to be a state. But equally because it *is* a state, this monopoly is only a relative one. States only successfully claim this monopoly because others successfully challenge it.

Territorality, nationality and law

The state is, I have argued, both logical and illogical. Its 'inherent logic' is a contradictory one. I have looked at this problem in relation to the state's claim to exercise a monopoly of legitimate force, but this logical contradiction is also vividly demonstrated in relation to the territorial dimension of state power. Here (as we have seen) the exercise of force requires rulers to assert their prerogatives over one group of inhabitants in particular and this group acquires its specific identity as the inhabitants of a given *territory*.

With modern states, this territorial identity, as Parekh puts it, becomes 'overarching and dominant',[7] and it might be supposed that as a consequence territory is now clear and coherent as an attribute of the state. Yet in modern as in traditional states, there is challenge and contestation. All states are confronted by those who do not accept the territorial identity ascribed to them. The more radical the dissenters, the less likely they are to see themselves as members of the 'nation' and subscribe to the dominant political culture in terms of which the state identifies itself.

Challenge and contestation do not only occur within territories. They occur also *between* territories and both the champions and the detractors of the territorial identity link the two. Those who see themselves at war with the state seek allies abroad while states find it impossible to resist the temptation to connect internal dissidents with external enemies. Indeed the more vigorously the state asserts its territorial integrity and identity, the more manifest is the challenge from within and without. Vincent is reluctant to identify the state with territoriality since, as he notes, states will often disagree on boundaries and claim quasi-jurisdictional interests beyond these boundaries. This means that territory is 'not an entirely safe or definite guide'. He makes a similar point about the problem of nationhood. Despite its common usage, he argues, there is no 'theoretical warrant' for the concept of a 'nation state'. 'Whereas States do exist and can be explained juridically, nations are emotive artifices.'[8]

Two points are particularly worth noting here. The first is that there is certainly a link between territory and nationality. What gives a territorial identity its overarching and what Parekh also calls its 'quasi-ontological significance'[9] is the relationship between the two. Once sovereignty in its modern form develops as a power which is impersonal and abstract, then the territorial 'container' for this power begins to assume a national form. As Giddens comments, nationalist symbols provide the 'moral component' of sovereignty,[10] for clearly loyalties do not exist in the abstract. They must be given cultural content and linguistic focus. This is why sooner or later the state is compelled not only to territorialize its subjects but also to 'nationalize' them.[11] The people comprising a nation became the source from which the state derives its legitimacy so that in terms of its 'inherent logic' the exclusivity of the state in its jurisdiction over its territory is counterpointed by the exclusivity of the nation.

It is therefore misleading (to make my second point about Vincent's comment) to assume that states have 'firm' identities whereas nations do not. On the contrary, if nationalism is the 'emotive artifice' which Vincent suggests, its theoretical incoherence arises as part and parcel of the incoherence of the state itself. Nationalism asserts an ideal unity which is continuously contradicted in practice. It is perfectly true that states do not coincide with nations. The single 'national' language which generally characterizes the nation state is invariably superimposed upon a variety of local languages and dialects which might be harshly repressed or slowly uprooted by an expanding public education system.[12] In other words the national unity in terms of which states increasingly assert their identity is of a contradictory kind. Beetham has commented ruefully that it is only the exceptional nation state that does not have within its borders minority nations or sub-nations.[13] We would go further. The problem of nationality is not simply empirical: it is also a logical one. The assertion of national identity through the state signals both external and internal challenge and division. As nation states find themselves beset with dissenters and rebels, increasing emphasis is placed upon the 'national' character of their territorial exclusivity.

National identity is therefore a problematic part of a problematic whole. The fact that nationality like territory seems slippery and 'artificial' does make it any the less 'essential' as a defining attribute of the state. On the contrary, it is precisely because territory and nationality are always to a greater or lesser degree contested that they have to be underpinned by the state's monopoly of legitimate force. Vincent believes that, while nations may be fuzzy and emotive and the territorial principle unreliable, the state itself is a coherent entity. Why? Because it defines itself juridically – in terms of the *law*. Yet the contradictory character of the state embraces all its attributes, and the law is subject to the same problem of contradiction which afflicts the principle of territoriality and nationhood. Whereas Rousseau speaks grandly of obeying a law one prescribes to oneself, he also notes that laws (at least in the state) exist only because people *break* them.[14] How stable and unambiguous, it is tempting to ask, is the law when it is imposed in a statist way? The apparent uniformity, homogeneity and universality which particularly characterize laws in their modern form belie their 'fuzzy', contested and contradictory character.

Structural versus functional views of the state

The notion of 'success' in the way the state claims a monopoly of legitimate force raises logical problems (I have suggested) which extend to the state's identity as a whole. Once this point is grasped, it becomes possible to see why we also need to challenge Weber's insistence that the state should be defined 'sociologically' in terms of its means rather than in terms of its ends. Weber commands quite widespread support[15] in arguing for a 'structural' definition of what the state *is* as opposed to a 'functional' definition of what the state *does*. What is peculiar to the state (Weber argues) is its 'means' – its use of physical force – whereas its 'ends' are common to many organizations in society.

In one sense this 'structural' definition seems helpful since states can indeed undertake many activities (i.e. serve many 'ends') which are not inherently state-like in character. They can run health services, manage post offices and own industries as well as organize the army, police and prisons. It is true, as New Right critics readily point out, that the state's involvement in welfare functions is funded from the public purse and at the end of the day people *have* to pay their taxes. But, on the face of it, it seems perfectly possible for the state to hand many of its 'functions' to social or private bodies while continuing to exercise its monopoly of legitimate force. Stressing means rather than ends – structures rather than functions – appears necessary if we are to focus on the specificity of the state.

This argument seems to be strengthened by the unsatisfactory character of definitions of the state which simply emphasize its *functional* character. If for example the state is defined as an institution which 'functions' to secure order and social cohesion, then logically *any* institution which pursues this end becomes part of the state. Defined in this way, the state acquires an almost infinite institutional elasticity and the distinction between state and society (let alone state and government) is obliterated as a consequence.[16] Some 'functionalists' like Easton prefer (as we have seen) not to speak of the state at all, but even those functionalists who continue to analyse political processes in terms of the state are unable (as Vincent rightly complains) to tell us what the state is. By identifying the state in terms (say) of the differentiation, autonomization, institutionalization and universalization of political processes, the problem of differentiating the state from other administrative and social bodies becomes extremely acute.[17]

However it does not follow from this that we have the choice of defining the state *either* functionally in terms of its ends *or* structurally in terms of its means. On the contrary, the fact is that we cannot understand what the state *is* unless we also understand what it *does* and vice versa. If there is a 'specificity' problem with regard to functionalist or 'ends oriented' definitions of the state, this is no less true of structural definitions which emphasize means. To define the state adequately, attention needs to be paid to both ends *and* means. After all Weber himself accepts that other bodies and individuals also exercise force and it is precisely because the 'means' (like the ends) are shared by others that the state has to assert its monopolistic claims.

It is revealing therefore to see that in practice many 'Weberians' find that they are unable to speak of the state's structures without importing a functional dimension into their analysis. Thus, while

Barker defends Weber's structural argument, he also comments that whereas many institutions claim legitimacy, they do so 'for different purposes'. Only the state claims authority so as to (as Barker puts it) 'legitimize coercion'.[18] It does not simply pursue order: it pursues order through vanquishing its adversaries. This is the *end*, as Barker's language makes clear, which the state pursues, and it is a distinctive end which is intelligible only in relationship to the state's distinctive means.

It is for this reason that Hall and Ikenberry present their essentially Weberian definition as one which is both institutional and functional in character. It is true that they find that history sometimes makes it necessary 'to decouple the linkage' since in Latin Christendom in the early Middle Ages the provision of order, rules of war and justice was made by the Church rather than 'by the puny and transient states which existed within its boundaries'.[19] But this is really a terminological problem which does not affect our argument. The state has to be identified in both structural and functional terms, and, if the puny and transient institutions to which Hall and Ikenberry refer were unable to function as states, it becomes questionable whether they can be called states at all.

Vincent has argued that when the state is defined purely in functional terms, not only do we blur the distinction between state, government and politics, but we ignore the state's inherently problematic character.[20] Indeed (as we have seen), if we define the state solely in terms of its functions rather than its structures, we are in danger of obliterating its identity altogether. This is also true when we seek to define the state in purely structural terms. Emphasizing structure at the expense of function leads to an abstract view of force which identifies it with politics in general and thus distracts us from the peculiarity of the state itself. Once we abstract the structural dimension of the state from its functional one, the definition as a whole loses both its specificity and its problematic character. Many institutions seek order and, as the anthropological argument acknowledges, self-help bodies in stateless societies also exercise force. The point about the state is that it pursues order and exercises force in a particular and distinctive manner.

What makes both the ends as well as the means of the state specific is the fact that the institution claiming a monopoly of legitimate force imposes a *kind* of order on society which no other institution is capable of doing. The state concentrates and centralizes force in a way which is monopolistic and exclusive and it seeks order through methods which can never be more than partially successful. Only a definition which focuses upon *both* structure and function can capture the curious reality of the state as an institution which claims an end which its very means prevent it from actually realizing.

Poggi's ingenious attempt to defend a purely functional characterization of the state demonstrates the problem. The state, Poggi tells us (quoting Heller), organizes and activates social processes 'grounded in the historical need that some modus vivendi be achieved among the contrasting interests operating in a given section of the globe'. This is however a bland and uncritical definition since in reality, as we have seen, the 'modus vivendi' which the state achieves among 'contrasting interests' is under continuous challenge from those who feel excluded and who are the particular targets of state force. The social processes which are 'activated' by the state (as Poggi puts it) are in part the same processes which necessarily threaten this modus vivendi. In other words the function is also a dysfunction – i.e. it works in a contradictory manner.

Poggi misses this point because he does not define the state in terms of 'the institutional patterns governing its operations'. He specifically declines to do this, he tells us, because there is a 'wide discrepancy' between the undertakings and the outcomes (the aims and achievements) which characterize the emergence of the state historically. He is determined to present the state functionally without actually defining it structurally since a definition in terms of both structure and function would necessarily lead him to the unpalatable conclusion that states pursue ends which always elude them. Given Poggi's general view that the state is a 'good thing', he is anxious to avoid an analysis of the state which presents it in this problematic and contradictory manner.[21]

Indeed this is precisely why, as we noted in chapter 2, that some political theorists declare the state indefinable, for the paradox is that a coherent definition of the state must identify the organization as an incoherent institution. The problem is not solved by trying to avoid a definition: it is solved only by confronting the institution's inherently problematic and contradictory character. An abstract structuralism like an abstract functionalism makes this point impossible to grasp.

Modernity and the state and society divide

We have argued that all states are public, monopolistic, legal, territorially focused and sovereign bodies, even though we have readily conceded that in pre-modern institutions these attributes are particularly inchaote, incoherent and incomplete. We are now in a position to see why the modern state plays such a central role in illuminating the character of the state in general, for it is only in the modern period that the state can be explicitly identified as an institution which is recognizably separate – an institution which appears to be distinct, independent or autonomous.

It is the modern state which proclaims its institutional and conceptual divorce from society (and indeed from government as its executive agency). It is only with the modern state that law is declared to be an impersonal act of will in which, as D'Entreves notes, the stern, solemn figures who wear the gowns and uniforms are mere office-bearers or functionaries whose competence is conferred by laws.[22] The modern state is distinctive and autonomous because it is also highly abstract. Its abstract and impersonal character is graphically expressed in the notion of sovereignty as a power which is absolute, illimitable and concentrated. It is the state's character as a sovereign body which encapsulates its radical separation from society.

Hence it is clear that the limitation thesis, as I have called it, is right to emphasize the distinctiveness of the modern state. A 'state tradition' (as Dyson describes it) is not well developed in the political culture of countries which either stress the importance of dividing powers in federal structures or see the state simply as a synonym for the nation or community as a whole. A 'disposition' towards identifying the state requires an historical tradition which emphasizes its 'primacy, autonomy and sovereignty'.[23]

It does not however follow that, because the distinction between the state and society is sharply and explicitly developed only with modernity, this distinction corresponds to social reality. On the contrary, as we shall now see, the 'abstraction' of the state is a mystifying appearance. The more the autonomy, impersonality and sovereignty of the state is stressed, the more sharply its problematic and contradictory character is highlighted. Sovereignty, as it has been well said, means that all power comes and goes from one source.[24] Essential to the notion of sovereignty is its *universal* character. It applies to, superintends and underpins a territorially demarcated society *as a whole*. As a logical concept, sovereignty cannot be limited and hence, though distinct from society, it also embraces society. It is separate from individuals and yet it also 'constitutes' them as citizens – 'abstract' individuals who are equal before the law as the common members of a common territory. Though distinct from church and family and all other social organizations, the sovereign state regulates these organizations, forbidding them to act in any way it disapproves.

On the one hand we have a development which seems highly positive and which (as we shall see) contains the key to unlocking the problem of legitimacy. The state now has an identity which sets it apart from society. This separatism means that the state cannot claim to encompass and control the totality of social existence. Posts are not to be given to favoured individuals on the basis of wealth, rank or religion, but what Poggi calls 'a set of filters of significance, of standards of mediation, of coding and decodings' blocks off such direct linkages.[25] Criteria for state employment are publicly sanctioned, and legally embodied frameworks are laid down for individuals to pursue diverse private interests.

On the other hand this separatism is made possible only by a notion of the state which is more explicitly absolutist and univeralist than ever before. The notion of sovereignty can only imply that what is private is itself constituted by what is public. Because the state is sovereign, the status of the individual as the bearer of rights and obligations must be a formal creation of what Hobbes called the 'mortal god' – the sovereign state. The individual is thus 'autonomous' only in the sense that the state recognizes and authorizes this 'autonomy'. Public law is separate from private law, but at the same time it is this very separatism which allows the state to provide the framework in terms of which autonomous individuals pursue their own private interests. Essential to the uniqueness of the state is that it has (potentially and formally) a hand in everything.

Even if we accept (as some proponents of the limitation thesis argue) that a state can exist externally without existing internally, the same logical problem still emerges. As Giddens comments, the consolidated independent sovereignty of each individual state in the seventeenth century was at the same time a process of overall inter-state integration. States *depend* for their autonomy upon the recognition of other states. There is a persistent tension between the absoluteness of the sovereign state and the continuous and inescapable presence of other states limiting this 'will to sovereignty'.[26] The full implications of this problem will be looked at later in relation to the concept of an international society but here it is worth stressing that, both externally as well as internally, the modernist concept of the state as a distinct, separate and sovereign institution serves merely to accentuate the problematic and contradictory character of its identity.

Barker describes sovereignty as 'a normative rather than a

descriptive or explanatory concept'. But the problem of the state/society divide is not resolved by confining the concept of sovereignty to an ethereal realm of normative metaphysics. In the same way Watkins has argued that the legal concept of absolute sovereignty is a necessary fiction while from the standpoint of a 'descriptive' political science sovereignty is always limited.[27] It is true that states in practice are not able to exercise the power to make commands which cannot be countermanded. But this fact does not prevent them from trying, and the notion of sovereignty expresses acutely an identity problem which afflicts the state as a whole. Parekh is right therefore to argue that this identity problem is one which arises out of the state's own institutional reality. Because the state is separate and independent from society, it does not (as he points out) encompass the totality of social existence. If it did, then presumably the state and society would not be separable at all. On the other hand, Parekh insists that the state is not just an *aspect* of society, nor one of its many institutions: 'it permeates all areas of society and structures and reconstitutes it in a particular manner'. Those who say that the state stands above or transcends society are only partially right since the state is also very much in society. Once the state emerges, the whole society itself 'with the possible exception of the most intimate private realm' undergoes a total and subtle transformation.[28]

Vincent, like Parekh, makes it clear that this is not simply a 'normative' problem. It is a 'descriptive' one as well which arises out of the practice as well as the theory of the state. The state seems to be distinct as well as all-embracing.[29] No wonder Parekh describes the state/society relationship as 'complex and elusive' – a relationship which has continued to baffle politial theorists for the past four centuries and still resists adequate conceptualization.[30] Here indeed is Easton's elusive Pimpernel and Poulantzas's 'undecipherable mystery' embodied in an actual institution! In reality therefore sovereignty is more than an abstract right: it is also a concrete power. The assertion of sovereignty is vital to understand why states believe they are entitled to punish dissidents, crush rebels and go to war. It is a concept of great practical relevance. If the state seems impossibly abstract, expressing a curious combination of absolutism and autonomy in its relationship to society, this conceptual problem arises because the institution itself is contradictory and problematic.

Nor – we reiterate – is this a problem peculiar to the modern state. The modern state emphasizes a problem which has existed all along for, as we have argued, the question of imposing order in the name of community through force characterizes the state in all its forms. The sharpness, explicitness and abstraction of modern concepts expose a problem which was previously buried in a communitarian rhetoric that blurred the distinction between state and society. It is natural that many proponents of the Weberian definition should emphasize the importance of the modern state since it is only the modern state which explicitly 'abstracts' the monopolist from its social competitors and radically divorces public form from private content.

Nevertheless the modernist emphasis upon a public impersonality and sovereignty demonstrates the contradictory character of the state in general and demonstrates the absurdity of its inherent logic. It also accounts for the fact that (as we shall see) it is the modern state (and only the modern state) which provides the conceptual framework for looking beyond the state itself.

SUMMARY

- Weber argues that state merely 'claims' a monopoly of legitimate force. In fact, in exercising this monopoly, states never enjoy more than a partial success.
- All states have a contradictory nature since they assert a monopoly of legitimate force only because this monopoly is challenged and congested. A state therefore which accomplishes its objectives is a state which has no reason to continue existing.
- This contradictory identity manifests itself also in the state's assertion of a territorial and national unity which necessarily presupposes disharmony and division. An inherent gulf between ideals and reality explains why the state must be defined in terms of both its 'functional' ends and its 'structural' means.
- The more the state differentiates itself from society as an explicitly public and sovereign body, the more troubled and confusing its identity becomes. Hence the modern state provides the key to a critique of the state in general.

6

The Problem of Legitimacy

We have argued that just as pre-modern states have ill-defined and embryonic attributes of territoriality and sovereignty, so too is this true of legitimacy. The question of legitimacy requires a more detailed treatment however because of all the state's attributes identified by Weber it is the most contentious. The concept of legitimacy links force with morality, coercion with freedom, power with authority.

The argument that there is a 'differential' in the way rulers and ruled view legitimacy is a tempting one but it fails to engage the character of legitimacy as a *relationship* in which the subordinate appear to submit willingly to the powerful. In order to sustain a contrast between legitimacy and force *and* grasp legitimacy as a relationship, it is necessary to distinguish between force and coercion. The state, I will argue, undermines legitimacy because it employs force, whereas governmental processes (however coercive) are compatible with legitimacy.

This makes it possible to see why it is that legitimacy is not only a problem for the state, it is a problem *of* the state. Indeed it is the attribute which raises the state's problematic identity in its acutest form.

Legitimacy as a contested attribute

Weber is right in my view to insist that legitimacy is a necessary part of the state's overall identity and that no state can be logically defined without it. Just as traditional political theory raises the notion of rule by force, so too does it tackle the problem of rule as an imposition which is just and morally defensible. There is a general recognition that the state cannot merely impose brute force – it has to impose a force which rightfully commands the obedience of subjects and works for the good of all.

As I have argued elsewhere, even definitions of the state which emphasize the centrality of force still create conceptual space for the notion of legitimacy.[1] The human mind, Laski once wrote, 'revolts from the notion that the possession of coercive power can be defended regardless of the ends to which it is devoted'.[2] To say that a state is not legitimate is to deny its right to enforce its commands: it is to assert that these commands should not be obeyed. Legitimacy is not therefore an attribute which states may or may not have. It constitutes what Barker calls 'an historically observable component' of the state's relationship with its subjects.[3]

This argument however evokes much unease. It is revealing that some Weberian-inspired definitions of the state prefer to leave undecided 'whether the population of a society regard the state as legitimate'.[4] Others complain that Weber appears to be arguing that the mere fact that a state can ensure compliance with its commands is enough to make it legitimate. In De Jasay's view, the vulnerable part of the Weberian definition is 'the circularity of its idea of legitimacy'. Are we to suppose, De Jasay asks, that the state is legitimate simply because, as the definition asserts, it successfully claims a monopoly of force? In a society where masters can flog their servants at their discretion or union militants threaten workers if they cross picket lines, it seems perverse indeed to suggest that force possesses a kind of built-in legitimacy.[5]

This argument raises the question examined earlier in our exploration of the 'success problem'. Weber (as we have noted) argues that the state successfully *claims* a monopoly of legitimate force and in some versions of his definition the word 'successfully' is placed in parentheses. This is precisely Barker's response to De Jasay's criticism. If the parenthesis is indicative of an aside, a hesistancy, a qualification, then Weber's definition, while less neat, 'is both more realistic and more complicated'. Barker quotes Weber as saying that the legitimacy of a system of domination suggests only 'the probability' that appropriate attitudes will exist, and the corresponding practical conduct ensue.[6]

All this underscores the point that states claim something which they only partially and imperfectly realize, but it does not follow from this, as Barker contends,[7] that the attempt to achieve legitimacy is not a 'defining' characteristic of the state. The whole point about the state which Weber rightly stresses is that it must *aspire* to legitimacy, and it is unlikely to aspire to legitimacy unless it partially obtains it. The claim to legitimacy is a crucial part of what the state is and must be deemed a *defining* attribute of the state. Legitimacy is of course highly problematic since, as Weber's formulations imply, complete success is elusive and we can argue therefore that the state is both legitimate and illegitimate at the same time. To the extent that it fails to impose its monopoly of legitimate force, its legitimacy (like its monopoly) is a contested one. Indeed, this point is put well by Barker when he comments that 'the contours of legitimacy can most clearly be viewed when it is contested'.[8] Even in the modern state where the claim to impose a monopoly of legitimate force appears most successful, here as elsewhere there is imperfection and incompleteness.

Legitimacy must therefore be interpreted as a contested concept. This point particularly concerns Beetham in his fierce critique of Weber. Weber's arguments represent 'an unqualified disaster',[9] he argues, since Weber appears to define legitimacy simply in terms of what people *believe*. What is legitimate is that which is considered legitimate and there appears no objective or rational standards in terms of which legitimacy can be assessed. Legitimacy is a matter for report rather than for judgement. This, Beetham insists, will not do. Legitimacy denotes not merely beliefs but the *justification* of beliefs, and he argues for a definition which embraces three characteristics.

These are the following. Legitimacy has to be linked to legality – whether conduct occurs according to rules. It has to be justified in terms of beliefs which are shared by rulers and ruled alike, and it must be accompanied by a demonstrative expression of consent. Hence Beetham is unhappy also with Weber's celebrated analysis of legitimacy in terms of tradition, charisma and rational legality since if, as Weber presents them, these are separate types of legitimacy, then the impression is created that power in the traditional order is not validated in terms of rules.[10] In fact, Beetham argues, each of these elements is involved in legitimacy taken as a whole, and this reinforces the point that legitimacy is more than a belief. It is a belief which has to be specifically justified.

Once we emphasize the tentative character of Weber's definition (in the way Barker does), we can see that, despite Beetham's sharp strictures, Weber does in fact allow for relative rather than complete success in the state's claim to legitimacy. His notion of legitimacy therefore (implicitly at any rate) presupposes a degree of failure. There is more room here than Beetham supposes for noting that people challenge as well as accept legitimacy, and that legitimacy can exist only in the context of the state because it is a contested legitimacy. But interpreting Weber in this way, as I believe we must, still leaves open the problem of what legitimacy can actually mean in practice if it is always challenged. How can we employ such a concept in the context of a society in which the attempt is continuously made to impose order through force?

Legitimacy and the differential argument

We have already contended that distinguishing the state from government turns upon our analysis of physical force. Force is necessary to the success of the state but signals the failure of government. It is the use of force by the state which lies at the root of its contested legitimacy. Force has to be used because people cannot resolve their differences through negotiation and arbitration alone, and therefore it is the tension between force and legitimacy which highlights its contested character.

It is however one thing to assert the opposition between force and legitimacy: quite another to demonstrate coherently the co-existence of legitimacy with the state. When Rousseau explores the question as to how the state can be made 'legitimate', he starts from the premiss that 'force is a physical power; I do not see how its effects could produce morality'.[11] But this does not lead him to present the case for a polity bereft of physical force. Instead he argues for a concept of the general will which forces people to be free. The relationship between force and legitimacy creates grave difficulties for Weber as well. If force and legitimacy are mutually exclusive, then 'legitimate force' as a defining attribute of the state seems to be a contradiction in terms – at best an ideological pretension which we cannot possibly take seriously.

One way of salvaging Weber's concept of legitimate force is to argue that legitimacy extends to those who either coerce or benefit from coercion and excludes those who are the targets of force. In this way legitimacy is divided. States are legitimate in the eyes of the rulers (broadly speaking) and illegitimate in the eyes of the ruled. A version of this argument is hinted at by Barker when he complains that the concept of the state as legitimate sometimes assumes that legitimacy is 'equally distributed' and therefore its absence is equally spread. Take the case of Northern Ireland, often regarded as a situation in which legitimacy has disastrously failed to take root. Certainly a large minority contested the legitimacy of the Stormont state up to 1972, but what of the Unionist majority?

'A legitimate relationship with some citizens', Barker argues, 'can be more important to the state than a legitimate relationship with others.' The state will generally evoke legitimacy among its own personnel and among those who enjoy social privileges but, for the masses, the very concepts and institutions which give legitimacy meaning 'are dim or absent'. The erosion of a legitimate relationship with its tank commander may be of more significance for the state than a similar failure with its political philosophers.[12]

In essence Barker's argument is that an affirmation and a rejection of legitimacy exist side by side. Legitimacy is the condition in which those who are not coerced or threatened with coercion are able to place a cordon around those who are coerced. With a few subjects, legitimacy has an importance out of all proportion to their numbers, while with a large number of subjects, it can be of disproportionately small significance. Barker does argue, it is true, that 'physical coercion and legitimacy cannot be separated as "mutually exclusive". On the contrary they sustain one another'. But this argument is premissed on the assumption that it is possible to separate sharply those who are the targets of force from those who accord this force legitimacy. Physical force, he argues, works partly because of the coercive superiority of the coercer but also because of the assumption (by those not coerced) that coercion will be accepted.[13]

This argument is a tempting one. It meets our insistence that legitimacy is a contested concept and it appears to fit pre-modern states where rulers may have little contact with the ruled. It also takes account of the problematic character of the state in general where, as argued above, unless some break the law and challenge the state's monopoly of force, then the state has no *raison d'être* at all. It is true that Barker argues that coercion in itself does not erode legitimacy, and he makes a distinction between criminals and rebels. Criminals do not threaten the state, whereas rebels break laws and resist enforcement in a way that indicates that they reject the authority of the law and its enforcers. The phrase 'it's a fair cop' enables a line to be drawn between crime and rebellion.[14]

But this distinction should not be drawn too tightly. As the experience of the Thatcher government after 1979 has shown in Britain, a sharp increase in crime was at least for a period accompanied by urban rebellion, and (as I have argued earlier) criminals at least embryonically and selectively challenge the legitimacy of the law they break. Weber's own comment that the thief both recognizes and resists the criminal law[15] captures the tension between simultaneously acknowledging and yet contesting legitimacy. If criminals themselves at least implicitly challenge the legitimacy of the state, this makes the differential argument even more plausible, for this would mean that, in any given state, some would see the authorities as having a lot of legitimacy, others less, and (let us say) outright rebels virtually none at all.

But for all its superficial attractiveness, the differential argument is ultimately unsatisfactory. It sees legitimacy purely as a practical problem: a state must not alienate too many people too much of the time or its coercion will crumble and it will increasingly rely upon open terror. But the problem with this argument is that no judgement is possible about the legitimacy or illegitimacy of the state as such. All states are both legitimate (for the powerful) and illegitimate (for the coerced). In fact, as we shall now see, what makes legitimacy a particularly contested concept is that it poses a theoretical as well as a practical problem. It is, as noted above, a problem not merely for the state: it is a problem of the state as well.

Legitimacy as a relationship

In my view Beetham is right to express dissatisfaction with what I have called the differential argument. He accepts that an obvious distinction can be drawn between those who staff the administrative and coercive apparatuses of the state and the population as a whole, and concedes that considerable pains will be taken to reinforce the support of those directly involved with the state.[16] But it would, he insists, be mistaken to conclude, as some have done, that legitimacy is chiefly of consequence for members of the state and of little relevance for the population at large.

Legitimacy, Beetham argues, can exist only when it extends beyond the political elite and embraces the subordinate as well. It is power which conforms to rules and involves consent from those who are ruled. Yet he immediately concedes that in most historical societies in the pre-modern world, only some of the subordinate have been qualified to give consent. In such societies it would be taken for granted that adult males can give consent on behalf of their wives, children, clients, tenants and even descendants.[17] But what does this tell us about legitimacy? Are we to assume (as in the differential argument) that here rule is legitimate for the adult males but not for those upon whose behalf they ostensibly act?

Beetham rejects such an inference. In the case of gender relations, he argues, legitimacy exists because a hierarchical division of labour is not only governed by rules but is justified in terms of common beliefs and confirmed by consent. Consent in this case derives from the presence of socio-psychic processes that internalize attitudes so that differential roles appear 'natural'. For the same reason legitimacy can be identified in paternalistic relationships in general even when these assume an even more starkly hierarchical form. Take the question of slavery. Beetham argues that where the performance of slaves matters to their owners and the supply of these slaves can be maintained only through reproduction (as for example in the southern states of the USA after the end of the slave trade), a paternalistic relationship can develop in which slaves are treated as the 'permanent children' within an extended family.[18]

Paternalism embraces a relationship in which the subordinate are deemed wholly or partially, temporarily or permanently incapable of defining their own interests. It embraces parents and children, male chauvinists and women, racial supremacists and their victims. Indeed it manifests itself in all states where rulers assume special expertise based on tradition, spiritual qualifications or ideological skills as in Marxist–Leninist systems.[19] In such cases the paternalism is legitimate provided it is governed by rules and involves the continued belief by the subordinate that common interests justify the hierarchical differentiation.

This is a potent argument and I shall argue that it embodies a relational view of legitimacy since it rests on the assumption that if there is a *relationship* between the dominant and subordinate, then this relationship can be sustained only if it is also legitimate. Beetham hints at this relational argument when he distinguishes between the legitimations of the powerful (where they rationalize to themselves their harsh treatment of subordinates) and what he describes as a 'legitimate *relationship* justified in terms of shared beliefs'.[20] Paternalism is legitimate to the extent that it is relational since it is hard to see how parents and children, (male chauvinist) men and women, slave owners and slaves can continue relating to one another unless there exists between them a sense of shared values.

This relational view of legitimacy is borne out by Beetham's argument that legitimacy involves limits. If legitimate power is power that is valid according to rules, then these rules must bind both parties if they are to be taken seriously. Hence the power of the rulers appears justifiable because it is in conformity with underlying norms to which both parties subscribe. Thus Beetham argues, 'one of the ways in which it loses its legitimacy is when the powerful fail to observe its inherent limits'.[21] In such a case a relationship loses its cohesion as the subordinate reject the 'naturalness' of their position and deference gives way to defiance.

Is pure coercion possible?

The problem with the relational view of legitimacy however becomes evident when we return to the basic premiss which is central to the problematic character of the state, namely the contradiction between legitimacy and force. On the one hand it is asserted that legitimacy is not some kind of lump or 'quantity' which is differentially doled out so that it is enjoyed by the rulers and denied by the ruled. Legitimacy is a relationship in which the subordinate acknowledge the right of the powerful to continue dominating them. Both sides recognise limits, rules and common values. On the other hand, despite the presence of normative elements here, it is hard to see a legitimate relationship as one which avoids force.

In none of the paternalistic relationships to which Beetham refers can we assume that the presence of legitimacy points to the exclusion of force, since Beetham can hardly deny that in such relationships parents chastise children, masters flog their slaves and husbands beat their wives, albeit in the name of a common interest which both parties supposedly acknowledge.[22] Yet the problem of reconciling legitimacy with force is one that clearly worries Beetham. Thus he comments that, where legitimacy is eroded, coercion becomes much more extensive and he instances the collapse of Communist Party states in Eastern Europe. Here a prior loss of legitimacy made these regimes so reliant on coercion, and they became hopelessly vulnerable once sufficient coercion could not be maintained.[23] Of course it is true that, when paternalistic relationships crumble, coercion becomes more obvious. But that is not the point. The point is that, while these relationships are sustained, they can be both legitimate and coercive. Indeed the paternalistic regimes of Eastern Europe are a case in point. These were (for a good many years) 'really existing' states and Beetham is unequivocally Weberian in the way he acknowledges the legitimacy of the state. The form of power which is distinctive to the state – organized physical coercion – is one (Beetham comments) that stands uniquely in need of legitimation, but, however problematic the legitimacy of the state, it is real all the same.[24]

Beetham's problem then is this. He embraces a relational argument that suggests that legitimacy is compatible with coercion. Yet he is still anxious to argue that the two are mutually exclusive. To defend his argument, he takes the example of slavery in a situation in which the supply of slaves can easily be replenished through conquest and trade. Here he contends that while the powerful may invoke legality and have justifications for their power, these legitimations are addressed to the powerful and not to their subordinates who are seen as mere objects rather than persons. In this case there exists what he calls 'a purely coercive, unlimited, arbitrary power of one group over another'. The 'purity' of the coercion means that legitimacy is absent. Elsewhere Beetham comments that in certain situations it is possible for the goals of the powerful to be realized on the basis of coercion alone and, where this occurs, there is no legitimacy.[25]

But the problem here is that this exercise of 'pure coercion' is difficult to square with the existence of relationships, and there is no doubt that, even in the more extreme kind of slavery instanced above, relationships are involved. It is true that a high degree of coercion is present and we need not doubt that when this coercion slackened (as when slave owners were away fighting) mass desertions would follow. But is it plausible to assume that in this more extreme form of slavery a 'pure' coercion is involved? On the one hand Beetham speaks of 'purely coercive, unlimited, arbitrary power' but on the other hand he acknowledges that, even with this extreme form of slavery, both legal and moral justifications are employed. It is because these justifications are not addressed to subordinates with whom the powerful share no common language that legitimacy is non-existent.[26]

But this argument is not defensible. After all masters could still address slaves through relatively privileged intermediaries (as in the power structures of concentration camps), and Beetham's point is contradicted by his own argument later that these highly coercive regimes would need incentives as well as sanctions 'to encourage cooperation'.[27] All this surely implies the kind of 'limits' found in other hierarchical and paternalistic relationships. The relational argument not only suggests that legitimacy can be present where coercion is involved, but it treats the interactions between the powerful and the subordinate as complex totalities in which it is impossible to focus upon one aspect of power in isolation from the others.

The point is underlined by Dahl in his analysis of power. In a continuum ranging from 'trained control' where people are free from any obvious external influence to physical force where their autonomy shrinks to zero, the different forms of power or influence do not have 'crystalline boundaries', but 'merge into one another'.[28] Beetham's argument is that it is possible to employ legal and moral justifications and even encourage co-operation through incentives without at the same time invoking some normative concept of common interests shared by oppressor and oppressed alike, but this ignores the structural totality of power as Dahl defines it. Dahl finds the intermeshing of both power and authority, rational persuasion and physical force to be 'one of the most poignant and troubling problems of political life'.[29] It is certainly not a problem we can get round by constructing relationships which are based either on pure force or on incentives to co-operate which do not involve the limiting acknowledgement of common interests. Indeed when Beetham criticizes the exponents of rational choice theory for assuming that agents can act purely out of self-interest, he implicitly makes the point which lies at the heart of the relational argument. When people relate, they necessarily do so both as moral agents and as self-interested actors. Co-operation must imply legitimacy as well as prudence and momentary advantage.[30]

The dilemma we are left with is this. The relational argument resists the view that legitimacy is simply a lump which can be divided in differential fashion so that what is legitimate for the coercers is illegitimate for the coerced. But by asserting that power can be exercised legitimately in hierarchical and despotic relationships, force itself appears legitimate not simply because it is advocated by the powerful but because it is accepted by the subordinate whose subordination depends in part upon coercive elements in the relationship.

Force, sovereignty and the abstract individual

The relational argument appears more convincing than the differential 'lump of legitimacy' thesis but it has a major drawback. By reconciling legitimacy with force, it suggests that the state's moral claims are unproblematic at least as long as the state itself is stable. It is true that states are likely to become spectacularly reliant on coercion when they are crumbling, but, as Beetham's analysis of paternalism suggests, as long as states exist, they are legitimate despite the fact that they have, as Weber rightly argues, force as their most distinctive feature.

Our problem then is this. In order to assert the problematic character of the state, we must demonstrate the contradictory relationship between legitimacy and force, but to do this we need to go beyond the relational argument which sees legitimacy as a dimension which exists even in the most coercive of relationships. Once again it is the modern state with its sharp public/private divide, its explicit notion of sovereignty and its emphasis upon the impersonal nature of rule which provides the key to unravelling the problem. To understand why, we need to note that as the state assumes a modern form, so legitimacy itself comes to acquire startlingly new features.

An increasingly public and visible state is counterparted by an increasingly private and atomized society. As the state 'withdraws' from society, so the notion develops of the market as an autonomous and impersonal mechanism which exists 'on its own'. Central to this concept of an autonomous market is the idea that the members of society can be conceived as abstract individuals who originally inhabit a state of nature from whence they derive their inalienable natural rights. The state itself is characterized as a social contract forged by rational individuals who have no relationships with one another. The force associated with repressive hierarchies in general and the state in particular is seen therefore as extrinsic to individuals. Abstracting individuals from relationships involves placing force outside freedom, obligations outside rights, and the state and hierarchy outside individuals as autonomous agents. This conception is vital for the notion of society as a collectivity of uniform citizens who obey the law because and only because it has been made 'legitimate'.

Legitimacy is rooted in a non-relational concept of the individual who is equal, rational and capable of self-government. Laws are legitimate only when they have been authorized through consent. Force is inimical to such an individual because it means a loss of autonomy, self-determination and rationality. A decisive step has been taken in asserting the opposition between legitimacy and force but this step has been made possible through the construction of a non-relational concept of the abstract individual. Although classical liberalism declares the state to be an artifice which represses the individual and compromises natural rights, it cannot resolve the problem of force and legitimacy.

The whole construct of the abstract individual and the asocial state of nature is a myth. It is a conception which arises ideologically as an expression of market relationships in which individuals appear to exist outside of society. Nevertheless it poses a crucial challenge. The contradiction between force and legitimacy lies at the heart of the state's problematic character. On the other hand, if this conceptual distinction between force and legitimacy is to be sustained in a way which is plausible and coherent, then individuals must be conceived in relational terms without embracing the paralysing consequences which flow from the relational argument.

The fact that an abstract juxtaposition between force and legitimacy cannot resolve the problem is evidenced if we look briefly at the treatment of legitimacy in Hobbes and Rousseau. Lacking a concept of a *relationship* between the individual and the sovereign representative who acts on his (rather than her) behalf, Hobbes simply collapses legitimacy into force. On the other hand Rousseau, who criticizes Hobbes for apparently equating might with right, is no more successful in analysing the relationship between force and freedom. His abstractly autonomous individuals are dissolved into the sovereign community so that even the most draconian forms of coercion enjoy legitimacy. When the general will speaks, all tension between legitimacy and force vanishes. The classical liberal tradition provides the key to the problem since in historically unprecedented fashion it declares force to be inherently immoral and makes it possible to analyse the state as a problematic and contradictory institution. At the same time its own abstract treatment of the individual and sovereignty leaves the problem of legitimacy painfully unresolved.

Legitimacy and the distinction between coercion and force

If the classical liberal juxtaposition between force and legitimacy is mystifyingly abstract, how is it possible to recast the distinction between the two in a way which is concrete? How are we to establish a relational view of power which demonstrates nevertheless the tension between force and legitimacy?

To do this we need to make a distinction which is implicit rather than explicit within classical liberalism. Up until now we have tended to refer to force and coercion as though the two were more or less synonyms. To tackle the problem of legitimacy, it is now necessary to differentiate them, for it is only when we do so that we can see why the liberal juxtaposition between force and freedom is so cripplingly abstract. Classical liberalism, through the theory of the social contract, links the force of the state with the development of social relationships. As a result no conceptual space exists for distinguishing between coercion on the one hand and force on the other. The contract is a product of autonomous wills in which there is deemed to be an absence of both force and coercion.

The abstract assimilation of the two is the product of an historical development in which those who are dominant economically cease to have direct access to the means of violence to sustain their rule. This 'withdrawal' of overt violence from society has positive as well as mystifying consequences. On the one hand it makes it possible to distinguish between force and legitimacy since the free individual is the individual who is free from force. On the other hand this 'withdrawal' of force from society creates the illusion that, since it is possible to avoid force, it is possible to avoid coercion, and the market (as the paradigm of the social contract) is seen as an institution which is legitimate only because it is free of coercion. Indeed some libertarians have argued that, as a consequence, power is absent from market relations altogether. The free exchange involved in the labour contract appears as the interaction between two autonomous partners.

If however we are to puncture (as Marx did) this libertarian illusion and emphasize the coercive character of the labour contract (as Beetham wishes to when he analyses the plight of workers in early capitalism), then we must distinguish coercion from force. For what makes the coercion of the contract particularly deceptive is that no direct force is involved at the 'private' level. Choice is constrained but only by the 'dull compulsion of economic relations'. Of course if the worker breaks the law, direct force comes into play through the action of the state, but that is another matter. The fact that the market itself can be coercive was linked by social liberals like Mill to an understanding of the coercive character of social pressures in general. Indeed, as I have argued elsewhere,[31] the concept of 'natural penalties' in *On Liberty* suggests that, since everything we do affects others (who naturally respond as a result), there is a sense in which all relationships involve an element of social coercion. In the case of natural penalties however, the sanctions are unintended and are implicit in all our relationships. Taken in this broad sense, coercion does not undermine autonomy: on the contrary, it is the precondition for its very existence.

Where does this leave the question of force? The term 'force' can of course be applied broadly as when we speak of the 'force' of circumstances or when Marx refers to the 'violence of things'. Here however it makes more sense to speak of force as 'physical force' where individuals directly rather than indirectly compel others. Physical force, defined in this way, must be sharply distinguished from coercion in general. Of course coercion takes different forms which also need disentangling. Natural penalties are very different from explicit moral or economic sanctions: in the one instant individuals are simply pursuing their own interests, in the other they are seeking to punish dissidents and offenders. The more 'concentrated' the coercion, the more deliberate and intentional it is, and coercion in its most concentrated form involves the threat to use physical force. It is in this context that it becomes most tempting to use force and coercion as though they were synonyms since a threat to use force would not be credible unless force itself on occasion was actually used.

But strictly speaking coercion is always relational, whereas force is not. A person is directly coerced when he or she is threatened with force. This in itself will not destroy a relationship provided of course the recipient of the threat, fearing the physically punitive consequences of disobedience, complies. Compliance is necessary to a relationship and implies some (although perhaps not very much) sense of mutual interest, some notion of legalistic limit, some sharing of normative expectations. Even where people are threatened with force in an explicitly coercive manner, this is still compatible with legitimacy. Only when the relationship is disintegrating and compliance actually *breaks down* can it be said that legitimacy itself (already somewhat residual) finally disappears.

Hence the distinction between force and coercion is absolutely crucial. When force is applied rather than merely threatened, relationships are disrupted. It is true that coercion itself may be unintentional but it is still relational in the sense that individuals subject to this coercion remain agents capable of making choices. Force however extinguishes agency, and Beetham is therefore right when he argues (as we have seen) that to treat a person as a mere object is to deny legitimacy. He is wrong however to assume that people can be treated in this way in the contexts of relationships. When force is actually used, the individual becomes the mere property of another – the object of their punishment, rage, lust, anger or whatever. The limits which necessarily attend relationships wither since force or violence (I use the terms here synonomously) involves (to a greater or lesser degree) dehumanizing or 'naturalizing' a person so that they become indistinguishable from any other 'thing'. Whereas in a relationship each sees the other as a subject (even when these relationships are hierarchical in character), when violence is employed the relationship is suspended since the victim is now 'objectified'.

The classical liberal tradition is thus correct to stress the opposition between physical force and morality, and historically speaking (as we have seen) this is an antithesis which can be made only when individuals are depicted outside of relationships as self-determining,

autonomous beings. This depiction, though historically momentous, is nevertheless problematic since the antithesis between force
and legitimacy is instantly mystified unless individuals are put back
into the context of relationships. However the only way in which
this can be done is to make the distinction of the kind I have
drawn.

Of course direct coercion is only analytically distinguishable
from force since if no force was actually used, the threat to employ
it would lose its credibility. But strictly speaking threats are
relational in a way in which the use of physical force is not.
Coercive threats therefore do not contradict legitimacy. Force
does. The slave who complies out of fear of consequences is
involved in a relationship and (as I have suggested above) this
relationship can be stable only if normative and legalistic elements
are also involved. The more a coercive relationship is sustained
through a significant number of acts of force, the more its legitimacy is attentuated since each act of force does indeed undermine
legitimacy and signal in a most graphic way the absence of
common interests and of a mutually limiting legality. Nevertheless,
strictly speaking, it is force, not coercion, which is incompatible
with legitimacy. The kind of coercion which threatens physical
force becomes problematic not because it is inherently illegitimate
in itself but because it takes place in a context in which force itself
is also used.

The differential argument and the sovereign state

We are now in a position to acknowledge the differential character
of legitimacy while accepting the logic of the relational argument.
Those subject to direct coercion are most likely to question the
legitimacy of the state precisely because they are also the most
likely to be victims of force. The opposition between force and
legitimacy subjects the state to an insoluble problem. On the one
hand the state rests ultimately upon force; on the other hand it
seeks to use this force to secure legitimacy. The one necessarily
contradicts the other.

However, two points have to be made in this regard. The first is
that, even in highly repressive systems, force itself may be used only
occasionally. It is costly and dangerous. States therefore use particular acts of force in order to sustain varying types and degrees
of coercion, and since, as I have argued, coercion is itself compatible with relationships, states have a partial and contradictory

legitimacy. Of course the use of what I have called 'direct coercion', i.e. the threat to use force, is likely to limit legitimacy, since those who obey purely out of fear are also likely to have experienced or be acutely conscious of the existence of the state's use of physical force.

The second point is one made by Beetham himself when he argues that a state can be perceived to be too weak as well as too overbearing. If an overbearing state is one which uses force to suppress deep-seated grievances, a weak state is one which fails to use force to quell disorder in others. What of the rights and liberties of those who may have good reason to believe that, unless the unruly are subject to the force of the state, property and personal livelihood will not be be secure? The relation between coercion and legitimacy, Beetham argues, is 'a complex rather than a simple one'. If the state uses coercion to protect its citizens, 'then the effective application of coercion to this end cannot necessarily be construed as either illegitimate in itself, or as evidence of a deeper-seated weakness in legitimacy'.[32]

But the issue goes deeper than this. If by coercion we mean the kind of direct coercion which is credible only because it also involves physical force, then (despite what Beetham says) there *is* a legitimacy problem. It may be that the use of force by the state is intended to prevent the use of force by the law-breakers, but this places the state in the unenviable position of using immoral means to achieve moral ends, of necessarily undermining the freedom of one in order to secure the freedom of others. The point is that, if force is illegitimate (as I argue it is), then it is not only illegitimate for the individual who receives it: it is also illegitimate for the individual who administers it. For force (as we have seen) violates social relationships by treating subjects as objects – people as things – and hence both the administrator and the victim of force are degraded as a consequence. The victim becomes a mere object: the administrator an 'objectifier', i.e. one who acts inhumanly since he or she treats another as a 'thing'. When force is applied, what might be called a 'natural' relationship replaces a social relationship as both parties become mere 'brutes'.[33] To treat a person as a thing is to dehumanize oneself.

The character of force as an act which destroys (social) relationships can be understood therefore only in terms of a relational argument. If force is mutually degrading and destroys legitimacy, it cannot be said to destroy legitimacy for one party while affirming it for another. When the state employs force, it undermines legitimacy in general – for the victim, but also for the administrator and indeed for the society as a whole. The sovereign state has universal jurisdiction and employs what Rousseau called a 'collective force'.[34] Every individual knows that the laws can be physically enforced when all else fails. Hence the very existence of this state's force necessarily compromises the existence of legitimacy for all the members of a society.

The differential argument is therefore unconvincing. It assumes that legitimacy is a problem only for the coerced and not for the coercer, whereas the truth is that in a state-centred society there is a *general* awareness that laws – whatever their moral standing – are backed by force. Who can say how many would continue to be 'law-abiding' if the force underpinning the laws was summarily withdrawn? Force therefore contaminates society as a whole. To the extent that they refrain from using force, states will enhance their legitimacy, provided of course (as Beetham notes above) they are not seen to condone or connive with the force of others. To claim to exercise a monopoly of legitimate force, as the state must, is to be responsible for force whenever and wherever it is employed. To increase its legitimacy, the state must diminish the overall use of force, and not merely displace public force into private channels. To the extent that it succeeds in doing this, securing order increasingly through persuasion and consensus, it becomes more of a government and less of a state. The force which makes the state a state renders legitimacy a seminal problem.

It is true that states maintain social relationships and a degree of order. The coercion they employ ranges from Mill's natural penalties to moral punishments. But all social bodies employ coercion of one kind or another. It is when this coercion is backed by force that legitimacy itself becomes contested and contradictory – not simply for those who fear or experience this force but for society as a whole.

SUMMARY

- Legitimacy is undoubtedly the most controversial element in the Weberian definition. All states claim legitimacy. At the same time it is clear that, like the other attributes in terms of which Weber identifies the state, this is a legitimacy which is always contested.

- It is therefore tempting to support the idea that a state is legitimate for its rulers and illegitimate for the ruled. The problem with this argument however is that it cannot explain how legitimacy can exist as a paternalistic relationship in which the subordinate accept the 'right' of the powerful to dominate them.

- The 'relational' argument extends the notion of legitimacy to despotic relationships which involve force. Yet the problematic character of the state arises from the violent manner in which it resolves disputes. To sustain the classical liberal distinction between legitimacy and force, it is necessary to distinguish between force on the one hand and coercion on the other.

- This enables us to see why the state has a built-in legitimacy problem which manifests itself every time it uses force. Moreover this is not only a problem for the recipient of force. Since it is mutually degrading, force compromises the freedom of the administrator as well as the victim of force, and, given the universal character of the state's jurisdiction, its use also undermines the legitimacy of the state for the society as a whole.

Part II

Challenges and Alternative Critiques

7

Liberalism

We have argued that it is possible to highlight the contradictory character of the state and the peculiarly problematic character of its legitimacy only if we take account of the state in modernity. Liberals, it has been said, stand firmly with the moderns,[1] and I shall argue that the modern state is essentially the *liberal* state.

Liberalism, I shall argue, is both a theory of and a theory against the state. This in essence is what defines its problematic character. Liberalism sees the state as 'unnatural' and postulates that all individuals are free and equal. On the other hand it suffers from a 'schizoid malady' since it asserts that individuals, who are naturally free, are obliged nevertheless to accept the force of the state. This problem leads subsequent liberals to abandon a theory of 'natural rights' but the dilemma still remains. For all liberals have to premiss their support for the state on assumptions which on the surface at least are profoundly anti-statist in character.

Our analysis of the 'challenges and alternative critiques' begins with liberalism since all the other challenges and critiques we will explore – the anarchist (in both its left and right wing forms), Marxist, feminist and postmodernist – are themselves responses to liberalism. But what is it? All acknowledge and emphasize the breadth and heterogeneity of liberalism, and one writer has even insisted that it is too ecumenical and pluralistic to be called an ideology.[2] Our concern here however is with liberalism as a critique of the state, and particularly with the proposition that an 'anarchistic element' has been implicit in the theory of liberalism from the start.[3] Of course not all liberals have been critical of the state, but our concern here (as with the other critiques and challenges we will consider) is to analyse not simply what particular adherents of particular standpoints say but what can be identified as the under-lying logic of their position. In seeking to probe the logic of liberalism, we will focus on the quality and depth of its critique of the state.

Challenging natural hierarchy

Political theorists have often been the beneficaries of the state structures they analyse. If we accept that political theory originates in ancient Greece, then it is not surprising that most political theorists of Greek antiquity regarded the state as natural, and subscribed to Aristotle's celebrated dictum that humans are 'polit-ical animals'. By this of course is meant that the state itself (and not simply government in general) 'belongs to a class of objects that exist in nature'.[4]

As long as division, hierarchy and the state appear natural, no liberal critique is possible. To challenge the state as a whole – and not merely in a piecemeal 'curate's egg' fashion – it is necessary to see the state as having a purely conventional or artificial character. Although Hobbes argues for autocracy in his *Leviathan*, he has (rightly) been described as the founder of liberalism because of the radical individualism and conventionalism of his political theory.[5] While there are dramatic differences between Hobbes and Locke as liberals, Locke's political theory also rests upon a natural egalita-rianism: all are born equal without subordination or subjection. The state of nature is a state of 'perfect freedom' in which people order their actions and dispose of their possessions as they think fit.[6] The state, as in Hobbes, is an artefact – the product of convention. This argument is pivotal since it represents an acknow-ledgement (however confused and implicit) that, because the state is *not* a product of human nature, a world without the state is in some sense conceivable. This conventionalism contains the radical kernel of liberal thought and it is here that we must begin if we are to locate its fundamental contribution to a critique of the state.

But how quintessentially *liberal* is this notion of the state as artefact? Ancient Greeks generally subscribed (as we have seen) to the concept of the state as a natural and ethical community, but what of the Sophists who (it is said) were the liberals of the ancient world? Indeed it has even been suggested that liberals like Hobbes, Locke and Rousseau are simply 'the modern representatives' of the Sophistic tradition.[7] The Sophists were itinerant educators whose scepticism, relativism and individualism led them to take the view that nature and law (conceived as a hierarchical and repressive institution) are antithetical.[8] Hence, like modern liberals, they see the state as having a purely conventional character. This conventionalism is not only radically different from Plato's and Aristotle's views of the state but sharply contrasts with medieval teachings as well.[9]

Set against the ancient and medieval emphasis on the natural character of discipline, obedience, hierarchy and the state, the Sophist argument seems radical and liberating. But it does not follow that because the Sophists regarded the state as conventional in character, they can be identified as *liberal* critics of the state. Protagoras, for example, is sometimes presented as a liberal champion of political equality, but he sees the state as a divinely sanctioned institution which is supremely responsible for educating society.[10] Other Sophists (who it seems press the antithesis between nature and law more vigorously than Protagoras) present a view which equates (as Plato himself points out) might with right. Thus Antiphon holds that, because the state is artificial and conventional, its laws should simply be evaded wherever possible. It is little wonder that Barker characterizes him as an anti-social thinker unable to accept the fact that people have to live together.[11]

Indeed this point brings us to a major problem with ascribing liberal credentials to thinkers like the Sophists. It is one thing to argue that the state is conventional, quite another to tackle the problem of how people might be governed in a way which respects their rights. Hence Strauss argues that the Sophists embrace what he calls a 'vulgar' conventionalism in which life according to nature involves exploiting the opportunities created by others. Philosophic conventionalists (among whom for example Strauss identifies Hobbes) by contrast deny that elitism is natural and they therefore raise the question as to how natural freedoms can be preserved through exercising rights and respecting institutions.[12]

Liberalism (strictly speaking) therefore does not only assume the state to be conventional: it also insists that it is possible to resolve the problem of government. For the Sophists by contrast political action is unnatural and inadvisable, and hence the problem of how a conventional society might be 'naturally' ordered is never addressed.[13]

Abstraction, subversion and the Pateman thesis

A liberal critique of the state cannot simply challenge the state's naturalistic credentials. It must also tackle the problem of order and government. At the heart of liberalism lies what Zvesper calls 'the political questioning of politics' but what I would prefer to call the statist challenge to the state. The ancient idea of the 'good state' gives way to the liberal notion of the 'legitimate state' – the state which has to be authorized through the consent of its citizens if it deserves to be obeyed.[14]

At this point it is useful to introduce the arguments of Pateman since she presents her important and influential analysis of political obligation as 'a critique of liberal theory'. Pateman is right to insist that even if arguments about consent and social contract can be found in ancient and medieval writings, what is particular to liberalism is its concern with the problem of *obligation*. Why is it that individuals who are 'naturally' free and equal have an obligation nevertheless to the state? The answer is that we are obliged to obey the state because these obligations are self-assumed – they are the product of free will and contract – and it is a response which takes us to the heart of liberalism. This voluntarism, as Pateman emphasizes, is not simply a conceptual position embraced by liberals in the seventeenth and eighteenth centuries. It is an argument which is basic to all liberal theory, and it remains central to the liberal political ideal today.[15]

Voluntarism and contractualism make liberalism a critical theory by posing the highly subversive question: if individuals are able to govern themselves, how is it possible to justify the existence of the state? It is true (as we shall see in more detail later) that towards the end of the eighteenth century (many) liberals began to abandon natural rights and social contract theory, preferring to justify the state in terms of utility or a reformulated notion of rights which no longer subscribes to a state of nature thesis. In practice the state becomes (as Pateman points out) a 'natural' and unproblematic 'fact' and the notion of consent is reduced simply to the voting behaviour of individuals in a liberal democracy. Nevertheless she insists that the liberal ideal of a constitutional state continues to rest upon individualistic, egalitarian and universalist notions which derive from (and only ultimately make sense in terms of) the abstractions of the contract tradition. However problematic it may be conceptually, voluntarism remains what Pateman calls 'a practical source of cohesion in the liberal state' which is why liberal democratic theorists cannot give it up, 'no matter how implausible their arguments may become or how many problems they engender'.[16]

There is therefore built in the very fabric of liberalism what Easton once called a 'schizoid malady', and this schizoid malady arises out of the attempt to justify the state with a logic which is subversive of the state. Liberalism is thus simultaneously statist and anti-statist in character and is constituted by the long history of a theory divorced from practice.[17] The problem arises not simply with later liberals who abandon the concept of the social contract and natural rights: it is evident from the start. Take the position of Hobbes. Hobbes may have been a conservative who supported the royalists during the English civil war but the postulates of his theory are radical and egalitarian, and hence his arguments could never have been accepted in royalist circles. If we are to understand how a theory with anti-statist premises can generate an argument for the state, Hobbes, as the illiberal founder of liberalism, is the theorist with whom to begin.

The key to this paradox lies with the question of abstraction. Ritchie complains of an 'abstractedness' or conceptual negativity which embraces theoretical postulates that are at odds with 'the concrete facts of social life and history'.[18] Humans are conceived as individuals who have been 'abstracted' from the social and historical relationships which make them what they are. The term 'abstraction' suggests not simply that a premiss is 'aloof' from concrete reality, since in that sense all thought is necessarily abstract to some degree or other. Abstraction means more than this: it implies that an abstract concept has a relationship to reality which is *contradictory* in character. Abstract theory is not just in tension with 'practice': it is theory which embodies within itself contradictory practical implications. An abstract *critique* of the state is therefore a concrete *apologia* for the state. Its premises are abstract because they necessarily imply their concrete 'opposite'.

Pateman illustrates this point graphically in the case of Hobbes. She insists that Hobbes's version of the contract (though it has singular features) establishes a pattern followed by subsequent liberal theory.[19] The task of the Leviathan is to bring not only the state but social life itself into being and, since individuals are free and equal and naturally govern themselves, society can emerge only through consent. To argue (to the contrary) that society comes about through force or command would be to assume the existence of hierarchies which are necessarily absent from Hobbes's state of nature.

A problem then arises which is particular to Hobbes. Why does a state which supposedly originates through consent demand unconditional obedience from its 'free' subjects? Surely a state which rests upon consent should be constitutionally limited, giving its citizens rights to criticize and dissent. Yet (as Pateman argues) Hobbes's extreme individualism meshes logically with his case for an absolutist state. When individuals contract to form a society and a state, they do not and cannot change their nature. They remain just as abstract as they were before and hence the sovereign represents the people only in the sense that he (the maleness is not incidental) is simply the individual writ large. Pateman quotes Hobbes: 'it is the Unity of the Representer, not the Unity of the Represented, that maketh the Person One'.[20] Since the contract is a simultaneous exchange of words, it is not a *relationship* between two interdependent, mutually enabling and mutually limiting beings. The voluntarism is abstract and so too is the sanction which sustains it. Only force can preserve consent. The atomistic individual in the state of nature is collectively re-expressed as the atomistic sovereign which is the Leviathan.

This explains not merely why abstract individualism is tied logically to absolutist sovereignty but why, as Pateman points out, the Leviathan is not an arbitrary ruler. His actions are those of his subjects. Hence it follows that subjects can legitimately refuse to do anything which endangers their lives (since no person can give up the natural right to self-preservation) and the Leviathan must apply law 'equally' to all. The gulf between everyday life and the political obedience of subjects is 'unbridgeable' so that space is created for individuals to pursue economic and cultural pursuits in a way which does not challenge the security of the state.[21]

Paradoxically then Hobbes's argument is both liberal and illiberal at the same time. The very extremity of Hobbes's liberalism – the consistency of his conventionalism and the abstractness of his voluntarism – makes it inevitable that the state which results will itself be absolutist and illiberal. Whether people obey through fear or brute force matters not for Hobbes since unconditional freedom in the state of nature can manifest itself only as unconditional obedience in society. Of course Pateman is right to insist that Hobbes's notion of freedom stands at the limits of what she calls 'hypothetical voluntarism'. There is no intermediate position between unconditional obedience on the one hand and arbitrarily acting individuals on the other. The notion of a limited constitutional state recognizing the rights of independent subjects cannot arise here since the construct of the *limited* state must imply (in part at least) that individuals are social beings who can act freely only through the relationships they have with one another.

Realism, hierarchy and the liberal state

Locke is generally regarded as a much more moderate, sensible and even coherent liberal than Hobbes. It is Locke who provides the classical argument that states must be restricted in scope and constrained in practice in order to safeguard the liberties of citizens who are the best judges of their interests. His state of nature is far more evidently a social state of affairs (even though Hobbes has also to ascribe social characteristics to his self-centred individuals in practice if not in theory), and Locke's laws of nature are divinely sanctioned norms which constrain people to behave in a sociable manner. Not only do people execute and enforce natural laws in the Lockean state of nature, but Locke even goes some way towards acknowledging what I have called earlier the anthropological argument. Government (as opposed to what Locke calls *political* authority) exists also in the state of nature as an institution which is 'hardly to be avoided among Men that live together'.[22]

But the greater realism of Locke does not avoid the problem of the schizoid malady in which abstract premises presuppose their concrete opposite. It is true that his account of the state of nature is far more historical than Hobbes's. He argues that initially all individual property holdings are equal since the law of nature allows no individuals to possess more than they can use. It is only when individuals agree to introduce money that property can be accumulated and the 'Possession of the Earth' becomes 'disproportionate and unequal'. Under these circumstances, 'inconveniences' degenerate into a situation of war pressing individuals to form a *civil* society and a liberal state.

But the greater realism of this account cannot resolve a schizophrenic relationship between theory and practice since Locke (like Hobbes) still contends that what makes the liberal state legitimate is the fact that it arises from the consent of naturally free and equal individuals. As a result, the social character of Locke's state of nature is more apparent than real.[23] The capacity which people have to promise and bargain and 'keep faith' derives not from society but from God as their creator, and it is this abstract individualism which allows Locke to present the state as the product of a contract freely entered into. The greater realism of the account serves merely to make these voluntarist premises increasingly implausible.

If the liberal state is conventional, government itself is not, and the existence of government in the state of nature is presented by Locke in a way which makes the natural freedom and equality of individuals highly problematic. On the one hand government can hardly be avoided when people live together: on the other hand it is seen as inherently hierarchical. Indeed Locke's account of the origins of government (as opposed to the liberal state) largely follows that of the patriarchalist, Filmer.[24] This means that, at least in the pre-monetary stage of the state of nature where the 'Honesty and Prudence' of the father-rulers can be relied on, absolute monarchy itself enjoys consent. It is not only in the state of nature however that voluntarism is problematic (where individuals are seen to consent to money and unequal political relationships). Once radical inequalities develop with capital accumulation and a market economy, a new form of government – a liberal constitutional state – is required which will protect property and limit the power of rulers. But here too (as Locke makes it clear) the bulk of the population consent tacitly rather than expressly. The support of the propertyless, resident aliens and visitors for the state (not to mention women) is simply inferred from the fact that the protection of a civil government makes it possible for them to walk freely on the highway.[25]

By seeking to analyse consent in socially concrete terms, Locke ensures that the postulate of a contract formed by naturally free and equal individuals is continuously compromised by proliferating hierarchies. Most subjects are in rather than of civil society, and they are deemed to consent to the liberal state in much the same way that people consented to the absolute monarch in earlier times. Locke's attempt to interpret abstract voluntarism in a more 'practical' manner throws into crisis the whole logic of the liberal project. If in reality consent is largely tacit and the liberal state rests upon deep rooted structural inequalities, in what sense can it be said that this state acts as an impartial umpire protecting the interests of all the members of society? In moving away from the subversive abstractions of an egalitarian state of nature,[26] the case for the liberal state becomes increasingly unconvincing.

Utilitarians, Gray and the schizoid malady

The very explicitness with which Locke tackles the nature of consent makes it relatively easy for theorists like Hume in the following century to ridicule the theory of the social contract. The state is the product of an incurable weakness of human nature (Hume argues) and it arises through habit rather than contract. On the one hand even the tribal chieftain must be able to employ force to 'reduce the refractory and disobedient'; on the other hand the exertions of rulers result in a 'sensible utility' and produce 'an habitual, and if you please to call it so, a voluntary and therefore precarious acquiescence in the people'.[27]

Hume's argument influences (as we shall see) the Scottish Enlightenment and the nineteenth-century utilitarians. In disposing of contract theory, it also renders liberalism itself more and more problematic. Hume's instincts may be described as 'liberal' in the sense that he supports 'free governments' which encourage commerce in moderation and conduct themselves according to general and uniform laws, but he also defends oligarchy in Britain for the same reason as he supports absolute monarchy in France. It is legal, had been established by custom and authority and (apparently) enjoys popular allegiance.[28] Such an argument can only exacerbate the problem of the schizoid malady, since this malady (as we have already noted) arises out of the endemic tension between liberalism on the one hand and reality on the other. The problem is this: if the values of liberalism – freedom, equality and self-government – are increasingly modified supposedly to take account of social realities, what then is left of liberalism itself?[29]

It is precisely at this point that Gray's account of liberalism runs into difficulties. Not only does Gray see Hume's defence of limited government as unproblematically liberal in character, but he characterizes Burke (who bitterly attacks the theory of natural rights) as developing a form of conservatism in which 'liberal values are preserved but liberal hopes chastened'. In the same way the economists of the Scottish Enlightenment are praised for providing the first comprehensive statement in systematic form of 'the principles and foundation of liberalism'.[30] But the thinkers of the Scottish Enlightenment not only reject the social contract thesis; they show little interest in Locke's concern with establishing the legitimacy of property and the state. Adam Smith, the most celebrated figure of this Enlightenment, takes the 'realist' view that humans are naturally social in character and projects an evolutionary account of social development progressing from hunting, through pasturage, agriculture and finally commerce. It is true that in a society of hunters, Smith argues, there is little or no property and therefore no regular form of government. But such a society is not one in which people are naturally free and equal.

Humans, as Smith famously argues, have an inbuilt propensity to truck and barter, and this 'natural liberty' (as he calls it) can arise only from the development of exchange, the division of labour and acquisition of property. In short the 'natural' condition of society is to be attained only with the development of the highest stage of human history i.e. through commerce. The 'obvious and simple system of natural liberty' presupposes hierarchy and 'laws of justice' enforced by the state so that the notion of nature has been stripped of its anti-statist connotations. The liberal state, which must somehow transcend the class biases of civil society and apply laws equally and impartially to all, reflects the full development of human nature and the realization of this natural freedom.[31]

The problem then is this. By characterizing the (relative) conservatism of Smith and the Scottish Enlightenment as classically liberal in character, Gray simply dissolves away the anti-statist content of liberal ideals, and suppresses the notion of a schizoid malady – the built-in conflict between abstract theory and concrete practice. It is true that Gray continues to identify liberalism with (among other values) an individualism which asserts the 'moral primacy of the person against the claims of any social collectivity'. But if this is one of liberalism's defining attributes, how is such a 'moral primacy' to be established if all individuals are naturally members of hierarchical and statist societies?

This point is underscored by the utilitarianism of the nineteenth century which (it should be remembered) develops out of the work of Hume and the Scottish Enlightenment. Utilitarians like Bentham not only reject the 'anarchical fallacies' of natural rights theory, but they argue that individuals obey the state simply out of *interest*. This is an argument which (as Pateman stresses) strips liberal theory of its moral grounding. While it can account psychologistically for obedience, it cannot (nor does it try to) explain *obligation*. It explicitly abandons voluntarism, but without some kind of voluntarism (however hypothetical) the liberal emperor is indeed naked.[32]

Hobhouse puts the liberal case against utilitarianism memorably when he argues that, if rights depend upon utility, it becomes possible to envisage the complete subordination of the individual to society. Should the state maintain the rights of private property? Yes, if the community judges this to be useful; no, if it does not. True, the 'natural' pursuit of pleasure and the avoidance of pain affects all individuals equally as evidenced in the aggregative principle of the greatest happiness of the greatest number. But this makes liberty a mere means to a utilitarian end. Two equally illiberal possibilities, Hobhouse argues, might follow. Either a wise despot could govern if that seemed more conducive than popular rule to the greatest happiness of the greatest number, or conversely it might be possible for a majority to act tyrannically by insisting on slight inconvenience to itself at the expense of real suffering of a minority.[33]

Indeed Gray himself sees utilitarianism as providing a warrant for illiberalism, and characterizes J. S. Mill as affecting a rupture in the liberal tradition that begins with Bentham and James Mill.[34]

But the 'illiberalism' of the utilitarians itself derives from the rejection of the abstract individualism engineered by Hume and the Scottish Enlightenment. Utilitarianism exacerbates a schizoid malady which is inherent within liberalism itself. When abstract premisses come into collision with concrete social and statist realities, the former are simply abandoned in the interests of the latter. The utilitarians not only reject the notion of inalienable right: they also begin to argue that the capacity for pleasure is likely to be greater in the 'higher ranks of men'. In J. S. Mill's case it becomes even clearer that what divides individuals is more important than what unites them, and the attempt to differentiate between high and low pleasures in a revised theory of utilitarianism opens the way for a good deal of paternalistic interference. As Bellamy has argued, Mill's various proposals for rectifying block-ages on the road to improvement suggest that despotic methods suited to barbarians abroad might become permanent measures to keep people at home as well on the straight and narrow.[35]

Indeed Bellamy offers his own version of the schizoid malady. He distinguishes between 'ethical liberalism' in which market relations are idealized and an 'economic liberalism' which takes market-generated social inequalities and a coercive middle-class elite for granted. The tension between two can be found *within* individual liberal thinkers (and not simply between them), and it is a tension which is inherent in the liberal project. During periods of economic decline, political reaction and social unrest, 'ethical' optimism tends to desert liberals and 'economic' liberalism comes to the force. In the case of Mill and Green, the movement away from the 'ethical' pole expresses itself as an even more strident insistence on state intervention to realize liberal ideals. Hobhouse is spared the potentially authoritarian conclusions of his own theory until less prosperous times bring the two liberalisms into conflict.[36]

In Bellamy's view, ethical and economic liberalism presuppose each other in their mutual one-sidedness. In his analysis of Italian liberalism, he shows how Pareto (like many of those on the New Right today) starts as an ethical liberal and then, confronted by hierarchical 'facts', embraces a version of liberalism simply concerned with the pursuit of power for its own sake.[37] Moreover (as Bellamy points out) when Croce (for example) abandons his 'realist' welcome for fascism and makes the ethical case for a liberal state, he continues to reject classical doctrines of natural rights and sees the state as a utilitarian entity. In his section dealing with German liberalism, Bellamy argues that with Weber a commitment to liberal values co-exists with despair at the seeming inevitability

of bureaucracy, domination and elitism. Natural rights have lost
their credibility, and only outstanding individuals can overcome
the enervating and stultifying hierarchies of modern society.[38]

Kantians, Rousseau and Pateman's problem

The problem posed by the schizoid malady then is this. If liberalism abandons its (abstract) values in favour of supposedly
concrete realities, what happens to its distinctive identity? In the
period after the Second World War a positivistic liberalism
becomes difficult to distinguish from conservatism. The classical
heritage is explicitly abandoned as 'normative' and 'unscientific'
and, broadly speaking, the influential behavioural and linguistic
schools which come to dominate political theory are Humean and
utilitarian in temper. From the 1970s however there is not only (as
we have seen in chapter 2) a revival of interest in the state: the
ethical liberal tradition itself, which has received such a drubbing
from elitists like Schumpter, behaviouralists like Dahl and the
empiricist voting analysts, is resurrected. Utilitarian disdain for
classical political theory gives way to a concern with morality and
ethics, and we witness the development of a rights-based liberalism
looking to Kant rather than Hume for its theoretical inspiration.

But where does this Kantian liberalism stand in relation to the
critical (indeed subversive) insights of the natural rights tradition?
It is true that Kant himself advocates republicanism, a doctrine of
universal consent and the social contract. But he presents the
contract simply as an idea – as part of a noumenal and spiritual
world of reason which stands outside of the empirical and natural
world where humans remain egoistical and ineradically evil.[39] With
Kant the antinomies of the schizoid malady become conceptually
explicit. If we take reason as an *ideal*, then people should consent
to laws which treat them as ends. But what if they don't? Whatever
ought to happen in theory, Kant argues that in practice people
must obey laws whether they are consulted or not – a proviso (it
has been noted) which was 'no doubt convenient for the European
monarchs of his day'. His liberalism leaves people bound to their
governors hand and foot.[40] This combination of an a priori defence
of liberal principles on the one hand, and a practical willingness to
compromise with the tyranny on the other, points to a paradox
which arises within liberalism itself.[41]

This paradox is apparent also in what is generally regarded as the
most influential text of rights-based liberalism to appear in the

twentieth century. Rawls, it has been argued, brings together in his *Theory of Justice* some three hundred years of theorizing about the liberal state. Rawls asks his reader to imagine individuals in an 'original condition of liberty' in which they have no particular knowledge either about themselves or about anyone else. Rawls contends that this condition corresponds to the state of nature thesis in traditional social contract theory, but Pateman insists that it does nothing of the kind. For Rawls's argument derives from Kant rather than Locke. It is not intended, even hypothetically, to provide an account of the origins of the liberal state, and makes no attempt therefore to show *why* the state is justified. Rawls simply agrees with Kant that it is improper to regard the liberal state as if its right to be obeyed is open to doubt.[42] Like Kant's contract, the original condition is merely an 'idea' of rationality. This 'idea' expresses itself in terms of Rawls's principle of justice as fairness, and it is one which people will choose if they are rational even though they might refuse to accept it when actually consulted!

The original condition as conceived by Rawls is therefore quite unlike the traditional state of nature in classical liberalism. It is not a condition which people can 'leave' since the assumption (as in Hegel) is that the state *qua* state is unproblematic. It is there simply as a natural and necessary feature of the world, and requires no justification. Lacking a critique of the state, Rawls's argument is therefore (unsurprisingly) hierarchical in character. An elite with superior wisdom and judgement has an 'obligation' to the state, while the rest of society merely has a natural duty to obey – a duty which 'requires no voluntary acts in order to apply'.[43] The revival of a rights-based argument by Rawls simply underlines the extent to which modern liberalism even in its Kantian form has become uncritical of the state.

Although Hayek repudiates the kind of social justice advocated by Rawls, he is seen by Gray as a figure who has done more than anyone else to revive classical liberalism in the postwar period. Yet with Hayek the schizoid malady takes an even more virulent form. It has rightly been argued that his 'bizarre' liberalism has only superficial similarities to Locke and Kant and is best understood as a liberalism 'purged of all its classical truths'. Hayek argues that there is no material basis for equality at all, and cultural and spiritual freedom may well flourish better under autocratic than under popular rule. A bizarre form of liberalism indeed![44] I will consider Nozick's libertarian critique of the state (which is often compared to Hayek's) in the chapter of anarchism. Here I want to conclude by tackling Pateman's contention that a solution to liberalism's schizoid malady can in fact be found in the particular version of social contract theory presented by Rousseau.

Rousseau, Pateman contends, denies that the liberal state can be justified through voluntarist arguments. He should not be described as a liberal thinker at all. She rightly stresses the remarkable realism of his conjectural history of the state of nature where he sees individual characteristics and social relationships as mutually reinforcing. His natural condition (unlike that of Hobbes and Locke) consists of sentient beings, some of whom are potentially (but only potentially) human. This human potential involves the capacity to act on the basis of rational deliberation and on moral principles, and it is realized only as humans increase in numbers, start hunting and settle down into family groupings. As this occurs, the seeds of a self-interest (an *amour propre*) are sewn, and with the discovery of metallurgy and agriculture, social inequalities deepen, war develops between rich and poor and a liberal social contract results.

For Rousseau (as Pateman rightly emphasizes) this liberal social contract is a fraud. It does no more than stabilize inequality and gives an appearance of legitimacy to the domination of some over others. The formation of the state sees people running headlong to their chains thinking they have secured their freedom. The formal nature of a liberal contract as an abstract egalitarian device merely conceals real inequalities in power. Rousseau argues for a form of social contract in which individuals will not passively *obey* the dictates of another, but are obligated by laws they have made themselves. Here is a contract which provides (Pateman argues) 'an actual foundation for a participatory political order of the future'.[45]

Rousseau's celebrated argument is certainly radical and challenging, and Pateman is right to suppose that dramatic social and political change would be necessary if each individual citizen was to be in a position to think of his or her own interests in terms of the good of each member of the community. But can we assume that Rousseau's argument takes us beyond the schizoid malady of classical liberalism in which an abstract anti-statism presupposes the 'concrete' necessity for the state? Pateman presents Rousseau as a consistent critic of liberal theory, but where (we must ask) does Rousseau stand on the state – the sovereign institution which claims a monopoly of legitimate force for a given territory?

The use of force is central to the mechanism of the state, and it is on this point that Pateman falters. Rousseau famously refers in his *Social Contract* to the need to force people to be free, but this celebrated phase, Pateman argues, might better be rendered as 'strengthened' to be free in order to capture the moral and educative effect of political participation.[46] The argument is not persuasive. Pateman herself notes that when making the case for a 'civil religion' Rousseau insists that the severest penalties up to and including execution must be imposed for non-compliance. Physical force is to be used against law-breakers in general so that murderers consent to die, the galley slaves are in chains and adulterous wives are deemed guilty of treason, presumably a capital offence. Pateman concedes further that, for Rousseau, minorities in general can be forced to comply with the will of the majority, and she protests that 'this argument contradicts the basic principles of his theory'.[47]

But Pateman's problem arises because she fails to see Rousseau as a theorist who takes the state ultimately for granted. His argument can be understood only if it is located within its liberal framework. In the first place, humans for Rousseau enjoy a natural independence as abstract beings – so abstract indeed that their humanity is merely potential – and it is this natural independence which endows them with their absolute freedom as individuals. Crucial to Rousseau's argument is the assumption that individuals derive their capacity to will not from society but from their creator,[48] and this absolute sovereignty of the individual translates into the unconditional freedom of the general will.

Of course Rousseau insists that the individual right to property is one which must be enjoyed by all so that a legitimate social contract rests upon a substantive rather than a purely formal equality. Nevertheless his argument is still liberal in character. The individual desire for property is seen in practice as part of human nature, and so is the market. Hence the graphic dictum that, while the force of circumstance tends always to destroy equality, the force of legislation ought always to tend to preserve it.[49] As a liberal Rousseau assumes that inequality is inherent in society. Chains may be legitimated but they can never be eradicated, and it is on the basis of these premisses that there follows the classic statist scenario. Radical conflicts of interest are ultimately endemic and irremovable. Hence force is necessary to try and resolve them.

In effect, Rousseau ultimately endorses Hobbes's argument for the necesity of the state. Like Kant, he believes that human nature resists putting reason fully in control so that an apparatus employing force will always be with us. As Levine puts it crisply, some of the people all of the time and all of the people some of the time will need to be 'forced to be free'.[50] Prominent among the recpients of state force are likely to be women, dissidents and (since social circumstances make substantial equality impossible) the poor and dependent as well. Pateman has to concede that, for all the brilliance of his critique of liberal theory, Rousseau shares in the 'liberal failure to include everyone in the argument for political equality'.[51] But this failure arises precisely because Rousseau's critique of the liberal state is itself liberal in character. He never succeeds in transcending a schizoid malady (symptomatic of liberalism as a whole) in which an abstract view of the individual ultimately necessitates concrete support for the state.

SUMMARY

- All modern critiques of the state are responses to liberalism as a theory which holds that the state is unnatural and yet argues that naturally free individuals are obliged to accept its force.

- This accounts for the 'schizoid malady' which lies at the heart of liberalism. An abstract view of the individual both opposes and yet presupposes the need for an institution which secures compliance to laws through force.

- Liberals subsequently have sought to soften this paradox by accepting the sociability of individuals and denying the existence of abstract natural rights. But this stance simply perpetuates the problem. Liberalism is distinct from conservatism only if it continues to defend the right of individuals to authorize the laws they are expected to obey.

- The postwar revival of rights-based liberalism exemplifies rather than resolves this problem by arguing for ideas of justice and freedom which take the force of the state for granted.

8

Anarchism

A critique of the state must address itself to the relevance of anarchism since anarchism more than any other creed explicitly sets itself against the state. Anarchism is of course a highly disparate doctrine embracing positions (as we shall see) at both extremes of the ideological spectrum. It is also a very old theory but as a systematic critique of the state anarchism really emerges only in the eighteenth century as part of the European Enlightenment and in the wake of the French Revolution.[1]

Although anarchism is sometimes presented as an extreme form of socialism, it is with its relationship to liberalism that we must begin, since anarchism (as it has been well said) 'owes more to conventional liberalism than some of its exponents are willing to admit'.[2] We have already seen that liberalism suffers from an incurable schizoid malady born of abstract premises which necessarily imply concrete and statist hierarchies.

Anarchism, I shall argue, despite its vigorous opposition to the state, cannot escape the same fate since anarchists embrace an abstract individualism which makes a coherent critique of the state impossible. Philosophical anarchists are unable to account for co-operation and community, while those who postulate a stateless society as an extension of the free market cannot plausibly tackle the problem of division and inequality. Even anarchists who explicitly identify freedom in 'communitarian' terms espouse notions of spontaneity which lead in practice to an authoritarian politics and an uncritical view of violence.

The individual and society: the philosophical argument

There is widespread agreement that the first comprehensive exposition of anarchist principles is to be found in Godwin's classic

Enquiry Concerning Political Justice (1793). Godwin embraces the conventionalism central to the liberal critique, but he had (like most other thinkers of his day) abandoned the state of nature thesis. Humans are social beings and, as such, they have no inalienable natural rights. However although Godwin is a utilitarian, he links his utilitarianism with what he calls the 'right to private judgement' – a sphere of discretion which is inviolable. Individuals alone can decide what is conducive to their own happiness, and hence any compulsory restraint violates a privately determined pursuit of happiness. On this basis the state is necessarily vicious, evil and tyrannical.[3]

Godwin's theory is rooted in (and demonstrates the extraordinary implications which flow from) a commitment to abstract individualism. Pateman is right to suggest that he ends where Hobbes begins,[4] since, despite his view that humans associate for the sake of mutual assistance, society is never more than the sum of its parts. It is merely an aggregation of individuals who view the world through their own subjective viewpoints. If this atomism leads to radical insecurity and arbitrariness in Hobbes, for Godwin it generates the 'unspeakably beautiful' vision of a world in which individuals freely exercise their private judgement. Hence social institutions stand in the way of individual freedom, and everything normally understood by the term 'co-operation' is in some degree an evil. Even the act of promising violates the sphere of individual discretion, since promising binds our future conduct and would distract us from the consequences of our particular actions. Like obligations, laws are inherently oppressive because they are necessarily general in character whereas every case (like every individual) is 'a rule to itself'. Even laws passed in a direct democracy deprave understanding and character, binding people to decisions reached collectively as a 'fictitious' and corporate community.[5]

Godwin may have been opposed to property, the market and acquisitiveness in general, but his anarchist assumptions derive from the abstract individualism of Hobbes and (I would argue) Rousseau.[6] His opposition to the state extends to social relationships in general. However sociable and perfectible individuals ought to be, they retain a sphere of private judgement that is essentially atomistic and non-relational in character. Godwin may have hoped that small face-to-face communities would replace the state (with temporary co-ordinating bodies being transitionally necessary to resolve disputes and repel invaders), but he has rightly been called a 'philosophical anarchist' since his main preoccupation is with principles rather than with practice. Indeed it is not clear how *any* solution to the problem of the state can derive from Godwin's arguments, given his insistence that co-operation, organization and even direct democracy all infringe personal autonomy. His is a theory which, as Pateman comments crisply, takes away from individuals the means of transcending their own subjectivity.[7]

The problem of trying to sustain a critique of the state based on abstract individualist assumptions is revealed also in the arguments of Stirner. Stirner is often bracketed with Godwin as a 'philosophical' anarchist, but, unlike Godwin, Stirner does not see individuals as benevolent and rational, and he enthusiastically embraces the Young Hegelian argument that alienated consciousness is the source of all our oppression. The logic of his argument however is still rooted in the atomistic premises of classical liberalism. The state of nature may be social in character, but individuals constitute the highest level of reality and Stirner exhorts them to depart from their natural condition! People have no rights of any kind. As a conscious egoist, the individual (in Stirner's view) is beyond good and evil and the oppressiveness of the state is no different in essence from the oppressiveness of social relationships. Both subject the ego to some 'generality or other'.[8]

Like Hobbes, Stirner sees the natural world as a war of all against all. To escape, what is required however is not a powerful state but an association of sovereign individuals – a union of conscious egoists – who would spontaneously and voluntarily come together out of mutual interest. As with Godwin, direct democracy is out. In fact all 'teleological' categories – goals, purposes, ends – are oppressive even if they are imposed by individuals upon themselves. The union of egoists would nevertheless enable individuals to accomplish more than they could on their own, and, given Stirner's (again Hobbesian) assumption that all individuals are more or less equal, this union would create security and end poverty even though Stirner's egoistical world is one without rights or morality. The logical extremism of Stirner's argument (like that of Godwin's) is revealing because again it demonstrates the impotence of a critique of the state based on abstract individualism. As Marx and Engels comment in their lengthy critique of *The Ego and His Own*, Stirner employs a concept of uniqueness as a norm which morally obliges other individuals. Like all philosophical anarchists, he is in the hapless position of having to attack authority from moral premises which are not supposed to exist.[9]

This problem doubtlessly accounts for the muddled and contradictory stance embraced by Wolff in his much more recent but frequently cited defence of anarchism. If Godwin's premisses are utilitarian and Stirner's egoistical, Wolff argues his case from a neo-Kantian position. All adults are responsible beings who exercise a capacity for choice and have a potential for autonomy which they lose if they obey the dictates of another. Since a person's primary obligation is to be autonomous, legitimate authority of any kind is a contradiction in terms. However so disabling is the logic of this argument that Wolff feels that he has to accept that, in the case of a direct democracy at least, people can be bound by decisions they have been involved in making. At this point his argument takes on a positively Rousseauan turn. The authority to which each citizen submits, he suggests, 'is not that of himself simply, but that of the entire community taken collectively'. Each person now encounters 'his better self in the form of the state, for its dictates are simply the laws which he has, after due deliberation, willed to be enacted'.[10]

The argument is all-revealing since it demonstrates the problem of trying to justify authority from a non-relational view of the individual. From the assertion that all authority is equally problematic, Wolff moves to an assertion that (in conditions of direct democracy at least) all authority is wholly *unproblematic*. The 'police power of the state' (as Wolff calls it) ensures that individuals obey laws they have ostensibly imposed upon themselves – precisely the kind of statist mystification that (as Dahl comments) Wolff's 'defence' of anarchism was surely intended to rebut. The authoritarian character of his argument arises out of (abstractly conceived) anti-authoritarian premisses.[11] As another of Wolff's critics has noted, the concept of a moral judgement must imply the existence of some kind of authoritatative public arena without which the conduct of an individual cannot be assessed. If autonomy and authority are linked in this way,[12] then this can only reinforce the argument that abstract individualism is powerless to provide the philosophical basis for a coherent critique of the state.

A Lockean state of nature without inconveniences?

While the philosophical anarchists we have looked at all subscribe (in some form or other) to individualism, they say little about the kind of stateless society which might flow from these abstract premisses. In contrast, what are generally called individualistic anarchists combine their indictment of existing states with a dogged and developed attempt to construct an alternative model.

Individualistic anarchists have (as we would expect) a close relationship to classical liberalism. They start from the premiss that the individual is sovereign, and many 'individualists' (as I shall call them) embrace a philosophy of natural rights. If, as one of their leading postwar exponents warns, utilitarianism is preferred to natural rights, statism itself becomes relatively easy to justify.[13] The individualists generally identify with Locke's state of nature as an anarchic order where market relationships provide the cohesion and discipline which renders the state redundant. This involves an element of mystification since (as noted earlier) Locke's state of nature embraces government and (in its later phases) even absolute monarchy. What it simply lacks is a *liberal* state! Moreover Locke's construct is a conceptual device to justify the rise of the (liberal) state so that individualists need to explain why the inconveniences of the state of nature, which Locke believed would inevitably degenerate into war, can somehow be avoided.

The nineteenth-century exponents of 'Lockean' anarchism were often critical of the structural inequalities generated by the market.[14] However, the more recent individualists can legitimately be called 'anarcho-capitalists' since, like Rothbard, they insist that exploitation and coercion are simply the product of the state.[15] Substantial inequalities between capitalists and workers are inevitable in a free society. State welfare is as pernicious as state warfare, and all attempts to regulate production deny consumers access to the commodities which *they* wish to buy. Goods which everyone wants – sanitation, roads, street-lighting for example – are best provided by private enterprise, while groups like the elderly, the unemployed and the disabled should be catered for by charity since state provision is invariably wasteful and open to abuse.[16]

But it is not only the 'positive' functions of the state which ought to be left to the market. Anarcho-capitalists argue that the market can take over the state's 'negative' functions as well so that Rothbard contends that people could privately insure themselves against bodily assault, for example, in the same way that they currently insure their possessions against theft. Aggrieved parties would then seek compensation and redress for injury through private tribunals, and the free market would see to it that arbitrators and judges with the best record in settling disputes would prosper according to their reputation for impartiality and efficiency.

But how would judgements be enforced? Recalitrants could be subject to boycott and ostracism, and in the case of more serious 'crimes' private agencies could hire guards and police both to defend themselves and their clients, and to tackle those who failed to pay compensation or accept imprisonment for their misdeeds. As with tribal blood feuds, an individual might even decide (perhaps with the help of friends and relatives) to retaliate in person, and killing a murderer would become the legitimate concern of a private court only if the wrong person was obliterated![17] Getting rid of the state – 'the great legalized and socially legitimated channel of all manner of social crime' – would (Rothbard believes) strengthen the good in 'human nature' and discourage the bad,[18] but humans remain possessive individualists by nature. It is precisely this assumption which leads his fellow libertarian Nozick to argue the case for a minimal state.

Nozick's *Anarchy, State and Utopia* (1974) is significant in this context since it attempts to construct a non-anarchist case on the basis of individualist anarchist principles. Nozick starts from a 'Lockean' position of natural rights, and he sees protection as a good like any other which (as in Rothbard's scenario) competing protective associations seek to provide. However, Nozick unlike Rothbard assumes that, as a result of this competition, one dominant protective agency will necessarily emerge which excludes other defence associations from acting in its area. Nozick describes this dominant protective agency as an *ultraminimal* state: it acts exclusively but protects only those who pay for its services. It becomes a *minimal* state when it provides protection for all within its 'domain' whether they pay privately or not.

Nozick argues that the state emerges as the consequence of an invisible hand which violates the rights of no one in the process. Hence he insists that his case for the state rests upon anarchist principles.[19] The argument is however vulnerable even on its own terms. Anarcho-capitalism must assert that, if one agency restricts the activities of others, it violates their property rights. To get round this problem, Nozick has to contend that other agencies risk 'rights violation' if they continue to protect their clients. But, as Paul notes,[20] this is an extremely dubious rabbit to pull out of the hat. After all 'procedural rights' on Nozick's own admission are not natural in character, and each party can legitimately invoke its own version of such rights in defence. Only *force majeure* can resolve the issue, and Nozick seeks to sweeten this coercive pill by arguing that, since competitive agencies act in a risky way, they merit compensation. This they receive when the minimal state provides protection for all citizens free of charge.

But this argument only exacerbates Nozick's problems for if the state is to be justified on the basis that certain activities are too risky to be undertaken privately, then (as I have pointed out

elsewhere) this is a principle capable of an almost infinite extension.[21] What *is* plausible about Nozick's argument is the admission
that, in a free market, competition generates monopoly with a
dominant protective agency coming to look suspiciously like a
dominant protection *racket*. It is true that Rothbard contends that
a rogue agency would face public wrath and retaliation from other
private agencies, but this is hardly convincing. After all it is
precisely because the classical liberals of the past believed that
spontaneous competition yields concentrations of power, that they
insisted that individuals should leave the state of nature and place
themselves under the protection of the 'monopolistic' state.[22]

The problem of how people might protect themselves in a purely
individualistic 'society' raises a more general difficulty. Protection is
a example of a 'public good' – a good which by definition cannot
be supplied to one person without being supplied to all. The
provision of these goods is possible only if free riders can be
persuaded to conform. They in turn exemplify the wider problem of
'externalities' which arise from the unintentionally *social* consequences of individual acts. Whether these externalities are negative (when say a factory pollutes the environment) or 'positive'
(when protecting your property protects your neighbour's as well),
they reflect the vulnerability of the 'invisible hand' thesis in a world
in which the social interdependency of individuals has become
increasingly difficult to ignore. One of Rothbard's critics has rightly
noted that, unless we assume the existence of 'shared interests and
common peers',[23] it is hard to see how we could prevent individual
actions from undermining order or expect 'courts' to enforce their
decisions in a stateless society. But the assumption that individuals
are the members of an egalitarian community of shared interests
and common peers is one which (needless to say) anarcho-capitalists
are vehemently committed to deny!

Spontaneity, coercion and the problem of government

The inclusion of the 'individualists' in the camp of anarchy is often
rejected by those who regard the values of solidarity and co-
operation as central to anarchist ideals.[24] But even if we accept that
communitarian anarchists (as I shall call them) are the authentic
representatives of their tradition, we still need to explore the
question as to whether these theorists have succeeded in overcom-
ing the abstract individualism which stands in the way of a
coherent critique of the state.

On the face of it 'communitarians' espouse a social rather than an individualistic analysis of hierarchy and power. Bakunin, Marx's political rival during the battles over the First International in the 1860s, declares with an anti-Hobbesian fervour that 'man is born into society, just as an ant is born into ant-hill or a bee into its hive.'[25] Freedom itself arises 'positively' as the satisfaction of needs and wants within a solidaristic community. To a greater or less extent communitarians oppose not only the repressive hierarchies of the state but the inequalities and exploitation identified with capitalism. The co-operative character of humans is conceived in terms of the concept of *spontaneity*. To act spontaneously, anarchists argue, is to act without restraint or restriction, and hence, if it *were* possible to have a 'pure anarchy' (most anarchists concede that it is not), this anarchy would involve the complete absence of social controls and hierarchical power. Spontaneous activity, communitarians argue, is possible because society is a self-regulating order which develops best when least interfered with. It does not, in the words of Proudhon (another of Marx's nineteenth-century socialist adversaries), have to be wound up but carries its own pendulum and spring within itself.[26]

But why should society have this self-regulating character? Spontaneity is natural, law-governed, instinctual and unconscious. It is grounded in what Marshall calls a kind of 'cosmic optimism'.[27] It is true that Malatesta challenges Kropotkin's view of nature as a providence in which there has to be harmony in all things, and argues that throughout history solidaristic and exploitative instincts have co-existed. But the point is that the proclivity towards spontaneity is still as instinctual, absolute and (in this sense) as natural as its opposite. It provides the basis for establishing what Malatesta calls 'perfect solidarity among men of the whole world'. If, for Bakunin, humans are naturally beasts and slaves with an instinct for power, they are also naturally sociable and autonomous beings with an instinct to revolt.[28]

Spontaneous individuals are therefore (as anarchists see them) people unrestricted by hierarchical dependencies of any kind. Since this sociability is instinctual in character, it is not a sociability born of human relationships. Malatesta argues that 'men must love each and look upon each other as members of one family',[29] but family relationships (taken generically) are surely *involuntary* in the sense that children normally do not choose their parents or parents their children. This involuntary dimension within human life is arguably symptomatic of social relations in general in the sense that individuals constantly find themselves in contexts which confront them as givens. This is not to say that we lack freedom to change this world. It is merely to assert that we can express this freedom only through our relationships with others, and the point about relationships is that they restrict as well as empower. Both dimensions are incompatible with the splendid isolation of the abstract individual.

This point explains why liberals in the seventeenth and eighteenth centuries placed individuals outside of society in order to ascribe to them absolutist notions of freedom and autonomy. While an anarchist theory of spontaneity is easy to understand in terms of the abstract individualism which underpins the philosophical and anarcho-capitalist traditions, it is rather more problematic when it is invoked to support communitarian arguments. For if the communtarians are serious in asserting that humans are social in character, then logically they cannot link spontaneity with an absence of hierarchical dependencies of *any* kind. A social view of individuals is a relational view, and the essence of social relationships (as we stressed in chapter 6) is that they necessarily locate freedom within specific constraints.

This leads to a further implication of the relational argument. A relationship of any kind must imply that activity is to a lesser or greater degree *organized*. A relationship involves the adoption of *roles*, and roles can be defined only in terms of mutually limiting and enabling rules and expectations. Of course individuals act through a multiplicity of roles, and they may jettison one in favour of another (or create new roles altogether). But while organized activity allows (and is indeed a precondition for) freedom, it cannot be reconciled with a notion of spontaneity which is absolute and unconditional in character. If sociability is instinctive then it is not relational, since human nature itself is not the product of predetermined 'instincts'. It is a relationship which expresses microcosmically the way in which humans *relate* to nature through their technical, economic, social and cultural organizations. An anarchist view of 'instincts' ignores the dynamic character of sociability which has become obvious since the middle of the nineteenth century.

A relational (as opposed to an anarchist) view of spontaneity has crucial implications for the concepts of coercion and government we need to employ in our critique of the state. While anarchists rightly emphasize the importance of stateless societies in the past, they fail to embrace the full implications of what I have called in chapter 3 the anthropological argument. On the one hand Marshall notes that stateless societies employ sanctions of approval and disapproval as 'instruments of social control'. But to speak of 'sanctions' is to speak of social and moral coercion. Yet Marshall is unwilling to concede that stateless societies are societies which are *governed*. He argues that all anarchists 'whatever their persuasion' believe in a concept of spontaneous order which compels them to oppose not only the state and government but what he calls 'the coercion of imposed authority'.[30]

The point is that some concept of coercion is (as I have argued elsewhere) inherent in all social relationships. It is impossible for the freest person to be unaffected by Mill's natural penalties, the opinion of society or (rationally persuasive) arguments which refer to the unpleasant social and natural consequences which follow if we fail to pursue a particular line of action. Although Taylor does not allow for what I have referred to as the 'coercion' of social and natural circumstances, he defines coercion as the making of substantial and credible threats. A society in which individual did not possess the ability to make *any* credible threat is almost inconceivable. In other words Taylor himself (despite his sympathies with anarchism) emphasizes that the absence of an organ imposing concentrated force on society (i.e. a *state*) should not be taken to imply an absence of coercion in general.[31]

If, as I have argued, humans are social because they are relational beings, then they cannot survive without coercion or government. Here Marshall's position is most revealing. He comments that, in solving disputes, public opinion and social pressure can operate in a stateless society as powerful deterrents and sanctions. He characterizes these deterrents and sanctions as a 'political and moral coercion' but insists that they would give way to freely adopted customs and norms as a new social order made disputes 'increasingly unlikely'. In other words, it is only because Marshall believes that *disputes* themselves would become unlikely in the future that he suggests that coercion itself would disappear.[32] This surely does acknowledge (leaving aside the idea that a form of society can be envisaged without any disputes whatsoever) that the state is not the same as government, and that sanctions can be considered coercive even though they do not employ physical force.

There is a further problem with the anarchist view of spontaneity. To link the state with government as the twin enemies of freedom is to ignore the extent to which government even within state-centred societies has a positive role to play. It has been frequently noted that, with the rise of new liberal and socialist administrations, significant programmes of social reform have been introduced, strengthening the power of the trade unions, for example, improving the security and health of the most vulnerable sections of society and implementing a modest redistribution of income and resources. This has led one radical theorist to protest that if the state vanished overnight, 'there would an orgy of unlimited repression and exploitation by capitalism'.[33] We will return to the question of the 'welfare state' in the chapter on democracy, but it is worth reiterating the point made in chapter 3 that, once we distinguish between government and state, it becomes possible to see that many activities undertaken in the name of the state are not necessarily and intrinsically statist in character.

Anarchist attacks on the 'welfare state' as bureaucratic and oppressive can be described as *anti-statist* only if they are able to show that the governmental provision of welfare and security has to be underpinned by a body which possesses a monopoly of legitimate force. The mere fact that administration 'interferes' with or constrains individuals does not in itself imply statist oppression since these activities could assume a purely governmental character. Indeed this kind of 'interference' is inherent in relationships in general.

Carter is therefore right to argue[34] that the existence of administration does not in itself raise the question of violence directly, although bureaucracy may create psychological remoteness and (I would add) is often linked empirically to radical conflicts of interest which create the need for the state. Nevertheless we need conceptual tools which make it possible to keep state and administration separate, and, while it is understandable that anarcho-capitalists vigorously object to any regulation of the market whether it is governmental or statist in character, it is surely odd that theorists who link freedom with community should continue to embrace concepts of spontaneity and government which derive their logic from the abstract individualism of the liberal tradition.

Ends, means and the question of violence

The problem of how to move from a state-centred to a stateless society is one which is not merely acute for anarchists, but insoluble. By equating state violence with government and coercion in general, they make it impossible to develop a coherent argument for transcending the state.

It is true that some anarchists acknowledge the need for a preparatory period before a full fledged stateless society can emerge. Godwin, for example, believed that it would take a considerable time before society became sufficiently enlightened to adopt anarchist institutions, and Marshall has suggested that different types of anarchist organization could be taken to represent stages of progression towards an anarchist goal. Thus Proudhon's mutualism (involving the social regulation of competing private producers) could give way to Bakunin's collectivism (where people are rewarded for the work they do) which in turn might yield to the more comprehensive idea of Kropotkin's communism (where reward is according to need).[35]

But however we conceive an anarchist society, the problem still remains: can we get rid of the state without (at the very least) utilizing governmental means to do so? This is a difficulty which confronts all anarchists, even conservative pro-capitalist libertarians who seek no more than a radical extension of existing free market practices. Miller argues that all revolutionary ideologists are caught in a trap: the assumptions necessary to make their ideals plausible also make it impossible to understand past and contemporary developments.[36] If, as anarcho-capitalists argue, the market is a source of freedom, how is it that certain beneficiaries of the market have a vested interest in perpetuating concentrations of state power? The very 'terrorism' and 'invasiveness' of the state adds to our difficulties since in Rothbard's view the state faces no limit except for 'the extremely difficult course of revolution against a power with all the guns in its hands'. Rothbard declines to elaborate the tactical implications of this argument since clearly the 'extremely difficult course of revolution' is hard to square with the continuing sanctity of the exchange relationships of the free market.[37]

For communitarians the problem of matching anarchist means to an anarchist end is even more acute since here our concern is with replacing hierarchical capitalism with an egalitarian community. I have spoken elsewhere of the problem of what I have called Rousseau's paradox: people are to govern themselves in a world in which they are everywhere in chains.[38] On the one hand they are enslaved, but on the other hand the ideal of self-government forbids recourse to special assistance from leaders and rulers 'on high'. It is true that Marshall argues that anarchists reject only authoritarian forms of organization[39] but it is far from clear how this meets the paradox since (as we have seen) organization itself becomes inconceivable if we reject coercion and government along with the state.

Miller cites the sad reflections of Goldman as she compares the weaknesses of Russian anarchists when set against the organizational strengths of the Bolsheviks. The work of the anarchists, she remarks, 'would have been of infinitely greater practical value had they been better organized' but she fails to ask whether these failures are implicit within the theory itself.[40] The problem is – as Rousseau's paradox suggests – that it is impossible to move beyond abstract spontaneity without contradicting anarchist ideals. These contradictions take a particularly sharp and colourful form in the theory and practice of Bakunin. Bakunin insists that the instinct for revolt is natural, and therefore political organization constitutes an intolerable inroad into autonomy and freedom. However, this raises the difficulty: what is the anarchist to do if the popular masses fail to rise up in revolt?

Two responses are possible. Either anarchists (as in Godwin's case) simply wait for the spirit of rational enlightenment to seep down to the ignorant masses however long this process takes, or (as in Bakunin's case) the people need some kind of helping hand. A general staff must act as intermediaries between 'the revolutionary idea and the instincts of the people'. This at least is a practical rather than a 'philosophical' response but the ensuing problem is formidable since the general staff (as their title suggests) resort not only to organization but to organization with an authoritarian vengeance. Bakunin is notorious for his secret societies, manipulation, deceit and 'invisible dictatorship'. The Bakuninist dictatorship is to be invisible presumably because (as the Jurassian Federation of Anarchists specified under Bakunin's influence in 1874), this is a 'dictatorship' which the insurgent masses exercise without the mediation of any committee or government![41]

An anti-authoritarian end co-exists not simply with coercion and government but with the kind of force which is unambiguously authoritarian in character. The argument points to two distinct problems with the anarchist scenario. The first is the one already noted with anarcho-capitalists. If the state is organized as a repressive hierarchy with formidable and comprehensive powers, how do you remove it without becoming statist as well? The problem has been frequently noted with regard to anarchist activities during the Spanish Civil War. Miller argues that in Spain during this period the much vaunted ideal of spontaneity proved a liability and had to be abandoned as anarchists adopted military methods of organization. He cites Borkenau's comment that in one of the villages of Aragon the agragian revolution was the 'almost automatic consequence of executions' carried out by the anarchist militia, and records that between September 1936 and March 1937 the militia were incorporated into the regular Republican army.[42]

The second problem which faces anarchists seeking to transcend the state is even more arresting. For this raises the question of whether, in using organizational (and even statist) means to combat the state, there is not, as one sympathetic commentator has ruefully argued, 'a streak of psychopathic violence' which runs through anarchism.[43] We see for example how after the crushing of the Paris Commune in 1871 anarchists resorted to a tactic of 'propaganda by deed' – dramatic action designed to shake the masses out of their passivity – and these propagandist 'deeds' often degenerated into acts of terror. The agonized slogan of the radical black youth in the South African townships in the 1980s – 'liberation before education' – echoes comments by Italian followers of Garibaldi and Proudhon in the 1870s. A belief that 'everything is right provided it is not legal' leads to support for a terrorism which is justified as a way of avenging wrongs against the people, inspiring fear in the enemy and highlighting the evil practices of the state.[44] It has often (and rightly) been observed not only that this violence is counterproductive in that it increases both the repression and apparent legitimacy of the state, but that it flatly contradicts anarchist values of individual autonomy and freedom.[45]

Even Kropotkin, whose personal life has often been described in saint-like terms, displays what Marshall has called 'an uncomfortable mixture of quietism and aggressive elements' typical of many anarchists. Indeed at one point in his life Kropotkin supports the arguments of the anarcho-syndicalist Sorel that violence is the revolutionary whirlwind which energizes 'sluggish hearts'.[46] But is this 'psychopathic streak of violence' *inherent* in anarchist opposition to the state? Carter certainly finds elements within anarchism which are 'peculiarly receptive' to the appeals of violence. Its utopianism, she argues, encourages a belief that a golden age might be realized through one final apocalyptic outburst, while the emphasis upon a natural and instinctual desire for revolt can only promote what Bakunin calls 'the poetry of destruction'.

By shunning the 'contamination' associated with political organization in its conventional form, anarchists (Carter argues) put themselves in the bizarre position of suggesting that it may be worse to cast a ballot than fire a bullet, 'even if the ballot is intended to undermine the existing regime'.[47] In other words, the very refusal to compromise with existing organizations may lead to violence and, in Bakunin's case for example, to political manoeuvring of a highly authoritarian kind. The key to this extraordinary paradox lies (it seems to me) in an abstract concept of spontaneity which rejects the relational and organized character of human activity itself.

It is revealing that it is Michels as an anarchist turned authoritarian who finds all organization to be despotic, for the point is that anarchists make it impossible to conceptualize organization in ways which involve coercion and hierarchy but not physical force. They may comment (as Malatesta did) that the greater part of life in state-centred societies takes place without state intervention, but by identifying state intervention as 'government intervention' it becomes difficult to make sense of the constraints and restrictions which all associations (and indeed relationships in general) impose upon their participants. Godwin considered public opinion as a force no less irresistible than whips or chains; Orwell (cited sympathetically by Marshall) found Tolstoy's pacifism potentially coercive, while Gandhi's non-violence exerted (we are told) a moral force over people which has coercive overtones.[48]

The point then is this. It is one thing to warn (as Mill did) against opinion becoming intolerant and needlessly intrusive. It is quite another to suggest that ultimately moral coercion is as unacceptable as brute force. For, as we have seen, the relational character of society cannot be squared with a spontaneity which identifies individual sovereignty with an absence of all restraint. If the limits imposed by natural penalties and moral coercion are deemed authoritarian, then constitutionalism and the rule of law have to be rejected even if these institutions were to operate in a purely governmental rather than in an oppressively statist way. Sorel demonstrates graphically how an abstract contempt for political organization can be linked to the glorification of violence and elitist rule.

As I shall argue in my next chapter, if the constitutional and legal 'ideals' of the liberal tradition are rejected as oppressive, then the struggle to move beyond the state necessarily takes an authoritarian form (with all the grotesque paradoxes that that involves). To prevent emancipatory ends from being continuously sabotaged by authoritarian means, it is necessary therefore to transcend the abstract notions of individual sovereignty and spontaneity which anarchists uncritically appropriate from the liberal tradition.

SUMMARY

- Anarchists reject the state but the assumptions upon which they base this opposition are essentially liberal in character.

- In the case of philosophical anarchists like Godwin, Stirner and Wolff, an absolute autonomy for the individual is postulated which makes it impossible to explain the need for co-operation and the reality of community.

- Individualist anarchists seem to be more practical since they offer accounts of what a stateless society might actually look like. However since they see the free market as the mechanism which supplants the state, the kind of private arbitration they advocate could protect only individuals who were all members of an egalitarian community – the very assumption individualist anarchists seek to avoid.

- Anarchists who do accept the need for community identify freedom as a natural instinct rather than as the product of social relationships which can coerce as well as liberate. These 'communitarians' are unable to distinguish government from the state, unwittingly embrace authoritarian forms of organization and may even extol the virtues of violence.

9

Marxism

Marxism shares with the anarchism the idea that freedom and emancipation require the disappearance of the state. It is true that on occasion Marx and Engels refer both to the 'state forms' of a future communist society and to states which institutionally embodied the common interest of societies in the past.[1] But these references are (as we shall see) atypical and misleading. However much Marx and Engels may have dissented from anarchist concepts, they endorse the idea that a free society is a stateless one.

It is also true that it was Engels who specifically referred to 'the withering away of the state' whereas Marx (particularly in his early writings) speaks of the abolition, the dissolution and the 'transcendence' of the state. But in my view the differences here are stylistic rather than substantial.[2] Both took the view that a future communist society would be stateless in character, and both distanced themselves from those forms of socialism which aim simply to see the state 'reformed'.[3]

I shall argue however that Marxists have to explain why a theory which is extremely critical of the state leads in practice to the formation of repressive political regimes. To claim that this development is simply the product of unfortunate circumstances ignores the irony of a socialism which claims to do no more than 'scientifically' articulate historical circumstances. A contradiction between theory and practice is not incidental but derives from the way in which Marxists postulate communism as the predetermined outcome of events and the proletariat as the preordained agent of revolution.

Introducing the despotism thesis

We have already noted the problems which a schizophrenic relation between theory and practice poses for liberalism. What I wish to call the 'despotism thesis' asserts that Marxism also suffers from a schizoid malady which presents itself as 'the persistent discrepancy' between Marxism's emancipatory ambitions and the repressive actuality of its practice.[4]

The recent collapse of the Communist Party states of Eastern Europe and the former USSR has given a dramatic edge to the despotism thesis since these upheavals appear to confront Marxism with the sternest possible judgement of history. But it might be argued that history is merciless to all ideologies so that the rise and fall of Communist Party states tells us no more about Marxism than the reign of a Borgia does about Christianity.[5] The regimes of 'existing socialism' demonstrate merely that backward social conditions produce backward and repressive forms of society. Indeed some Marxists have sought to rebut the despotism thesis by emphasizing that tragic circumstances rather than theoretical deficiencies account for what has been described as a 'qualitative break' between Marx and Lenin on the one hand and Stalinism on the other.[6]

But the proponents of the despotism thesis are sceptical. They note for example that as early as 1921 (before Stalin became party leader) the Kronstadt rebellion in the USSR was crushed, and, if Kolakowski's dictum that 'Stalin was Trotsky *in actu*'[7] seems too stark to be plausible, it is not difficult to see that both leaders were contemptuous of the liberal tradition. Moreover it was Lenin himself who offered an authoritarian defence of the suppression of the Constituent Assembly in 1918. Supporters of the despotism thesis are not therefore persuaded by what I will call a 'circumstances argument' which seeks to drive a wedge between the emancipatory theorists and their authoritarian practitioners. On the contrary they contend that this argument leaves Marxists peculiarly vulnerable to the charge of inconsistency. Femia notes that it was Marx's plain intention to unite theory and practice,[8] and Marx and Engels's argument that communism can arise only as 'the real movement which abolishes the present state of things' suggests that a Marxism which is found wanting by the world of historical practice is a Marxism which stands condemned by its own historical premisses.[9]

The supporters of the despotism thesis acknowledge the role played by 'environmental' factors in accounting for the authoritarian character of Marxism, but insist that contingent historical circumstances have merely made a bad theory worse. A 'genetic' link between Marxism and despotism exists all the same.[10] In this they draw sustenance from Bakunin's classic prediction that the Marxist revolution will concentrate production in the hands of the state in a way that creates 'the most aristocratic, despotic, arrogant and contemptuous of all regimes'.[11] Anarchists are of course opposed to all states, but they support the despotism thesis on the grounds that the Marxist state will always be particularly authoritarian in form. The 'dictatorship of the proletariat' is not a 'transitional' state dissolving itself into society but a despotic polity distinguished only by its militant refusal to wither away.

The post-liberal logic of Marxist political theory

This despotism thesis however confronts us with a difficulty. If Marxism suffers from a paradoxical anti-statism which has repressive political consequences, how do we explain the development of Marx's own theory as an argument which (in my view) is post-liberal rather than anti-liberal in character? To understand this distinction, we need to recall that Marx began his political career as a nineteenth-century liberal steeped in the ideals of the French Revolution and European Enlightenment. He consciously identified with what he called 'the ever new philosophy of reason', and characterized the state as the 'great organism' in which legal, moral and political freedom must be realised. The individual in obeying the state obeys only 'the natural laws of his own reason'.[12]

It was Marx's commitment to this ideal which brought him initially into collision with the Prussian authorities. In the pages of the *Rheinische Zeitung* he eloquently champions the case for a free press, freedom of speech, trial by jury and extended parliamentary presentation. By 1843 Marx had become critical of 'politics' itself and in his critique of Hegel's *Philosophy of Right* he identifies what he calls 'a political state' with the particularistic interests of the police, judiciary and administration as bodies standing 'over and against society'. Marx contrasts the 'political state' with a 'true state' as a form of self-government in which people are able to determine their own lives. In the 'true state' (which can be realized only through electoral reform and the dissolution of a civil society riven by conflicting private interests), the political state is 'annihilated'.[13]

What is clear from Marx's argument here is that he seeks not to reject the liberal state but to *transcend* it. The true state does not jettison the abstract ideals of the political state but aspires to realize them concretely. As Marx puts it (in somewhat Hegelian fashion): 'the completion of the abstraction is at the same time the transcendence of the abstraction'. The argument is rooted in the 'subversive' premisses of the liberal tradition: free and equal humans can govern their own lives. What makes these premisses 'abstract' is that they are contradicted by the class divisions and statist hierarchies of liberal practice. Shortly afterwards Marx ceases to distinguish between the political and the true state, and refers instead to (liberal) democracy itself as the 'real state' – the 'complete state' whose abstract idealism can do no more than perfect the egoistic materialism of civil society. Liberal democracy (as Marx and Engels will later write) represents the 'last' and 'highest' form of the state – the form of the state in which the old order goes to pieces.[14]

The logic of the argument is post-liberal rather than anti-liberal since it presupposes that the liberal state has to be realized in order to be 'transcended'. This notion of transcendence, as Hunt's detailed analysis of Marx and Engels's political ideas makes clear,[15] implies a positive rather than negative view of the liberal tradition. The abstract premisses of liberal theory must become 'concrete' but this is possible only if repressive political and economic hierarchies disappear. Humans can be emancipated only in a classless, communist society in which the state itself has withered away.

What this means therefore is that the despotism thesis is not supportable unless it can demonstrate that Marxism is a theory which *necessarily* frustrates its own post-liberal logic. It is true that liberals might warn of the dangers of a 'spiritual despotism' under stateless communism, and anarchists argue that a regime can be stateless but repressive if it maintains itself solely through brainwashing citizens from the cradle to the grave. But, as Carter rightly points out, this scenario is 'both practically and logically impossible' since no regime can successfully indoctrinate its citizens without censorship, restrictions on freedom of movement and the 'forcible elimination' of rebelliousness.[16] In other words if Marxism has a viable critique of the state, then the despotism thesis falls since a 'spiritual despotism' is conceivable only when it is underpinned by the concentrated force of the state.

It is also true that Marx and Engels differentiated between the state and administration. Engels refers famously to a stateless society as one in which the government of persons is replaced by the administration of things and Marx, in a specific response to

Bakunin, insists that had his anarchist adversary understood 'the position of a manager in a co-operative factory, all his illusions about domination would go to the devil'.[17] But while this analysis accounts for a certain possible ambiguity about the 'legitimate functions' of a 'state' under communism, it does not support the despotism thesis since it assumes that the withering away of the state would involve the disappearance of institutionalized physical force. The administered society is not necessarily repressive, and Femia is right (in my view) to reject Hayek's contention that a planned society is itself authoritarian in character. There is no reason (Femia notes) why socialist planning should not accommodate a diversity of independent power centres – local government, trade unions, churches, industrial and professional associations.[18]

As far as Femia is concerned, the despotism thesis arises from what he calls Marxism's 'holistic' conception of 'man'. Femia argues that because Marx sees 'the essence of man' as the 'ensemble of human relationships', he simply 'reduces' the individual to society. The abstractions of liberalism are merely 'theoretical fictions'. Individuals, for Marx, lack the capacity for personal choice and are no more than the 'passive imprint of social forms'. His view of humanity is not only holistic, but since this 'holism' is anti-liberal, elitist, intolerant and monolithic in its conceptual absolutism, it necessarily creates the political and social basis for despotism. This dream of 'perfect unity' (in the words of Kolakowski which Femia cites approvingly) is likely to be realized as an 'artificial unity imposed by coercion from above'.[19]

The textual support for this argument is however problematic. If Marx rejects rather than transcends liberalism, as Femia suggests, then why does he identify the political emancipation of the liberal state as 'real progress', indeed as 'the final form of human emancipation within the present world order'?[20] Of course *On the Jewish Question* (in which these comments are made) is highly critical of the atomism of the liberal tradition but Femia misconstrues the concept of abstraction which Marx employs in these early texts. Abstraction (as in the critique of Hegel noted above) does not imply sheer fiction or pure unreality: on the contrary, it means incompleteness, insufficiency, and a one-sidedness which needs to be overcome. Because he misinterpets Marx's concept of abstraction, Femia misses the anti-authoritarianism of Marx's critique of liberal rights. For Marx is not just critical of the abstract view of society as a 'framework exterior to individuals'. He is also critical of the abstract view of the state which, as he points out, makes it possible for the French Constitution of 1793, for example, to assert freedom of press as a natural right, and yet completely deny its existence when it supposedly compromises 'public liberty'. Both the 'abstract' state and the 'abstract' individual are equally pernicious. Jacobinism merely demonstrates (Marx argues) a political life 'in violent opposition to its own conditions' since in a crisis the 'abstract' (i.e. the liberal) state demonstrates its inherently authoritarian character.[21]

In the same way Femia misses the post-liberal logic of the *Economic and Philosophical Manuscripts* which characterizes 'crude' communism as a society whose coercive egalitarianism negates (rather than transcends) private property and thus systematically denies 'the personality of man'.[22] Marx's argument is not that humans are the passive product of society. On the contrary, individuals are active (the point for which Marx later praises idealism)[23] but this activity can be explained only in terms of the relationships individuals enter. It is revealing that Femia, in criticizing Marx for an abstract (and authoritarian) holism, ignores the text which particularly emphasizes the voluntary and individual character of human activity. As Thomas has argued in detail, Marx and Engels in *The German Ideology* seek to rebut Stirner's 'egoistical' critique of communism by insisting that communists by no means want to 'do away with the "private individual" for the sake of the "general", self-sacrificing man'. The point is rather that it is the division of labour, private property and the state which prevent individuals from freely determining their own existence.[24]

Indeed, Femia's analysis would make it impossible to understand why *The Communist Manifesto*, for example, should present a veritable hymn of praise for capitalism as a system whose contradictory premises are embodied in the subversive abstractions of the liberal tradition. It is capitalism and capitalism alone that provides workers with their communist 'weapons'. A negative attitude towards capitalism (and its liberal ideology) would rob workers of the material development, political culture and theoretical enlightenment that makes communism conceptually and historically possible as a classless and stateless society. The logic of the theory in other words is positive rather than negative – 'transcendental' rather than dismissive – in character.[25]

The circumstances argument and the commune-state

If, as I have argued, Marxism is imbued with a post-liberal rather than an anti-liberal logic, then the despotism thesis is credible only if it can show that Marxism necessarily frustrates the post-liberal logic of its own theory. Femia argues that Marx's holistic theory lays the groundwork for the notorious distinction between the actual consciousness of workers and their 'true' or 'imputed' consciousness. He quotes the oft-cited comment by Marx and Engels that it is not a question of what this or that proletariat 'or even the whole proletariat' momentarily imagines is its aim, but it is a question of what the proletariat is, and 'what it consequently is historically compelled to do'. This argument, Femia contends, cannot but imply intolerance and elitism.[26]

Yet the compulsion referred to here is the compulsion of capitalist circumstances which educate and enlighten workers – it is not the compulsion of commissars or party cadres who claim to think and act for the proletariat. The logic of the argument is post-liberal since it is premised on the assumption that workers will turn to communism only when they have experienced capitalism for themselves. Revolutions are (as Engels puts it) the 'necessary outcome of circumstances quite independent of the will or guide of particular parties', and this would seem to imply that the role of communists is merely to help the workers (and the wider popular movements they lead) to help themselves.[27] But it is here that the post-liberal logic of Marxist political theory runs into difficulties. For if, as Engels argues, revolutions are the product of impersonal circumstances, he also argues (in a later polemic with the anarchists) that a revolution is the most authoritarian thing there is.[28] Revolutions inevitably concentrate power and create illiberal political institutions. Will they not inevitably generate states which refuse to wither away?

The post-liberal logic of Marxist theory appears to face in two antithetical directions at the same time. On the one hand the workers must emancipate themselves. Enlightened leaders are not to act on their behalf. On the other hand, what are Marxists to do if they find themselves in circumstances where they feel obliged to do and say things that are in tension with the post-liberal logic of their own theory? As Engels told the German socialist Weydemeyer, 'we shall find ourselves compelled to make communist experiments and leaps which no-one knows better than ourselves to be untimely'.[29] An anti-authoritarian logic seems to vindicate prostatist standpoints. Throughout Marx and Engels's writings on the revolutions of 1848 (for example) we find invocations of terror, panegyrics to violence, and perhaps what is most significant of all, a theory of 'permanent revolution' that dramatically anticipates the events of 1917 by suggesting that a proletarian revolution may 'immediately follow' a bourgeois revolution in a backward country. Texts like these have provided a fertile source for later handbooks on Marxism–Leninism and short histories of ruling communist parties, but if (as I have suggested) the politics of authoritarianism is in conflict with a post-liberal logic, why does it arise?

The problem in essence is this. The circumstances which 'compel' workers to resist capitalism may also 'compel' Marxists to take practical standpoints which contradict the emancipatory thrust of their own theory. Thus the *Manifesto* is written under 'circumstances' in which an alliance with Blanquist-minded artisans is possible only if Marx and Engels placate (in part at any rate) anti-liberal theoretical stances.[30] But perhaps the most dramatic example of the contradictory logic of this 'circumstances argument' can be seen in relation to Marx and Engels's analysis of the Paris Commune. In *The Civil War in France* Marx presents the Commune as the appropriate political form under which to secure 'the economical emancipation of Labour'. The analysis is celebrated for its militant anti-statism – so much so that it has even been argued that for Marx the Commune had ceased to be a form of the state at all.[31] The text forms the basis of Lenin's blueprint for the new Soviet state in 1917, and those who believe that the Russian Revolution might bring about the withering away of the state base their anti-statism on the successful realization of this commune model.

Yet it is not difficult to see that Marx's defence of the Paris Commune stands in radical tension with what I have called the post-liberal logic of Marxist political theory. The theory (as we have seen) assumes that, since capitalism is a global system, it can be transcended only through a political process that forges common interests between nations as well as within them. The Paris Commune however was confined not merely to a single country but to its capital city, and it is clear that Marx and Engels do not believe that in these conditions the communards could actually abolish the standing army, institute an egalitarian public service 'at workmen's wages' and supplant a privileged caste of bureaucrats by popular government. The radicalism of the communards (it would seem) stems from anarchist and Jacobin traditions and not from a conception of communism that transcends capitalism. The leadership of the Commune (Marx comments later) was 'in no way socialist, nor could it be', and the uprising hardly receives a mention at the Hague Congress of the First International a year later.

Yet although Marx and Engels privately regard the attempt to take power as a 'desperate folly', the work of the Commune was extolled nevertheless. Marx approvingly refers to the Commune as a 'working' rather than a 'parliamentary' body which combines executive and legislative activities and divests judicial functionaries of their 'sham' independence.[32] Avineri and Hunt suggest that these passages are much less anti-parliamentarian than they sound,[33] but as they stand, Marx's comments do appear to reject rather than transcend liberal constitutionalism and in particular the idea of the separation of powers. The analysis seems to imply that administrators should themselves be elected politicians, directly involved in policy-making and subject to immediate recall. But such a development can only (as Polan has persuasively argued) accentuate rather than diminish the problem of careerism. The 'collapse' of politics into administration would also make it difficult for an opposition to judge the performance of the executive critically and in general, any blurring of the distinct and differentiated roles of executive, legislature, administration, government and opposition, works against attempts to subordinate the state to society. Marx's analysis reflects what Polan calls 'an unsophisticated anti-bureaucratism' that in practice can end up only conspiring with the bureaucracy in the maintenance of its power.[34]

It has to be said therefore that the argument in *The Civil War in France* derives from a tactical solidarity which generates political stances of a pre-liberal rather than post-liberal kind. They were stances which proved (as we shall now see) of momentous historical significance in inspiring those who did not merely take theoretical positions but pursued practical policies of a notoriously illiberal kind.

The authoritarian legacy of 1917

The Russian Revolution stands as a particularly poignant example of an 'untimely' event which 'compels' Marxists to embrace a practice in apparent tension with the logic of their theory. It is surely significant that Rosa Luxemburg defends the revolution in the same way and for the same reasons that Marx and Engels praise the Commune. The Bolsheviks have acted with heroism, she argues, in circumstances in which they are bound to fail. On the one hand she sees the event as an act of great proletarian courage; on the other hand she is sharply critical of Lenin and Trotsky for making a 'virtue out of necessity' by imposing limitations imposed on political freedom in the name of a 'higher form of democracy'.[35]

The groundwork for this slide to authoritarianism had in fact become particularly clear after February 1917 when Lenin presented the 'democratic republic' not as the political basis for an advance to socialism but as a quintessentially bourgeois creation. It is at this stage that the Paris Commune becomes a model for the socialist state.[36] Marx's strictures on the limited parliamentarism of his day are presented in *The State and Revolution* as applying to democratic republics in general. In Lenin's view the Commune serves as a substitute for a 'venal and rotten parliamentarism' and his account is underpinned by what Polan calls a 'subterranean authoritarianism' that can only frustrate its anti-statist aspirations.[37] Although Lenin argues that unpropitious historical circumstances – isolation, civil war, cultural and political backwardness – have bequeathed a 'bureaucratic twist' to the workers' state, it has to be said that this 'workers' state' derives from a political model which is basically illiberal and authoritarian in character. What now divides the party leadership from its 'left' critics is simply the question as to when and how the supposedly libertarian promises of the commune-state are to be realized. Bukharin as a Bolshevik with anarchist sympathies exemplifies the irony of the situation.

In April 1918 Bukharin declares that the proletarian dictatorship is not a parliamentary republic but 'a commune-state, without police, without standing army, without civil service'. He draws extensively upon the anti-statist sections of Lenin's *State and Revolution*, moving effortlessly from pleas for the draconian use of force to a passionate advocacy of proletarian 'self-government'. While it is true that the New Economic Policy which Bukharin later champions does involve a recognition of market forces and a relaxation of political terror, it remains firmly entrenched within the framework of an authoritarian state.[38] Polan has argued that the Soviet state bears the stamp of Lenin's *State and Revolution* in all its phases – before and after the Bolsheviks secured a monopoly of power, before and after the decline of Soviets as significant institutions and before and after the rise of Stalin.[39] His argument is borne out (for example) by Stalin's defence of forced collectivization as a contribution towards creating the agrarian components of a commune-state.

It is true that after 1930 the 'withering away' thesis is increasingly identified with the 'chatter' of opportunists, and Stalin argues that, as long as the USSR is surrounded by hostile countries, a state is not only necessary but needs to be continuously strengthened. But the Marxist credentials of the 'withering away' thesis are never formally denied, and Stalin can still present the Paris Commune as the 'most suitable form of the dictatorship of the proletariat' – just as Lenin had done.[40] All the Bolsheviks paid homage to a model whose anti-statism is ultimately illusory in character, a point which is tellingly made if we compare the comments of two bitter political rivals.

In 1930 Stalin declared that the higher the development of state power, the closer it comes to disappearing. Ten years earlier Trotsky had argued (in a famous passage in his *Terrorism and Communism*) that just as a lamp shoots out in a brilliant flame before it is extinguished, so a state about to disappear will assume its 'most ruthless form' embracing the life of the citizens in every direction. Stalin's language may have been more prosaic but the sentiment is the same. The uncomfortable truth is that that the 'mightest and most powerful state that has ever existed' (as Stalin describes the USSR in 1930) has evolved logically from a political model whose libertarian form simply masks its authoritarian character.[41]

After the twentieth congress of the Communist Party of the Soviet Union in 1956, Khrushchev revived the withering away thesis in order provide theoretical rationale for his reforms. Between 1961 and 1963 far more is written in the USSR on the withering away of the state than had appeared during the whole of the Lenin and Stalin eras put together. But what clearly emerges from Tarschys's invaluable survey of Soviet literature during this period is the futility of trying to project the disappearance of the state while uncritically accepting the continuation of an illiberal political culture and institutions. While a number of useful points emerge, like the need to distinguish the state from administration and the force of the state from wider coercive pressures, the thrust of the arguments here as elsewhere is ultimately authoritarian. Some Soviet writers at the time argue that elections themselves might wither away 'like all juridical norms' while the party itself would continue to exercise a leading role even in a stateless society![42]

With Khrushchev's fall from office in 1964, speculative interest in the withering away thesis largely ceases. Yet Brezhnev can still comment that the new constitution of 1977 envisages the transformation of statehood into 'communist self-government' while Article 62 of the constitution obliges the citizen to safeguard the interests of the Soviet state, and (in a classically Stalinist formulation) 'to further the strengthening of its might and authority'.[43] But the emphasis is increasingly laid upon modernizing Soviet political institutions and under Gorbachev's reforms the notion of a 'law governed' state or *Rechtsstaat* receives official blessing. In the last years of the Gorbachev era (before the USSR itself finally disintegrates) it is argued by at least one Soviet writer that the country must return to the mainstream of human history. The attempt to abolish the state after 1917 may have led to the disappearance of the state as that institution is understood in the West, but it has simply created in its place a totalitarian monster that has swallowed up both 'the individual and society'.[44]

This brief historical account of the rise and fall of the withering away thesis graphically bears out a problem which is already evident in the positions of Marx and Engels. Under particular historical circumstances Marxists seem compelled to say and do things which contradict the post-liberal logic of their political theory. The question which we must now tackle is *why* such a contradiction arises and whether it is a problem which is inherent in the whole Marxist project.

The statist elements of an anti-statist theory

Marx and Engels's critique of the state arises (as we have seen) as an integral part of their theory of emancipation. Their response to Rousseau's paradox – how can people in chains become self-governing? – is to insist that people must make history for themselves. There is a striking similarity between this position (as Geras has noted with particular reference to Rosa Luxemburg) and Mill's argument that 'action can only be learnt in action'.[45] The argument is fundamentally anti-statist in the sense that it has self-activity at its core.

Yet (as we have seen) the anti-statist logic of this argument is continuously frustrated by the same historical circumstances which supposedly educate workers as self-active participants in political struggle. The argument implies (as Geras points out) the absence of a detailed map – an abstract blueprint to be imposed from above – and therefore provides an arena for the diversity, experiment and negotiation 'through which alone socialism can be created'.[46] But it is precisely at this point that the 'circumstances argument' appears to come adrift. If people are to emancipate themselves, what is to prevent them from making mistakes and blunders? Luxemburg considered this inevitable, and I have already cited Engels's comment that communists will find themselves compelled to make experiments and leaps which are untimely in character. This is the nub of the problem. Untimely leaps are likely to result in authoritarian political strategies and authoritarian political systems. The illiberalism of the commune model and the despotism which followed in the wake of the Russian Revolution bear this out. If then these 'untimely' events are an *inevitable* consequence of the circumstances argument, then Marxism does indeed espouse a theory of emancipation which leads unwittingly (but unavoidably) to despotism. It is true that a theory of emancipation must allow people to make mistaken and 'untimely leaps' which result in authoritarian political practices. But why are Marxists (as Engels suggests) 'compelled' to justify, applaud and idealize these mistakes?

The question posed by the despotism thesis can be reformulated thus: is there anything in Marxist theory which prevents Marxists from critically appraising the activities of popular movements and perhaps even seeking to discourage actions which work against the post-liberal logic of Marxist theory? There are three 'democratic deficits' (as Geras calls them) which deserve our consideration. The first is the notion that emancipation is not simply a possible end which a political movement might achieve but a 'unique destination' in which inexorable laws guarantee the working class its final victory. However 'open' the process of struggle, the result must be socialism – and socialism as defined by Marx and Engels.[47]

This argument injects into the circumstances argument a messianic dimension since it implies that revolutions are part of a 'natural' process of history and they must ultimately succeed. It is true that Rosa Luxemburg warns that barbarism rather than socialism might triumph, and the *Communist Manifesto* itself notes that class struggles might 'end in the common ruin of the contending classes'. But this still ties historical development to only one *thinkable* option and all other outcomes (and the liberal and conservative theories which envisage them) appear pathological and mischievous by contrast.[48] It is a position which can only encourage Marxists to support untimely events even if these have authoritarian consequences.

The second 'deficit' relates to the notion that political struggle has to be 'class struggle' in which industrial workers, as the producers of surplus value under capitalism, have a leading role to play. This argument not only creates difficulties in explaining the part taken by revolutionary intellectuals (like Marx and Engels) in 'proletarian' struggles but it limits an emancipatory project to a particular constituency with a 'privileged' position. Of course workers are exhorted to build a popular movement 'of the immense majority' but as a particular class they already have ascribed to them a predetermined destiny to build socialism. It is one thing to argue that those who suffer from repression are likely to be especially concerned with emancipatory movements since they are the victims rather than the beneficaries of statist hierarchies. It is quite another however to suggest that one class in particular has the inevitable role of 'leading' such movements. Such a stance can only make it easier to justify authoritarian measures when these are taken either against non-proletarians in general or indeed against those proletarians who do not accept the role which Marxism prescribes for them.

Trotsky links these two deficits – a mechanistic determinism and class dogmatism – when he comments in his debate with Dewey that the 'liberating morality of the proletariat' is necessarily endowed with a revolutionary character, and its rules of conduct are to be 'deduced' from the class struggle, the 'law of all laws' of social development.[49] Emancipation is not a political process in which concerned individuals seek to establish an alternative to repression and exploitation: it derives simply from an historically privileged theory enacted by agents with a prescribed role to play. This is an anti-statist argument whose monopolistic, elitist and 'deductive' features give it a pronounced statist character.

It is not surprising therefore (to take the third of Geras's 'deficits') that classical Marxism has never really been able to justify the struggle for emancipation in *moral* terms. Lukes gives numerous examples of Marx and Engels's apparent contempt for 'morality', and Hunt has drawn attention to what he calls a chronic 'moral constipation' – Marx and Engels's stubborn reluctance to endorse explicitly moral principles.[50] Trotsky's reference to the 'liberating morality of the proletariat' makes it impossible to conceptualize rules of conduct as they apply to people as individuals. The argument ignores the fact, as Geras has commented, that people other than those who produce surplus value also suffer as a result of the unjust social and economic relations of capitalism, and they are (rightly) concerned with emancipation as agents in their own right. Moreover what makes the exploitation experienced by proletarians repressive is not the technical fact that workers create surplus value for capitalists but the disparities of effort and reward, suffering and enjoyment which an inegalitarian society involves.[51] By placing a particularistic emphasis upon class and workers, Marxism not only weakens its wider theory of emancipation but it fails to show why the exploitation of workers should be unjust.

'Moral constipation' is integrally linked to a messianic view of circumstances and a monopolistic concept of agency. These three 'deficits' make it impossible to transcend liberal theory. In so far as they are integral to Marxism as it is expounded (even) in the works of Marx and Engels, these deficits suggest that the theory is a contradictory amalgam of post-liberal and anti-liberal positions, and that the latter are sufficiently potent to turn the circumstances argument in an authoritarian direction.

Towards the end of his life Engels confessed that the mechanistic and one-sided way in which he and Marx had presented their theory of historical materialism created serious misunderstandings in the minds of their followers. Indeed these misconceptions led Marx (so Engels tells us) to declare that he was not a 'Marxist'. This oft-cited comment provides a fascinating insight into the relationship between Marxism and what I have called its logic of post-liberalism. There can be little doubt that in presenting Marxism as an economic determinism – a 'reductionism' – Marx and Engels engendered dismissive attitudes towards liberal political institutions as the 'mere' expressions of a derivative 'superstructure'. Characteristically Engels points to 'circumstances' as the source of the problem. This one-sided presentation (he notes) arose out of polemical and partisan pressures which made it imperative to dramatize the discontinuity between their own theory and those of their 'idealist' and 'liberal' rivals.[52]

But how much of the one-sidedness (to which Engels confesses) is the product of extraneous pressures, and how much of it is inherent within Marxism itself? Materialism as a theory seeks to provide empirically verifiable explanations as to why people behave in the way they do, and the argument that people are social beings who can only survive through their relations with others is (I have argued) central to a coherent critique of the state. Moreover the 'consequentialist' argument that individuals express moral ideas in relation to their interests is perfectably acceptable if it takes us beyond abstract concepts of 'good and evil' as expressions of 'will' and 'sin'.

These materialist premises are indeed post-liberal in their logic since they generate a version of the circumstances argument which meets Rousseau's paradox and looks beyond the state. But Marxism as classically formulated is more than this. It is also a theory that these circumstances have a predetermined end which is unique and unavoidable; that this end is to be prosecuted by a particularistic agent – the proletariat – through a particularistic form of politics – class struggle – in the light of a theory which monopolistically presents itself as 'omnipotent because it is true'.[53] Morality becomes irrelevant and even contemptible when particular agencies have particular roles prescribed to them and they move to a particular outcome which has a predetermined character.

It is these elements which account for the fact that Marxists feel 'compelled' to take stances, embrace policies and construct forms of the state which can only frustrate the post-liberal logic of their own theory. They are positions which (as Dewey said of Trotsky but the words apply to Marx as well) lock up a brilliant intelligence 'in absolutes',[54] and they explain why even the Marxism of the classics is paradoxical in character. We have to concede therefore that the despotism thesis has a point. Marxism does ultimately embrace a theory of the state which is at once monopolistic, particularistic and absolutist, and these are the attributes which 'compel' Marxists to vindicate forms of the state which refuse to wither away.

SUMMARY

- Marxists argue that the state constitutes a barrier to a free society. However, they are vulnerable to a 'despotism thesis' which sees Marxism as an emancipatory theory which necessarily generates repressive political regimes in practice.

- The contention by Marxists that emancipatory ideals have been derailed by unfortunate circumstances runs up against the problem that Marxism rests its case for communism upon the unity of theory and practice.

- It is true that Marxism seeks to realize rather than reject liberal values and it emphasizes that workers should transform capitalism as the agents of their own emancipation. However the circumstances that educate workers also tempt Marxists to support movements which have a distinctly illiberal character.

- Marxism suffers its own form of the 'schizoid malady' which derives from an absolutist view of history; a monopolistic view of the proletariat, and a dismissive view of morality. These three 'deficits' account for the fact that once Marxist states are established, they resolutely refuse to wither away.

10

Feminism

Whereas liberalism, anarchism and Marxism are arguments which address themselves explicitly to the question of the state, with feminism this orientation is more complex. Feminism, like all ideologies, is highly heterogeneous, but the problem I wish to tackle here however is whether feminists have, need or can significantly contribute to a critique of the state. While some see the absence of a feminist theory of the state as a deficiency to be rectified,[1] others contend that feminists should not focus on the state at all.

This argument can be summarized as follows. The state either conveys the naive liberal idea of a neutral arbiter standing above society or the dogmatic Marxist notion of an institution which privileges class at the expense of gender. Insisting (as MacKinnon does) that the state is inherently male does not help since if society in general is pervaded by the practices of male power, what is specific about the state? The state is too aggregative to be of conceptual use in feminist analysis.[2] This is a 'redundancy' rather than an 'indefinability' thesis since it argues not that a definition of the state is impossible but that a specific focus on the state is unnecessary.

Clearly this redundancy thesis places a question mark over our inclusion of feminism within this book. I shall argue however that the feminist analysis of patriarchy does not simply offer an important understanding of the political dynamics of male power. It also provides invaluable insights into the nature of the state. Liberalism is rightly criticized for accepting a sexual division of labour which means that in practice the 'abstract individuals' who authorize the state are men. A naturalistic view of gender relations also weakens

Marxist theory but the link which Engels asserts between patriarchy, property and the state remains a potent one. An organization based on force is an organization which enshrines the domination of men. I will conclude that despite the position of some feminists to the contrary, patriarchal concepts like the public/private divide can be understood only as principles which are central to the sovereign state.

The problematic relationship between feminism and liberalism

It has been argued that 'all feminism is liberal at root',[3] and certainly feminism has both a close and a contradictory relationship to liberalism. Understanding this relationship, I want to argue, is crucial to rebutting the redundancy thesis. Feminism emerges historically as an argument against the naturalistic hierarchies central to pre-liberal thought, and this argument makes sense only if we locate the subordination of women within the wider structures of the state.

Thus Aristotle argues that 'the relation of male to female is naturally that of superior to inferior – of the ruling to the ruled'.[4] It is true that Plato allows women to become members of his guardian class, but his feminist credentials are suspect since only a tiny number of women would be likely to become rulers and those that did, would (as Rousseau commented sourly) have to become men. Feminist assessments of Plato (as of Aristotle) need to engage with particular views of the state. In a similar way, the position of women in medieval theory cannot be disentangled from explicitly hierarchical and statist arguments about the question of sin and (fallen) nature.[5]

Indeed it is significant that, when the classic liberals develop their arguments for a new kind of state, they do so in explicit opposition to patriarchalists like Filmer who hold that the divine right of kings derives from the absolute power which fathers have over mothers and children. Liberal rebuttals of classic patriarchy arise within the context of a wider argument about the nature of the state, and the liberal analysis of women embodies in particularly acute form the problem of what I have called the schizoid malady. This malady derives from a theory whose anti-statist premises generate support for the state, and this malady is graphically conveyed in the liberal assumption that men naturally dominate women. It is true that Hobbes (for example) sees men as indistinguishable from women in the state of nature. No matrimonial laws exist and only spontaneous acts of coitus occur. Since it is women who give birth to children, only the mother can be reliably identified as parent. Indeed Hobbes is unique among classical liberals in suggesting that the parental relationship is political, conventional and (initially at any rate) even maternal in character.

But the argument is deceptive. Hobbes also assumes (on some occasions at least) that individuals in the state of nature can only be *men*.[6] Moreover he takes the view that although women are (initially) 'lords' over their children, female power soon gives way to male power as men conquer women (rendered vulnerable by the need to nurture infants). If (as Pateman argues) this enforced submission were contractual, we would expect women to retain their natural right to self-protection. Yet they do not. This right is given up to men, and hence it is men who are the individuals who form the original contract which brings about both society and the state.[7]

Despite complexities which are peculiar to Hobbes, his view of family is – like that of the classical liberals in general – ultimately naturalistic in character. His abstract individual has to be a male represented in unitary fashion by the absolute state. If the founder of liberalism cannot avoid (despite his conventionalist logic) linking the state with a naturalistically conceived patriarchy, this connection is even more bluntly stated by Locke. Unlike Hobbes, Locke does not attempt to establish the family in conventional terms and argues that domestic relations inhabit a sphere outside of the state. Although 'conjugal society' rests upon a compact between men and women, this contractualism is vitiated by Locke's contention that domestic authority 'naturally falls to the Man's share, as the abler and the stronger'. It is true that women can keep the property they possess before marriage, but within the marriage itself all property belongs to the husband, and he alone can pass it on to his sons.

Butler's argument that Locke understates the feminist implications of his argument for fear of antagonizing a patriarchal-minded readership is thus misconceived. Locke's assumption that the inferiority of women has a 'foundation in Nature' is not merely tactical, but derives from his view of a society based on private property which confines women to a domestic sphere as 'the weaker sex'. The naturalism of his argument flows logically from the abstract character of his liberalism.[8] This schizoid malady is dramatically demonstrated by Rousseau, who argues in the *Social Contract* (despite what he has said about ungendered individuals in his *Discourses*) that the family is a 'natural society' in which the ruler corresponds to the father. For all Rousseau's obvious fascination with the patriarchal world of classical antiquity, his insistence that women must be confined to a private domestic world outside of the public realm is inherent in the arguments of Hobbes and Locke as well. Moreover his analysis reinforces our case against the redundancy thesis, for Rousseau contends with particular vigour that the subordination of women is inherent in the state. Patriotism can thrive only when it is rooted in that miniature fatherland, the home: the wife who is unfaithful to her husband commits a crime not simply of infidelity but of treason.[9] This not only subverts the Lockean argument that the power which husbands exercise over their wives is not political, but makes it clear that that the position of 'natural woman' in the patriarchal family is integral to the functioning of the liberal state.

Wollstonecraft's *Vindication of the Rights of Woman* (1792) has sometimes been described as a classic exposition of 'liberal feminism'. She argues that the 'divine right' of husbands should be challenged in the same way that liberals have challenged the divine right of kings, and she (rightly) contends that Rousseau's 'natural woman' is as much an artificial construct as Hobbes's naturally competitive and aggressive man. Like all individuals, women are rational agents capable of exercising autonomy through self-control. Wollstonecraft's abstract view of reason (as a universalizing principle that suppresses particularistic passion) clearly derives from the liberal tradition, and she takes the sexual division of labour to be natural. Most women, she assumes, will remain at home, and becoming rational and autonomous will simply make them better wives, mothers and domestic workers. Although she adds at this point, 'in a word, better citizens', in fact her support for women's representation in parliament is only tangential to her argument.[10]

Nevertheless Wollstonecraft does insist that as rational beings women must be free to choose their careers. They have a right to property, employment and to the protection of the civil law, and they must be reckoned as among the 'individuals' who form the social contract. Is she simply a 'liberal feminist'? It is true that the challenge she mounts to liberalism is limited, but it is unmistakable nevertheless. By making good motherhood a principle of 'citizenship' and conceptualizing the domestic sphere as one which ought to be governed by universal principles of rationality and justice, Wollstonecraft undermines the view of the family as a purely 'private' institution complementing the 'public' realm of the state. In rejecting the natural superiority of men (whose despotic behaviour should be curbed by law), Wollstonecraft challenges at least embryonically and implicitly the public/private divide and the sovereignty of property central to the liberal state.[11]

The same argument applies to another apparent classic of 'liberal feminism', Mill's *Subjection of Women*. Again the relationship of women to the state provides the crucial context to teasing out the tensions within his feminism. Mill supports the right of women both to education and employment, and to vote and hold public office. But is this anything more than an extension of liberal principles to women? Mill, as his critics readily point out, does not challenge the sexual division of labour. Although he denies that women are housewives and mothers by nature, he considers them 'most suitable' for this role, and even argues for female suffrage on the grounds that it will assist housewives in supervising domestic expenditure![12] However, as with Wollstonecraft, it has to be said that, if Mill's challenge to liberalism is muted, it is real all the same. His contention that the family should become the 'real school of the virtues of freedom' questions the very public/private divide which he tends otherwise to take for granted, and he acknowledges that women can be socially and economically *coerced* into marriage, even though he has no real answer to this problem.[13]

The relationship of feminism to liberalism must offer a challenge to the redundancy thesis therefore since this relationship can be explored only if we locate the analysis of women within the context of the state. Pre-liberal thinkers openly defend patriarchal structures on the grounds that rulers exercise a paternal power over their subjects, while (so-called) liberal feminists can condemn patriarchy only by implicitly challenging the liberal relationship between the family and the state. If the feminism is (in a troubled and problematic sense) liberal at root, then this proposition can be understood only through a feminist critique (however embryonic and implicit) of the state.

The spectre haunting Marxism

The liberal view of women is, as I have suggested, bedevilled by a naturalism which apparently contradicts (but emerges inexorably from) its abstract conventionalism. Marxism, by way of contrast, would seem to be in a much stronger position to banish naturalism from its analysis of women, since it is a theory which explicitly emphasizes the importance of assessing relationships in historical terms. Certainly Engels's celebrated work published in 1894 is particularly suggestive in the way it links the origins of the family and private property with the development of the state.

Engels argues that in early tribal societies men, women and children live together as part of larger households where production is for use rather than exchange. These are stateless societies in which decision-making involves both men and women and, since specific paternity cannot be established as a result of group marriage, collective property descends matrilineally. The 'world historical defeat of the female sex' (as Engels graphically describes it) occurs when men begin to domesticate animals and breed herds. At the same time women seek monogamous pairing relationships and the family is privatized. In the subsequent bourgeois family, female consent is neutralized by a woman's lack of economic independence, and in the working-class family the husband represents the bourgeois and the wife the proletariat. Only with the socialization of production under communism will male domination disappear. All women would be involved in paid employment outside of the home, and housework itself would become a public and collectivized activity.[14] The disappearance of patriarchy is integrally linked to the socialization of property and the withering away of the state.

Engels's account has been widely regarded as problematic. Central to the difficulties which concern us here is the way Engels relies upon naturalism at crucial points in his analysis. He assumes that it is simply natural that in the earliest societies men will be working outside the home and will therefore initiate (and of course benefit from) the domestication of animals. At the same time women are depicted as having a Victorian-like yearning for 'chaste' permanent marriages with only one man – a development which seals their fate.[15] Even though the involvement of women in the outside economy is seen by (the later rather than the earlier) Engels as progressive, no explanation is given as to why women should be paid less than men, and (like Mill) Engels never poses the question as to why men cannot share tasks in an egalitarian household. Women are generally characterized as 'surrendering' to men, and the implications of these apparently 'natural' differences for male sexuality, domestic violence and rape are not tackled. While it is true that the historicity of Marxism goes well beyond the abstract conventionalism of liberal theory, it is difficult to disagree with the criticism that a spectre of the 'natural' haunts Marx and Engels's treatment of women from the earliest writings to the most mature.[16]

In The German Ideology the family is seen to derive from a natural division of labour in the sex act, and what makes the argument 'thoroughly complicitous with patriarchal history and ideology' (in Di Stefano's view) is its privileging of production over reproduction.[17] This necessarily injects a gender bias into the Marxist account since production is defined in terms which exclude the traditional labour of women in the form either of reproductive activity or of the domestic activity of the household. The proletariat as the agent of historical change in the struggle for communism is not only monopolistic in conception, it is also male. It might seem odd to depict naturalism as a spectre haunting Marx and Engels when production is conceptualized as an activity in *conflict* with nature, and communism as a society which strips individuals of their 'embeddedness in nature'. But the point is that nature itself is characterized as a female adversary against whom man must wrestle, compelling 'her' forces to act in obedience with 'his' sway.[18] The celebrated comparison in *Capital* between the architect and the bee presents a 'voluntarist' view of unalienated labour which cannot account for the production, nurture and socialization of children.[19]

The concept of production is narrow, one-sided and ultimately patriarchal implying as it does that women are (natural) objects and men rationalistic subjects. Although it is true that Engels does on occasion suggest a non-instrumental view of production,[20] the problem here is that if Marxism does have a post-liberal (and thus post-absolutist) logic, this logic comes to grief on abstract, monopolistic and naturalistic assumptions about human activity. Women are subsumed into class just as reproduction is subsumed into production, and what Di Stefano calls the 'relational' and 'dialogic' orientation of Marx's view of dialectics is not sustained. Adverserial notions of conquest and class war under capitalism, followed by seamless unity and reconciliation under communism, suggest a subject – object model of human behaviour which is ultimately non-relational in character. A patriarchal disdain for mothers, child care and socialization prevents Marx and Engels from seeing that human activity is inter-subjective so that Marxism (in conflict with its own materialist premises) has to deny the sociability of the human species.[21]

In my view this naturalistic blockage can only strengthen opposition to the redundancy thesis, since it is an argument with crucial implications for the Marxist theory of the state. Just as a dictatorship of the proletariat is the state-form which cannot wither away, so the notion of class war has manifestly masculinist overtones, and even the classless communist society rests upon a conception of production which enshrines patriarchy. The Marxist society (at least as it is conceptualized in the classics) will inevitably be both statist and patriarchal since the same abstract and monopolistic concepts inform the analysis of women and of the state.

Patriarchy and the anthropological argument

The anthropological argument as we have presented it earlier asserts that humans governed themselves for thousands of years before they had states: government therefore is a process of securing order through social rather than statist sanctions. What then is the relationship between patriarchy and the state? Clearly if the relationship between the two is purely contingent, then the need for feminism to have a theory of the state becomes 'redundant'.

There can be no doubt that a sexual division of labour exists in stateless societies, and we have noted Engel's problematic argument that this sexual division of labour is natural in character. If we are to get to grips with the problem of patriarchy and the state, it is to this initial division of labour that we must return. Engels depicts a state of affairs in which men went to war, hunted and fished, while women cared for the house, cooked, weaved and sewed. But in what sense can we say (as Engels does) that this was 'a pure and simple outgrowth of nature'?[22] For what precisely does 'naturalness' mean in the context of a materialist analysis of social relations? On the one hand feminism is committed to the proposition that women are not naturally subordinate to men. On the other hand it is clear that while there have been societies in which men oppress women, there have never been societies in which women oppress men. It has been persuasively argued that matriarchy as the rule of women over men is simply a myth designed to vindicate its opposite.[23] So the question has to be posed: what is it about women which accounts for the fact that *they* rather than men are the victims of oppression?

In early societies women both bear and rear children. They work in households while generally speaking men hunt and become warriors. Why does this occur? Lerner argues that 'necessity' created this initial division of labour. In her view the survival into adulthood of at least two children for each coupling pair would necessitate many pregnancies for every woman. Since most nubile women devote most of their adulthood to pregnancy, child-bearing and rearing, Lerner concludes that the first sexual division of labour 'seems to derive from biological sex differences'.[24] Are we to assume then that this sexual division of labour (which had momentous social consequences for the subsequent creation of patriarchy) was ultimately natural after all?

Connell has argued that the natural qualities of objects like the biological properties of bodies clearly have 'practical relevance' to our understanding of human behaviour. But (and this is the point which Engels misses) this practical relevance does not have *causative* significance.[25] Thus on this argument biological sex differences make it possible to understand why in early societies it is women rather than men who work in domestic households, but at the same time these biological differences do not explain the social *relationship* which exists between them. Relationships are *constructs* infused with cultural and political assumptions which reflect the relative power each sex derives from its separate activities. They cannot be reduced to biological facts even where the latter have 'practical relevance'. Male dominance (in other words) must be seen as an *historic* rather than a natural phenomenon, which became (as Lerner puts it) a culturally created and enforced structure over time.[26]

Two important implications flow from this argument. The first is that we cannot assume that patriarchal domination exists simply because men and women undertake different activities. Male domination has to *develop* historically and it can do so only when men acquire the resources and power to control the lives of women. It is true that patriarchy is 'latent' within this differentiation but the mere separation of men and women is not in itself evidence that patriarchy has already developed. This is why Balbus's psychyoanalytical account of patriarchy deriving from what he calls 'mother monopolized child rearing' has to be challenged. Balbus argues that this practice generates great resentment so that, as a result, men dominate women even in stateless societies.[27] Yet this argument is curiously ahistorical. It derives in part from Chodorow's contention that female mothering always and everywhere produces male children with patriarchal attitudes. As Lerner rightly insists, this ignores the fact that in neolithic societies mothering and nurturing activities are identified with self-sufficiency in food gathering and competence in life-essential skills, so that here female parenting would be experienced by both men and women as a source of strength, even magical power. In hunting and gathering tribes where co-operation is emphasized and peaceful relations with other tribes are maintained, the relative status of men and women can be described as 'separate but equal'.[28]

The fact that male domination was not simply created by the initial division of labour is crucial to establishing the linkage between the patriarchal family and the birth of the state. Balbus himself acknowledges that the emergence of the state is possible only with the dissolution of kinship ties, and he accepts that the hierarchies of the state reinforce the authoritarianism of the father.[29] The point is that patriarchy requires male power, and this male power requires the development of a market economy, private property and above all the existence of slavery – what Lerner calls 'the first *institutionalized* form of hierarchical dominance in human history'. Thus the father in the patriarchal family in Mesopotamian society has (as Lerner points out) the power of life and death over children. He can give his daughters in marriage or consecrate them to a life of virginity in temple service. He can pledge his wife, concubines and children as pawns for debt. The patriarchal society requires not merely patrilineal descent but property laws guaranteeing the inheritance rights of sons, and a male domination sustained by military, political and religious bureaucracies. In short, 'in its earliest form patriarchy appeared as the archaic state.'[30]

This is not to deny that patriarchy develops out of the old kinship system where the initial sexual division of labour has already established distinctions between groups based on visible characteristics. Deference of the young to the old creates a model of group deference and the development of agriculture fosters an inter-tribal 'exchange of women' as a way of both avoiding incessant warfare and increasing the availability of child producers. As women's sexuality and reproductive potential becomes a commodity to be exchanged, it becomes clear that men have rights in women which women do not have in men. Patriarchal gender definitions are already in place before 'economic and political developments fully institutionalized the state'.[31]

As tribal societies become more 'developed', so patriarchy itself becomes more evident. Even within stateless societies, men have begun to embrace patriarchal stereotypes and male chiefs to acquire power. Among the Iroquois (a matrilineal and stateless society), men are consistently chosen as political leaders although women still play a decisive role in lineage and village politics.[32] But this merely confirms the historical character of the anthropological argument. Just as patriarchy develops as a process, so too does the state. Each is preceded by growing hierarchies within the old kinship system – the increasing subordination of women and the increasing power of (male) chiefs. It is these preliminary historical developments which make the birth of the state and patriarchy, or better the birth of the patriarchal state itself, possible.

Patriarchy and violence

There is a further reason for arguing that patriarchy arises as an inherent part of the state and that therefore a critique of the state should be central to feminist argument. In stateless tribal societies (as we have seen) violence is contingent to the process of government. It is tightly constrained by kinship relations, and it neither threatens nor constitutes an instrument of social order. In state-centred societies by contrast violence is pervasive and predominantly male. Connell points out that in the USA and Australia (for example) those convicted of violent crime and those who manage the 'institutionalized violence' represented by the police, the prison services and the military are overwhelmingly men. This is why he rightly argues that feminism does need to see the state as a crucial theoretical question since the state both 'institutionalizes hegemonic masculinity and expends great energy in controlling it'.[33]

Here the anthropological argument provides important insights into the link between patriarchy, male violence and the state. For patriarchy takes its first developed form as the capture of female slaves and indeed the first slaves are women. Prostitution, rape, concubinage and patriarchal marriage are linked both to slavery and to the institutionalized violence of the state.[34] Although formal slavery no longer exists (generally speaking) in contemporary liberal societies, the legacy of this slavery manifests itself in the widespread violence of men against women. Feminists are right therefore to argue that at the heart of male supremacy lies a violence that transmutes itself into a thousand shades of coercion and harassment.

MacKinnon's search for a 'feminist theory of the state' is premissed on the relationship between male sexuality and force. Although she sees force as inherent in pornography (for example), it is rape which is the defining paradigm of sexuality. Not only is this rape widespread – in the USA almost fifty per cent of all women are raped or are the victims of attempted rape at least once in their lives – but it can be understood only when sex and violence are confronted as acts which are 'mutually definitive rather than as mutually exclusive'.[35] It is true that MacKinnon is concerned specifically with the analysis of the modern *liberal* state, but she argues that in sexual relations the liberal 'appearance' of choice and consent, attributed as they are to differential 'natures', merely conceals the reality of force. Thus consent in rape trials is often invoked as a way of masking crude force so that even 'liberal' courts will assume that unless the force is sensationally explicit and particularly brutal, no rape has occurred. Consent (as Pateman has noted) may be inferred from enforced submission.[36]

Two points in particular arise from MacKinnon's analysis. The first is that the liberal state, like the state in general, sees and treats women in the way that men see and treat women.[37] The second is that the analysis of the state as an institution enmeshed in male violence provides important insights into understanding the relationship between force and compliance. Compliance with patriarchy can only function, Lerner argues, with the co-operation of women. It arises out of indoctrination, educational deprivation, a divisive distribution of privileges and punishments and what Lerner calls 'outright coercion'.[38] It is true that there is coercion in stateless societies where women choose occupations compatible with their mothering, thus linking 'biological function' and the initial sexual division of labour. But here the coercion is implicit (rather than outright) and it is the kind of coercion which (we have argued) is inherent in social relationships in general. It is a coercion of circumstances, for what other choice would women (and men) in these kinds of societies have?

With the exchange of women in marriage, men now (in Lerner's language) coerce 'unwilling women',[39] but even here the use of force is not as yet systematic or prevalent. Hierarchical arrangements are part of apparently 'natural' kinship structures, enshrined in custom from time immemorial, and the relative absence of physical force signals the undevelopment of patriarchal relationships. It is only with the state that slavery and, with slavery, patriarchy itself develops. Although slaves clearly comply with their masters through some degree of deference, ignorance and manipulation, in general the legitimacy of slavery is rendered problematic by the need to employ substantial and sustained physical force. It is true, as Lerner comments, that women have for millennia participated in the process of their own subjugation because they have been psychologically shaped to internalize inferiority.[40] But patriarchy as a legacy of slavery has to be underpinned by male violence in both its unofficial and official forms. Like the state (of which it is part), patriarchy necessarily has a contested or contradictory legitimacy, since ideological and psychological pressures have to be reinforced by the kind of direct coercion which requires periodic bouts of physical force to make it credible.

Here MacKinnon's analysis of coercion and consent in rape is illuminating. She argues that sexual intercourse may be deeply unwanted and 'yet no force may be present'. On this basis juries might find: no force, no rape. Yet this ignores (as she points out) the wider context in which unwanted intercourse occurs. Some women may 'choose' to acquiesce in preference to 'the escalated risk of injury' so that compliance arises out of a *fear* of the force which men are able and willing to exercise. Force, in other words, can be be contextually present if momentarily absent. Again some women may comply because they eroticize domination and this eroticization 'beats feeling forced'. But here too the contextual presence of force is crucial since, as long as domination is eroticized, force and desire are not mutually exclusive. If women are too *frightened* to refuse, then in what sense can be it said that sexual relationships are freely undertaken?[41]

Feminists would generally agree that patriarchy manifests itself quintessentially as male violence. But if this is so, then the link between patriarchy and the state is integral. States emerge in societies where an absence of cohesive common interests promotes violence in unofficial and official forms. Both the criminal perpetrators of violence and those who use violence to contain them are invariably men and this makes it impossible to analyse the nature of women's subordination without understanding the nature of the state.

The state and the public/private divide

We have argued that the state rests upon a naturalistically conceived public/private divide which assumes (as Aristotle so bluntly put it) that men are the rulers and women the ruled. Liberalism continues to embrace this public/private divide in apparent opposition to its own abstract egalitarianism, while Marxism cannot transcend such a divide as long as its notions of the proletariat and production are infused with naturalistic assumptions. It seems odd therefore that Allen (for example) does not include the 'public/private divide' among the list of categories like 'law', 'culture', 'subjectivity', 'violence', 'misogyny', 'the body' (to name just a few) which she sees as central to feminism.[42] Yet it is unlikely that she (or anyone else) would argue that the question of say 'violence' 'misogyny' or 'culture' can be discussed without referring (at least implicitly) to this most central of feminist concepts.

If it is accepted that the public/private divide is a crucial concept within feminist analysis, then this is a further reason for challenging the redundancy thesis. Although it is conventionally assumed that it arises only with liberalism, in fact the public/private divide is inherent in patriarchy, and therefore in the state itself. It is true that the family is seen in pre-liberal thought as a political unit, but this is because men as the heads of the household are also the rulers in the state. If the family is public, women are not. They are the 'private property' of fathers and husbands.[43] With the rise of capitalism, the domestic economy declines and the household loses its former productive significance. People leave the house in order to work and the family comes to be characterized as a private institution. As a result the public/private divide takes on a new meaning.

This raises a crucial question. What is the relationship between the public/private divide (as presented in ancient and medieval thought) and the public/private divide as it emerges within liberalism? Since individuals with inalienable natural rights are conceived as existing outside of society, the public/private divide now focuses on the relationship not between men and women but between 'individuals' and the state. Freedom is declared 'the privacy of private men from public actions', and as this comment of Crick's suggests,[44] it is a divide which extends only to males. What has happened to women? Whereas in classical patriarchy women, like children, slaves and servants, are explicitly identified as the objects of rule, liberal discourse deals with free and equal individuals enjoying natural rights. Patriarchy (it would seem) has vanished since the absolute power of men over women has given way to the representative relationship between the individual and the state. Alas, what has vanished is not patriarchy but merely what Dahlerup calls the explicit visibility of male domination as a norm of the state. Men as the abler and stronger by nature are still destined to rule.[45]

The public/private divide is central therefore to the wider schizoid malady which afflicts liberalism. A naturalistic public/private divide radically conflicts with a conventionalist public/private divide dealing solely with the relationship of individuals to the state. Yet the two 'divides' necessarily go hand in hand since possessive individualists can be possessive individualists only if they possess women. If feminists are to demystify the public/private divide (as I believe they must), then it is crucial that they should have a coherent view of the state. MacKinnon exemplifies this problem. She argues eloquently that the liberal state merely perfects the public/private divide, but it is not clear how she would demystify a divide which she rightly condemns as abstract and oppressive. Her solution would seem to be this. The distinction is simply a myth. Since women even in their most intimate experiences are subject to the domination of men, the public *is* the private.

To feminism, she argues, 'the personal is epistemologically the political, and its epistemology is its politics'. The public is the private because the personal is the political and indeed the subject is the object. 'Disaffected from objectivity, having been its prey, but excluded from its world through relegation to subjective inwardness', she writes, 'women's interest lies in overthrowing *the distinction itself.*'[46]

But this is a 'holism' which cannot take us beyond liberalism. If the public and the private cannot be distinguished at all, then one of the numerous halves of numerous dichotomies which characterize Western thought – reason and passion, form and content, culture and nature, universal and particular, men and women etc. – is collapsed into the other. What happens (for example) to the distinction between men and women? Do women (as Plato suggests) become men, or are we to assume (as radical feminists like Firestone argue) that women no longer need to bear children and (as a consequence) nature becomes culture? Indeed, if the very distinction between subject and object is rejected, how can the struggle for emancipation (which presupposes *some* differentiation between theory and practice) get off the ground? A 'holistic' solution to the problem can do no more than invert liberal patriarchalism. It is powerless to transcend it.[47]

MacKinnon's failure to resolve the public/private divide arises out of her failure to resolve the classic liberal dualism between society and the state. Just as she collapses public into private, so she seems to collapse state into society. Thus she argues that the Weberian monopoly of the means of legitimate coercion, thought to distinguish the state as an entity, actually describes the power of men over women in the home, in the bedroom, on the job, in the street, through social life.[48] This reductionism leaves her vulnerable to Allen's criticism that if the maleness of the state is a function of the maleness of everything else, then she undermines her case for the specifity of this 'male' state at the very moment she urges it.[49]

Clearly male violence is pervasive throughout patriarchal society (as MacKinnon suggests) but this does not rob the state of its specificity. The state seeks (as no other institution can) to monopolize violence in the paradoxical context in which this violence is also employed by the state's criminal 'competitors'. Weber's definition, we have argued, draws its specificity from the way it links the state with violence, and MacKinnon's problem arises because her notion of the 'political' conflates state with government. Because she accepts uncritically Dahl's (and indeed Millett's) definition of politics as a process which embraces not merely power but force, she presents the relationship between men and women in a patriarchal society as merely 'political' in character.[50] But what kind of politics is this?

All relationships involve an element of coercion (broadly defined) and thus an element of power. The social order is inherently governmental. Since people live in different circumstances and have different capacities and resources, conflicts of interest always arise, and the resolution of these conflicts (despite what anarchists say) requires governmental institutions and thus the employment of a wide range of social sanctions. It is precisely this relational and governmental argument which makes it important to stress that society is concretely differentiated rather than abstractly holistic, and it explains why (as Pateman rightly argues) feminism looks towards a social order, within which men and women are 'biologically differentiated but not unequal creatures'.[51]

Given what Pateman calls 'the social implications of women's reproductive activities',[52] it would be naive to imagine that all conflicts of interest between men and women (for example) could ever disappear. But in stateless societies these differences can be resolved governmentally with power and (in a broad sense) coercion – but not through the physical force characteristic of the patriarchal state (and the patriarchal society which this patriarchal state seeks to 'order'). If this is right, then the public/private divide continues but in a way which 'transcends' both the naturalistic conceptions of classic patriarchy and the abstract conceptions of liberalism. Individuals can only relate as men and women (and with an infinity of other identities as well). If they are to develop, their autonomy must be respected and nurtured, and the question of when and how the interference of others helps or hinders this development continuously arises. The tension between public and the private, in other words, is inherent in all social relationships.

Feminism thus contributes significantly to a critique of the state by linking emancipation to specific identity. It challenges the naturalistic character of the sexual divisions that are central to the state in general and stresses the importance of transcending the abstract (and thus patriarchal) individualism which is central to the liberal state in particular. Feminism (as we shall now see) also plays a crucial part in analysing postmodernist theory and in assessing the role played by democracy in the movement beyond the state.

SUMMARY

- Some argue that the state is 'redundant' to feminist analysis since male domination permeates social relations in general.

- However, the feminist critique of liberalism turns on the liberal view of the state as an institution authorized by men while women work in the home.

- Although Marxism suffers from a naturalistic view of women, the link which it asserts between patriarchy and the state is a telling one. Violence is at once central to the domination of by men and to the way in which the state resolves conflict.

- The prevalence of male domination through society as a whole does not downgrade but actually serves to highlight the importance of the state as a sovereign body whose universal jurisdiction permeates social relations as a whole.

11

Postmodernism

Marx once described the dialectic in its rational form as 'a scandal and abomination to bourgeoisdom and its doctrinaire professors'.[1] For postmodernists, however, rational dialectics have themselves become the outmoded prerogative of doctrinaire professors. A new scandal and abomination has outflanked the old. Postmodernism (along with feminism) has been described as one of the most important political–cultural currents of the last decade,[2] and post-modernists have certainly stirred up scandal and alarm by challenging the meaning of concepts generally taken to constitute the 'foundation' of knowledge.

For postmodernists, knowledge is to be conceptualized as a 'discourse', and discourses are theories which exercise power. We have already looked at the feminist argument that a theory of the state is unnecessary to analyse male domination, but with postmodernism the problem of whether a critique of the state is possible becomes even more acute. For the critique of the state we have looked at in this section are all rooted in 'modern' theories which derive from the Enlightenment. Yet postmodernism, we are told, comes not to 'complete' the Enlightenment but to displace and deconstruct (if not to bury) it.

The very notion of 'critique' (it might be argued) emanates from the Enlightenment, while Foucault, for example, as one of seminal figures in postmodernism, dismisses the state as 'a mythical abstraction whose importance is a lot more limited than many of us think'. Postmodernism celebrates diversity, dispersal and pluralism: the state is an institution which aggregates, concentrates and monopolizes.[3] One seems irrelevent to the other! All this makes it crucial that we should look not simply at what postmodernists say but at the *logic* of their position.

In fact postmodernism does contribute significantly to the argument of this book even though postmodernists appear to challenge the very concept of critique and seldom refer to the state. The postmodernist assault on what is called 'logocentrism' has potent implications for a critique of the state. The binary oppositions which postmodernists rightly challenge do not merely form the conceptual basis of 'Western' political thought: they also lie at the heart of an institution which claims a monopoly of legitimate force which it does and cannot have. However, if postmodernism is to constitute a credible post-statism, it requires an historical argument which conceptually 'privileges' the modern state. This means that postmodernism must jettison the kind of relativism and nihilism which bedevils the work of many of its practitioners so that it can defend a pluralist world of different individuals as the realization (and transcendence) of liberal modernity.

Logocentrism as a conceptual statism

Jencks in a wide-ranging analysis which embraces art, philosophy, literature, language and architecture produces a list of thirty-eight points which (he tells us) record the 'ambiguous slide and shift' from the modern to the postmodern agenda. It is revealing (in view of the reticence of many postmodernists to discuss the state) that the very first item of his 'list' contrasts the modern concept of 'nation-states' with the postmodern paradigm of 'regions/supra-national bodies'.[4] While Jencks has little more to say about this paradigm shift, the writer who provides a sustained analysis not merely of politics in general but of the state in particular is Ashley, and in seeking to assess the postmodernist critique of the state, I shall draw substantially upon his work.

To understand Ashley's critique of the state, we must first grasp the postmodernist critique of 'philosophy' or 'reason'. Rooted in Western thought (and going back to the ancient Greeks) is the idea that our institutions are structured around antinomies or dualisms. These dualisms can be expressed in an infinity of different ways – as mind–body, subject–object, form–content, culture–nature, the universal–the particular, etc.[5] Rational thought takes what postmodernists call a 'totalizing' view when it declares these antinomies to be in radical opposition to one another, and decrees that a thing can be known only by what it is not. Antinomies, in other words, are not simply different from one another: they are *mutually exclusive*. Postmodernists endorse the point particularly emphasized by Foucault and Derrida, that theory in this philosophical and rational form is authoritarian and intolerant. This authoritarianism is embodied in the notion of 'logocentrism' which features prominently in Ashley's analysis. A discourse is 'logocentric' or 'monological' when it sees binary terms as 'antinomies' or adversaries which confront each other in a 'zero sum relation'. One can win only if the other loses.[6]

Logocentrism is thus a theoretical activity with divisive implications, and Ashley follows Derrida and Foucault in employing not merely political but indeed statist metaphors in analysing the problem. A discourse is monological or 'logocentric' when it presents itself as a 'sovereign voice'. In seeking to impose order in an authoritarian way, a sovereign voice is conceptually static and absolutist because it cannot accommodate contingency and movement. Since one half of the binary divide is right and the other wrong, there can no 'interpenetration' or fluidity between them. Spatial and temporal diversity are 'threats' which need to be cabined, cribbed and confined by a sovereign voice which can brook no limitation, relativity, contingency or change. Sovereign voices impose 'narratives' upon unruly historical events, a narrative (or what Lyotard calls a 'metanarrative') being a story (as in biblical accounts) which is timelessly and universally true.[7]

Even when postmodernists do not actually mention the state, it is not difficult therefore to see that logocentrism is integrally linked to hierarchical and repressive political institutions. With Ashley, this link is made explicit. All the variants of modernist discourse have the state (he argues) as their unique and central focus. Sovereign and logocentric voices may be left-wing or right-wing, individualist or communitarian, humanist, Marxist, conservative or green. But they all in their different ways rely upon the metaphysical comfort of what he calls 'a pure and originary presence' – a compact with the state.[8] The state is thus the institution which above all others seeks to impose timeless order upon historical chaos. To think logocentrically is to act like the state – banishing, excluding, coercing, terrorizing, despising and marginalizing 'the other'. But logocentrism is not simply analogous to the state. It is the theoretical arm of the state since it would not be possible for rational agents to impose their will upon a protesting reality unless they could also call upon the power of the state to enforce their dictates. Hence logocentrist theory finds its most comprehensive expression (Ashley argues) in the 'totalizing' practices of the state.

Ashley does not refer to Weber's definition of the state but his argument clearly links it with logocentrism. Weber, as we have seen, defines the state as an institution which claims to exercise a monopoly of legitimate force for a particular territory. Certainly it is not difficult to see that each of the four elements – monopoly, territory, legitimacy and force – which constitute the Weberian definition have an 'inherent logic'[9] which is unambiguously logocentric in character. Ashley argues that modernist discourse sees the state as the agent of rational law, the subject of rational violence, and the reserve of rational administrative resources.[10] His analysis makes it clear that the Weberian definition fits the postmodernist critique like a glove. To claim a monopoly can only be logocentric since it self-evidently excludes competitors; the notion of territory shuts out outsiders and aliens, and the whole modernist logic of identity is rooted (it has been said) in an inside/outside distinction which seeks to keep borders firmly drawn[11] – a comment almost tailor made for the Weberian definition!

Lyotard, whose book *The Postmodern Condition* has become a classic text for assessing postmodernism, refers to logocentric propositions as 'grand narratives of legitimation'. Just as the state claims a monopoly of legitimacy, so grand narratives are privileged forms of discourse from which (abstract conceptions of) Truth and Justice emanate. States are the legitimators which do not stand in need of legitimation, and there is no doubt that what Lyotard calls 'a justice of multiplicities' cannot be reconciled with the kind of legitimacy claimed by the state.[12] Weber's comment (which we also noted earlier) that the state is 'the highest and ultimate thing in the world . . . the highest power organization on earth'[13] highlights the link between the postmodernist view of logocentrism and the monopolistic and absolutist character of the state.

Deconstruction and the metaphysics of force

For postmodernists, deconstruction is the conceptual process which challenges logocentric discourse. Clearly deconstruction cannot 'judge' authoritarian knowledge practices in an authoritarian manner: it must strive to be critical without being logocentric itself. As Ashley stresses, deconstruction cannot approach a 'text' (i.e. an institution or event presented in narrative form) by invoking some higher principle which is itself timelessly true and thus foundational in character.

Deconstruction (we are told) must work from within a discourse by 'appealing to its own terms'. Its task is to show that a discourse when 'interrogated' in postmodernist fashion undermines, undoes, subverts and displaces its own certain and central voices.[14] Connolly puts the point well when he argues that a (timeless) code of coherence and consistency must yield to what he calls a code of paradox.[15] The code of paradox compels a discourse to 'undo' itself by facing up to a number of unpalatable and painful realities. Under deconstruction, logocentric discourse has to accept that its 'pure and orginary presence' is in fact part of history, that its legitimations need legitimating and that its absolute truths have a relative character.

In particular, deconstruction involves demonstrating that the binary oppositions are 'relational' and interdependent. One has no meaning without the other. If logocentrism contends we cannot know what 'is' without knowing what 'is not', then the very identity of 'what is' must embrace its opposite. What is 'negated' becomes part of what is 'affirmed' and any attempt to banish and marginalize, displace and obliterate 'the other' necessarily fails. The state as the institutional embodiment of logocentrism is uniquely vulnerable to the deconstructionist's code of paradox. Each of the four attributes which make up the Weberian definition of the state depends for its very identity upon that which it would exclude. Thus to assert a monopoly is to acknowledge the existence of competitors; to claim an exclusive legitimacy makes sense only if this legitimacy is contested; to insist upon the 'sole' use of force must imply that 'the other' uses force as well. Take away the 'chaotic' and 'irrational' competitors – the anarchists, rebels, dissidents, terrorists and criminals – and the state's monopoly of legitimate force loses its entire *raison d'être*. The more the state asserts that it has a clear-cut territorial identity – 'here my writ runs not yours' – the more certain we can be that this fixity is in fact a fluidity: a contested terrain in which illegal immigrants, separatists, drug traffickers, etc. continuously 'transverse' the boundaries which have been so firmly drawn.

All four attributes of the state exhibit what postmodernists call an 'inter-textual' character. In other words the meanings of one text can be understood only in terms of the meanings which it seeks to erase and obscure. This paradoxical state of affairs is most dramatically demonstrated by the fact that the state relies upon physical force to impose its timeless and (abstractly conceived) rational order. For how can we be so sure that the state's mono-poly presupposes competitors; that its fixed territorial identities are in fact fluid, and that its sovereign legitimacy is always contested? The answer has to be that in each case the state demonstrates its 'pure and originary' presence through the exercise of *force*. This force has to be legitimated, legalized, nationalized, procedularized and territorialized, and these qualifying attributes reach their most developed form with the liberal state. But at the end of the day force, however qualified, remains force. Hence even the liberal state is still in the paradoxical position of declaring war on violence and the best it can do is to 'modernize' (i.e. rationalize) force. It cannot eliminate it. This force is the attribute which particularly under-mines the state's rationality as a sovereign voice since it cruelly exposes the critical 'limit' which (as Ashley puts it) all states necessarily place beyond criticism.[16]

In the eyes of postmodernists therefore the use of force by the state highlights its absolutism. It is the practice which seeks in a most totalistic way to obliterate difference, extinguish contingency and deconstitute the other. In chapter 6 I argued that force is incompatible with legitimacy since (unlike coercion) it involves treating individuals as mere things – natural objects who have no subjectivity and autonomy of their own. In that sense force seems non-relational in that it appears to deny the mutuality inherent in all human relationships.

But the postmodernist argument makes it possible to see why force is both non-relational and relational at the same time since force embodies the postmodernist's code of paradox in its most extreme form. On the one hand force is non-relational in that it seeks to resolve the problem of opposites once and for all by wiping 'the other' off the face of the earth. By treating its adversary as a mere object, force denies the inter-subjectivity of social relation-ships. However if force was *literally* non-relational in character, then the victim of this violence would cease to be not merely socially responsive but socially *significant* as well. He or she would have been robbed of all 'subjectivity', one opposite could exist without the other and rationality and logocentrism would appear vindicated!

The fact is however that humans can relate to each other only because they relate also to the wider world of nature (of which they are part). To dominate nature 'as a lord' is to impose a hierarchy that is oblivious to ecological (as well as to gender) consequences. Just as human activity is still relational even when it is directed primarily against non-human nature, so it is also relational when through the use of force it treats other people as things. You may physically obliterate your adversary but the presence of the extinguished 'other' nevertheless remains an integral part of your own identity, moulding your thoughts, fashioning your institutions and shaping your personality. If force is non-relational in a positive (social) sense, it is certainly relational in a negative (natural) sense. It demonstrates most graphically the futility of trying to assert identity by extinguishing difference.

It is true that it is possible to use force in order to end force, but if the use of force is to be self-annulling it must be tied to the postmodernist project of establishing the social and political conditions in which plural identities can replace a monolithic hierarchy. Here we are right to be cautious. For just as wars to end all wars can easily justify militarism, so a modernist (rather than a postmodernist) defence of force invariably perpetuates and aggrevates the zero sum games and radical conflicts of interest which make the *continuing* (and indeed escalating) use of force necessary. As states know to their cost, for every individual obliterated, tens are enraged, hundreds angered and thousands alienated. Force in other words is likely to 'extinguish' difference only by activating it in its most polarizing and contentious form. When the state expresses its sovereign monopoly through legitimate *force*, it not only confirms but at the same time multiplies the presence of violent competitors dedicated to challenging its force and contesting its legitimacy.

The postmodernist concept of deconstruction is crucial therefore to demonstrating why the state's use of force renders its identity intensely logocentric and catastrophically paradoxical in character. In confronting this problem, postmodernism necessarily subverts the 'metaphysics' of the state in terms of its own hierarchical and exclusionary logic.

Post-statism, feminism and the historical argument

Although postmodernism makes a persuasive argument for identifying the state with an authoritarian logocentrism and a mystifying metaphysics, its anti-statism is vulnerable to the following challenge. Can a radical critique of the state be sustained without presenting an argument at the same time for a world beyond the state? Ashley rightly rejects any (utopian) critique which identifies the 'end of the state' with the end of time, for this would project the stateless society as one in which difference and diversity had disappeared.[17] A coherent post-statism requires an historical argument.

Here the link between postmodernism and feminism deserves emphasis for it has been argued that the two arguments have complementary strengths and weaknesses. Feminists have at times found it tempting to make unwarranted and 'essentialist' assumptions about women which simply universalize the particular features of their own era, society, culture, class, sexual orientation, or ethnic or racial group. Some of the feminist critiques of the public/private divide assume that all forms of the sexual division of labour (even the very earliest) have the same patriarchal consequences, and, as far as Fraser and Nicholson are concerned, the postmodernist critique of ahistorical metanarratives can strengthen feminism only by acknowledging the existence of differences among women and by accepting axes of domination other than those of gender.[18]

A postmodernist feminism must attune itself to the cultural specificity of different societies and periods and to the different groups within these societies and periods.[19] Hence central to the feminist critique of patriarchy is an emphasis upon its historical character. If naturalism (as integral to statism) is to be criticized as logocentric in essence, then it has to be shown that patriarchy is a social construct and not a timeless reality. Feminists must acknowledge the fact that if patriarchy 'in general' involves the domination of women by men, this does not exclude but on the contrary *presupposes* an oppression which is different at different times in different societies.

In the same way postmodernists need to embrace this historical argument in their critique of logocentrism and the state. Ashley is right therefore to insist that the notion of the sovereign voice is not peculiar to modern discourse and that, in pre-modernity, statism takes the form of a 'mirror of God'. Whereas modern statecraft fixes the sovereign voice as rational, legal and human, medieval statecraft enshrines its narrative as the word of God which the king must serve.[20] Differentiating the historical phases of state development is crucial to the case for a post-statism. If (as the limitation thesis holds) the state is *only* a modern institution, then it would be difficult to resist the conservative rejoinder that a post-statist world might merely re-enact the repressive hierarchies of pre-modern times. A coherent post-statism must insist that all repressive and hierarchical polities *are* states so that a world beyond the state is a world beyond repressive hierarchies and the 'repressive hypothesis' embodied in the knowledgeable practices of the sovereign voice.

What is required is an analysis of the state which (in the memorable words of Gayle Rubin) engages in 'endless variety and monotonous similarity'.[21] The historical argument can support the case for a post-statism therefore only if it (*a*) asserts a general concept of the state; (*b*) does so in a way that presupposes particular differences between particular states; and (*c*) enables us to differentiate between the different forms of states in *developmental* terms so that states can be categorized as more or less progressive in character. If postmodernism is to be a post-statism, it must demonstrate how, within the specific form of the modern state, we can identify positions which, when deconstructed, acknowledge the case for a 'inter-textual' world of statelessness.

Again the feminist critique of liberal patriarchy is instructive here. Feminists contend that, in a liberal patriarchy, male supremacy ceases to be an explicit norm of the state and is subsumed under seemingly univeral and impersonal notions and procedures. Arguing that feminism is liberal at root involves 'privileging' (as postmodernists would describe it) 'modern' over 'classic' patriarchy since what is unique about the liberal patriarchal state is that it creates conceptual space (though not the social institutions) for women to become citizens and enjoy legal and political rights. A 'vision' of gender-free universality co-exists (in increasing tension) with naturalistic arguments for female domesticity and servitude. Hence even feminists who appear to embrace the liberal tradition find themselves challenging (if only embryonically) the sexual division of labour and the public/private divide. The liberal patriarchal state is not just one state among many: it is the state which 'perfects' patriarchy by presenting force as consent, domination as legitimacy and particularity as universality. It is therefore the first form of the state which invites its victims to look *beyond* patriarchy, since patriarchy (like hierarchy, inequality and exploitation) nowhere appears in its official and public norms.

Feminism points to the kind of historical argument which postmodernism must also follow if it is to deconstruct the state as a logocentric sovereignty. Putting the two theories together, the point (we may say) is this. Deconstruct medieval notions of God the father, and all you end up with is rational gender-free man. It is only when you are in a position to deconstruct rational gender-free man that you can articulate the prospect of a post-patriarchal post-statist world in which women and men, have-nots and haves, ruled and rulers 'change places', acknowledging their differences in an egalitarian and mutually empowering fashion.

Postmodernism and the refusal to privilege modernity

This invites the following question: can postmodernists privilege modernity in the same way that feminists privilege the liberal patriarchy they deconstruct? It is here that postmodernists encounter problems. Ashley argues for example that all theoretical positions (i.e. pre-modern, modern and postmodern) are 'equally arbitrary, equally the effects to decide the undecidable'.[22] The stance is one of radical scepticism. Lest the point be missed, Ashley reiterates irritably in a footnote, 'I am not raising here the tired question of whether theoretical assumptions are "true or false" '. All cultural practices are political practices and all political practices are 'arbitrary practices of power by which the proliferation of meaning is disciplined and narrative structure is imposed upon history'. Postmodernism (on this argument) is in the same boat as all other discourses.[23]

But this argument is one which threatens postmodernism as a credible post-statism. Take Ashley's point about knowledge as a political practice. We can surely accept that conceptual distinctions, criteria of legitimation and procedural rules are a form of power in the sense that they affect our practice. But why should we assume that knowledgeable practice is always tied to the kind of power which is arbitrary, oppressive and therefore (by implication) takes the form of violence or the threat of violence? Surely knowledge can exert a political power which is governmental (and thus not authoritarian) rather than buttress the kind of logocentric discourse associated with the state. Ashley's argument that postmodernism is *just as* arbitrary as every other discourse, can only mean that it too has a sovereign voice, imposes narrative structures on history, and embodies a statist logic which seeks to extinguish the diversity it presupposes.

Indeed even sympathetic critics have frequently pointed to the way in which particular practitioners of postmodernism fall victim to the code of paradox they are trying to expound. Ryan finds that Baudrillard's celebration of meaninglessness and his despairing assessment of the uselessness of all political action is intelligible only because it assumes the timeless authenticity of a 'silent majority' who stand outside language, simulation and semantic coding. In the same way Crook argues that Baudrillard has to resort to a 'transcendent physicalism' when he dissolves all dualisms into a single world-constituting substance like 'discourse', 'intensity' etc. Lyotard has been similarly deconstructed. The babies which he throws out with the bathwater – the large-scale historical narratives and the general analysis of domination and subordination – return as the integral part of a critique which has supposedly banished them.[24]

Ashley's problem is basically the same. By contending that all practices are equally arbitrary, he makes it impossible to pose an alternative to the statism and sovereign voices he criticizes.[25] The notion that all discourses are equally arbitrary expresses a relativism which is profoundly (one is tempted to say quintessentially) modernist in character. For relativism subverts absolutism only by continuing to presuppose it: it is rather like displacing God in order to enthrone the Devil. It involves 'taking sides' in precisely the way that all sovereign voices do.

Harding has argued (in support of a feminist concept of science) that some postmodernists merely invert the absolutism of the Enlightenment by assuming that, if we give up the goal of telling true stories about reality, we must also stop trying to tell less false ones. 'They assume a symmetry between truth and falsity.' In fact (as Kuhn's theory of paradigm shifts suggests) there is no reason why we cannot aim to produce less partial and perverse representations without having to assert 'the absolute, complete, universal or eternal adequacies of these representations'.[26] To identify diverse systems of meaning as arbitrary (rather than as *more or less* truthful or progressive in character) is to evaluate these discourses, as Yeatman has pointed out, in relation to 'a nostalgic elegy for the erstwhile "essentialist" and "foundationalist" loadstones of modernism: reason, progress, science, objectivity, (Western civilisation) and so on'. Her point is also a feminist one: 'postmodern relativism reveals itself as the last ditch stand of modern patriarchy'.[27]

In so far as Ashley is unable to make a coherent case for post-statism, he surrenders to the very modernism he is trying to deconstruct. Connolly puts the point gently when he chides Ashley for a 'post-ponism' which constitutes a recipe of self-restriction and implies 'binary oppositions' of a modernist type. Yet Connolly himself elsewhere resorts to the very 'strategy of reversal' he warns against by endorsing Nietzsche's attack on rationality and the Enlightenment.[28] The point is that, if we present deconstruction as a purely 'negative' activity, this makes it impossible to tackle problems like poverty, patriarchy, nuclear weapons, debt crises, regional conflicts, famine and impending ecological catastrophe – problems which taken together appear to place in doubt the entire future of the world, in all its pre-modern, modern and postmodern dimensions!

An absolutist attack on reason cannot but render ambiguous the political credentials of postmodernist practitioners. Lyotard's alternative to abstract rationalism seems to be a kind of concrete 'mysticism' which rests on the hopeful but undefended assumption (as Ryan points out) that 'release' from the authoritarian aspects of Western culture will give rise to a better world. White for his part warns that, while postmodern thinkers would not endorse explosions of violence associated with group nationalism in the former USSR, it is not clear that they have a normative discourse available to condemn such violence.[29]

We return, in other words, to the problem we have already noted with anarchism and Marxism. It is not enough to attack liberal absolutism: it is essential to transcend it. To criticize the Enlightenment-oriented Jürgen Habermas for 'scratching where it does not itch' (as Lyotard does) problematizes the whole notion of thought as *critique* and leads Rorty (for example) to espouse a postmodernism which is a bizarre combination of pragmatism and conservatism.[30]

Mapping out a logic of post-statism

Despite the scepticism, nihilism and relativism noted above, Ashley's own argument suggests that postmodernism can embrace a logic which looks beyond the state and the polarizing modernist discourse in which he (along with many other postmodernists) remains partially trapped. It is true that Ashley contends that postmodernism is an arbitrary political practice like any other. On the other hand he *also* insists that postmodernists cannot as it were take sides in the binary oppositions that constitute the dualistic structure of logocentrism, since to do so would be to 'do the business of the state'. Postmodernists must avoid becoming (in White's words) the ringmasters of otherness, reacting to the one-sidedness of modernity by embracing a one-sidedness of their own. The task of the postmodernist (Ashley tells us) is to seek a position which is drawn to the 'margins', the 'frontiers' and the border lines of modernity's central voices. The historicity of all subjects must be respected since each 'side' can be identified only through its differences with the other. In other words, the 'logical' Ashley argues a case which has implications that Ashley 'the nihilistic practitioner' cannot accept.[31]

To those who would insist that it is impossible to reject suprahistorical notions of rationality without at the same time presupposing them, the logical Ashley replies as follows. Post-structuralists (i.e. postmodernists)[32] must *invert* the 'logocentric hierarchy' so that they privilege historicity over the sovereign voice of reasoning man. This privileging of historicity over (narrative) theory does not mean rejecting reason or theory as such since it is clear that postmodernism is itself a theoretical discourse. No theoretical discourse can expose puzzles and paradoxes without the use of reason.[33] Postmodernism is therefore a logic beyond logocentrism. It is not a logic of metanarratives and foundationalism but it is *a logic of deconstruction*. Postmodernists approach texts from the 'model of the heterologue' (as Ashley calls it) and the heterologue is itself 'logical' (as its name suggests). Indeed, in so far as the heterologue seeks to capture the inescapable or essential historicity of subjects, it is arguably even *more* logical than the monologue.[34] For what makes the state (as we have seen) a supreme embodiment of *monological* discourse is the fact that it is in the hapless position of having to legitimate itself in relation to the very law-breakers and dissidents it is dedicated to suppress – a position which in the last analysis is not very logical at all! By way of contrast the heterologue acknowledges explicitly that its boundaries will be transgressed and that its grounds of legitimation are always in doubt.

It is precisely at this point that the logical Ashley clashes with the nihilist practitioner. If historicity is to be privileged over theory, then it follows that modernity must be privileged over pre-modernity. After all it is modernism (as Ashley himself accepts) which provides the conceptual tools of historicity, contingency and diversity which are crucial to the postmodernist critique. Pre-modernity (in its medieval form) subsumes diversity into theology, acknowledges no independent world of contingency and historicity, and (of particular relevance here) sees the state as an institution which is natural rather than 'constructed' or 'artificial'. Critical discourses of modernity are by way of contrast endlessly preoccupied, Ashley notes, with 'the problem of the state'.[35]

This can mean only, contrary to the notion that all knowledgeable practices are equally arbitrary, that the sovereign voice of reasoning man is a *more* subversive narrative than the sovereign voice of God the father. Because, in Ashley's words, modernity is 'a multifaceted regime of highly mobile knowledgeable practices',[36] it embraces notions of subjectivity and constructed identities without which postmodernism could not undertake its work of deconstruction at all. Logically therefore modernity like liberal patriarchy must be more progressive, more critical, more rational and more aware of historicity than the explicitly theological narratives of pre-modernity. If postmodernism is to be a coherent post-statism, it must privilege modernity over pre-modernity since it is within (and only within) modernity that post-statist perspectives can realistically arise. Indeed the logical Ashley acknowledges this point in his deconstruction of Waltz's view of international politics when he argues that it is the modernist discourse of a *multiplicity* of sovereign states which unwittingly subverts logocentric concepts of state and sovereignty.[37] Since pre-modern discourse has no conception of an international society composed of independent sovereign states, its metanarratives cannot be deconstructed in a way which promotes a heterological model of post-statism.

Taken together as 'scandalizing discourses' whose anti-statist logics interweave, a postmodernist feminism (or a feminist postmodernism) has remorselessly radical implications. It constitutes a logic which embodies an historicized concept of theory grounded on the irreducibility of difference. It embraces concepts of reason, truth and objectivity which have been freed from foundationalist limits, patriarchal stereotypes and absolutist prohibitions. It must theorize the universal in a way which links it coherently to particularity, and endorse a notion of critique which explicitly and self-consciously accepts its own permanent vulnerability to deconstruction. It is hardly surprising that (put in these terms) the 'logic' of postmodernism is one which intimidates and startles many of its practitioners.

For consider the practical implications of this critical logic. A coherent postmodernism requires an analysis of how, within the inconsistencies and paradoxes of liberal statism, a post-statist world is struggling to be born. Such a project has massive resource implications. Diversity can only be celebrated among strangers (as Young cogently argues), and not repressed through violence and tyranny, if people inhabit a decentralized plurality of self-managing groups and institutions whose members (in Fraser and Nicholson's words) 'problematize the norms of their practice and take responsibility for modifying them as situations require'. White captures the logic of postmodernism well when he argues for an ethic of 'care' which embraces a willingness to entertain difference in all its particularity. He endorses Heidegger's argument that we need to relearn our 'finitude', for it is precisely the refusal to bear witness to one's limits which creates the urge to dominate[38] – to act in a *statist* manner.

If postmodernism is to challenge modernity successfully, it has to project a world in which order and cohesion, pluralism and organization are forged through conciliation, arbitration, debate and argument. Sovereign voices of sovereign states with their monopolies of violence, patriarchal loyalties and logocentric identities must be subjected to egalitarian pressures sufficiently durable to dissolve (however gradually) these repressive hierarchies away. It is no wonder that some practitioners retreat from the logic of their own scandalizing discourses and, like Ashley, are inclined to take refuge in relativism and nihilism. But then as the feminists most enthusiastic about integrating the critical logic of the two discourses might be tempted to observe, the most ambivalent of the postmodernists are likely to be men.

SUMMARY

- Postmodernism appears to reject the notion of 'critique' as the absolutist concept of a rationalistic Enlightenment. Postmodernists seldom refer to the state.

- Yet the postmodernist attack on logocentrism has powerful anti-statist implications since the state itself rests upon the kind of conceptual oppositions which postmodernists seek to deconstruct. The argument that we must respect the position of the alien 'other' implicitly rejects the notion of force – an idea central to the state.

- In order to develop a credible post-statism, postmodernists need to embrace the kind of historical argument which feminists adopt when they stress the importance of liberal as opposed to classic patriarchy.

- Many postmodernists see all 'discourse' as equally arbitrary and adopt a relativist stance which makes it impossible to support a pluralistic world of different identities. This nihilism has to be overcome if postmodernism is to realize its post-statist potential.

Part III

The Practical Implications
of the Critique

12

International Society

An effective critique of the state must say something about the practical possibilities of realizing a stateless world. In analysing contemporary challenges and alternative critiques to the state in Part II, we have noted weaknesses in all the arguments we assessed. Liberalism in practice (if not in theory) takes the state for granted. While feminists and postmodernists *are* imbued with a *logic* which is post-statist in character, they do not explore the way in which it might be possible to move beyond the state. The hostility with which anarchists view organization and government undermines their efforts to tackle this problem seriously.

It is true that Marxism does emphasize that states are indispensable to statelessness, but Marx himself basically saw the state as a domestic actor in the context of the class divisions of a particular society. The socialist system which came into existence after 1917 was dominated by one state in particular, and authoritarian institutions made it impossible to grasp what Berki has called 'a whole world of societies' as the context for a withering away of the state.[1] This particular weakness brings me to the question which I wish to discuss in this chapter.

In an earlier work I dismissed the role which international institutions might play in 'getting rid of the state' on the grounds that sovereign states are the 'stateless actors' of the international community.[2] However this ignores the importance of *international society* as a system of 'stateless' institutions to which states have already yielded up their sovereign powers. As we turn in Part III to explore the practical implications of our critique, it is with this concept that we must begin.

The concept of international society is generally associated with the English school of international theory and with the work of Hedley Bull in particular – recently described as one of the most distinguished theorists of international relations since Kant. Bull is especially well known for insisting that a sharp distinction must be made between an international system and an international so-ciety.[3] Bull conceptualizes international society as an anarchic order which embodies notions of justice that conflict with the partisan interests of the state.

Unfortunately he proceeds to frustrate this positive view of 'anarchy' as a form of order by arguing that international society can be nothing more than a society of states. He embraces an uncritical view of sovereignty and he fails to see the extent to which a 'new medievalism' (which he presents as an unrealistic alternative to international society) has already begun to emerge. Despite Bull's pessimism, the link he makes between common interests and international society is a fertile one. Once common interests are conceived dynamically and historically, they become the basis for an order in which states themselves contribute to the formation of a stateless world.

The challenge of Hedley Bull and the 'English school'

According to Bull and the English school, an international *system* arises when states interact in a way in which the behaviour of each forms a necessary element in the calculation of the other. An international *society*, on the other hand, implies in addition that common interests and values exist so that the members of this society consider themselves bound by a common set of rules, and share in the working of common institutions. They are governed not merely by rules of prudence or expediency but by 'the imperat-ives of morality and law'.[4]

Bull accepts the argument of Martin Wight that the idea of an international society arose from within European Christendom and over the centuries radiated outwards. By the end of the First World War, international society embraced representatives from the Americas, Africa and Asia as well as Europe. Since the non-European states still laboured under the stigma of inferior status (with the partial exception of Japan), it is only after the Second World War that we can speak of the transformation of an international society of states into an international society of peoples.[5]

Critics have complained that the English school is animated by a conceptual hostility to sovereignty, and Bull himself argues that Wight rejected 'the intellectual prejudice imposed by the sovereign state'.[6] In Chapter Four of *The Anarchical Society* – widely acknowledged as his *magnum opus* – Bull argues that state necessarily violates all our notions of justice. It is quite inhospitable to cosmopolitan justice (i.e. a just world community); it offers only 'a selective and ambiguous welcome' to human justice (i.e. justice as it pertains to individuals) and it systematically affronts the most basic and agreed principles of international justice (i.e. justice between states).[7] Indeed Bull even appears to challenge the very permanence and morality of the state by arguing that order among humankind is wider, more fundamental than and morally prior to order among states. Towards the end of *The Anarchical Society* he contends that the anomalies and irregularities of the existing state system are so glaring that a 'time may come' when world order might be pursued by a universal form of political organization radically different from the existing states system.[8]

The concept of international society (as Bull expounds it) appears to question not only the morality and justice of the state but its very capacity to secure order – defined by Bull as the avoidance of violence, the keeping of promises and the stability of possessions. Moreover international society is explicitly characterized as a society which is anarchical in character. The notion that anarchy is compatible with order breaks with the traditional idea of the state as the rational antithesis of chaos, and highlights the centrality of common interests in charting a world beyond the state. By suggesting that alternatives to the states system should be explored; that states act in ways which are immoral and unjust, and that the pursuit of order is compatible with a society which is anarchical, Bull appears to be vigorously challenging the champions of the sovereign state.

Bull's inconsistencies and the sovereignty problem

However, things are not as they seem. In *The Anarchical Society* Bull also strikes a positivist note of pessimism. His purpose, he tells us, is not to advance any 'solution' to the problem of maintaining order in world politics and he argues that the states systems is (at least for the foreseeable future) here to stay.[9] This pessimism derives from an inconsistency which lies at the heart of Bull's conceptualization of international society. On the one hand, he presents international society as an 'anarchical' order in which common interests embody notions of justice which are in conflict with the state. On the other hand he argues that international society is nothing other than a society composed of sovereign states. Indeed what makes the anarchical society *international* is simply the fact that it links existing nation states together.[10]

If international society is more than a 'system' therefore, it is less than a *community*. It is Bull's acceptance of international society as a system of states which accounts for the acute difficulties he has with his account of order and justice. 'Serious ambiguity' (as Harris has recently pointed out) arises when Bull alternates between a positivist stance which sees order at odds with justice, and an ethical mood which suggests that international society can be orderly only if it is just.[11] This ambivalence also accounts for Bull's curious misreading of classical texts. He follows Wight in arguing that the notion of international society goes beyond Hobbes, halts before Kant and accords with the position of Grotius. Yet Hobbes, as it has been pointed out, also restricts the conduct of states through his notion of a natural right to self-preservation; Grotius has neither a notion of international society nor a purely procedural view of 'order'; while Kant's cosmopolitican society seeks not to go beyond the world of states (as Bull suggests) but rather to secure peace among them.[12] It would seem that this misreading of classical texts derives from an underlying uncertainty as to whether the state really does constitute a barrier to the pursuit of justice and (a moral notion) of order.

Bull's general inconsistencies are sharply focused by his treatment of *sovereignty*. Although the English school (as we have noted) is sometimes accused of hostility towards this concept, in fact sovereignty lies at the heart of Bull's (dramatically contradictory) definition of an international society. Not only is international society composed of states, but (as Bull makes clear) one of the identifying attributes of states is that they assert sovereignty in relation to a particular portion of the earth's surface and a particular segment of human population. Bull takes the notion of sovereignty as self-evident and unproblematic. It is simply inherent in the state properly so-called. Yet, since he is committed to the concept of an international society, he argues also that these sovereign states are bound by 'imperatives of morality and law' which embody common interests and common values. Like Wight, he endorses the view that a state can claim sovereignty only if its right is recognized by every other state.[13] The inconsistency of the argument is simply this: if states are constrained in the way Bull acknowledges, then the sovereignty which he ascribes to them has been stripped of its essential meaning.

In chapter 5 we explored the concept of sovereignty as an abstraction inherent in the contradictory relationship between state and society. The idea arises within the classical liberal tradition as the political and collective embodiment of the absolute and inalienable (i.e. the *sovereign*) rights of individuals. The fact that sovereign states themselves are seen to exist in an international state of nature mirrors the abstract and atomistic individualism which underpins classical liberalism as a whole. This individualism is incompatible with any meaningful notion of society. Just as the individuals in the state of nature have discrete and separate identities which derive from *outside* society, so sovereign states are similarly atomistic and self-referring in character.

Bull's problem is therefore this. On the one hand he argues that, as the members of an international *society*, states express their identity through their relationships with others. The very principle of statehood requires *all* states to respect the notion of non-intervention, the equality of other states and their right to domestic jurisdiction.[14] On the other hand international society, as Bull defines it, is nothing other than a society of statist sovereigns. The characterization is a contradiction in terms. For sovereignty, like the classical liberal notion of the individual from which it flows, is an absolutist and abstract notion that instantly crumbles when expressed in relational terms. Either the state is sovereign or it belongs to an international society. It is logically impossible to do both. Bull has (rightly) been described as defining sovereignty in classic power-as-control terms (along with theorists like Hinsley), and put in these terms sovereignty reflects all the limitations of both modernist and male thinking with its emphasis on domination and its penchant for absolute and dichotomous categories.[15]

But why do we have to accept an absolutist concept of sovereignty which derives from the classical liberal tradition? Bull himself protests that Hobbes's theory (for example) ignores 'the treatment of sovereignty as a complex of rights conferred by international law', and there is a substantial literature distinguishing between relative and absolute, positive and negative sovereignty. Why not define the sovereign state as an independent entity which *recognizes* the constraints which international society imposes?[16] But this argument is more problematic than it seems. For, if we redefine the classical liberal view in this way, a sovereign state then becomes a state which *self-consciously* shares power with others. What has happened to the concept of sovereignty as power which comes and goes from a single source – which is supreme or final? The more realistic our definition of sovereignty, the more the concept seems to fall apart. The point is that the notion of sovereignty is indissolubly linked to the state.

Bull argues that there is a sharp dichotomy between the domestic role of the state and its international relationships. He distinguishes between *internal* sovereignty which states exercise over their own territory and populations, and *external* sovereignty which means 'not supremacy but independence of outside authorities'.[17] This suggests that externally sovereign states share power, while internally they reign supreme. But to this argument an obvious objection presents itself. How can a state have supreme power over its own citizens if it does not have supreme power *vis-à-vis* other states? If it is constrained externally, is it not also limited in what it can do internally? External constraints have always existed in terms of trading relationships and treaty obligations between states but, as long as international law appeared to grant states a free hand to treat *their own* citizens as they wished, these constraints appeared relatively invisible. However once international law turns its attention (inter alia) to the question of human rights, and European citizens (for example) can petition the Commission on Human Rights to secure redress against their own governments, then it is clear that the division between internal and external sovereignty is untenable.

What was once merely latent becomes explicit. States limited externally cannot be supreme internally since no state has ever been able to insulate its domestic policies from the impact of external constraints. Almond has recently drawn upon the earlier work of theorists like Hintze and Seeley and later writers like Gourevitch and Tilly to underline the point that there is a 'constant collaboration' between the inner and outer worlds. The very character of the state and the extent to which it either centralizes power or develops forms of power-sharing linked to consociationalism and corporatism depends upon external developments. Almond argues that what is required is a model which recognizes that international security, economic, political and cultural environments shape and are shaped by the internal politics, economics and culture of individual nation states.[18]

Bull himself admits that, carried to its logical extreme, the doctrine of human rights and duties under international law 'is subversive of the whole principle that mankind should be organised as a society of sovereign states'.[19] But this 'subversion' arises because the whole principle of sovereignty is coherent only when tied to the atomistic logic of classical liberalism. The doctrine of human rights merely renders explicit the problem which is inherent in the concept itself. A consistent notion of sovereignty has to endow states with absolute attributes which cannot exist in a relational world. Once you begin to strip sovereignty of its abstract character, the state finds itself in the unenviable position of acting as a monotheistic creator in a pagan world of multiple gods.

Ordered anarchy as a frustrated concept

Domestic supremacy is not problematic only because states are externally constrained. The particular problem of sovereignty arises out of the general problem of the state itself. This is why Camilleri and Falk are correct to tie their critique of sovereignty with concern about the state as a 'metaphysical abstraction divorced from time and space'. Bull remains saddled with the problem of sovereignty because he uncritically accepts the state as an institution which exercises a force which is 'overwhelming'. He senses that the state has a paradoxical character but cannot look beyond its contradictions.

On the one hand he appears to argue that force and legitimacy work against each other; on the other hand he accepts that the members of the state give their moral blessing to laws which invariably have coercive consequences.[20] If Bull is conscious of the problems we have discussed in Part I, he sees no way through them. Yet the three values which lie at the heart of his definition of order – 'life, truth and property' – all render problematic the state's claim to exercise a monopoly of legitimate force, and it is particularly contentious therefore that Bull should identify the state with government and order.[21]

It is because he defines international society as a society of sovereign states that his sympathetic conception of anarchy is prevented from realizing its critical potential. Bull accepts the anthropological argument that tribal societies maintain order through non-statist means, and he defends international law as a body of 'anarchic' rules which secures compliance from states despite the absence of a central authority commanding a monopoly of legitimate force. This leads him to reject Kelsen's argument that the legal character of international rules derives simply from the fact that states can resort to violent reprisals, and that the sanctions enforcing international law are analogous to blood feuding in tribal societies. As Bull rightly insists, in both tribal and international society the resort to violence is not only occasional and circumscribed, but it is incidental to the mechanisms of the anarchical order which seek compliance through consensus rather than force.[22] By way of contrast, the violence employed by the state is integral to its very identity.

Yet despite his acceptance of anarchy as order, Bull is anxious to stress the limitations of what he calls the 'domestic analogy'. Anarchy, he argues, is far more tolerable between societies than it would be within them since 'states after all are very unlike human individuals'. He expresses a perference for Locke's conception of state of nature over that of Hobbes's (wrongly assuming that Locke's natural condition is a 'society without government'), and he takes it for granted that overwhelming force is necessary to secure order domestically. He suggests that states are not vulnerable to violent attack to the same degree that individuals are although he does concede (a point we shall return to later) that in a nuclear age violence could obliterate states in the same absolute manner that it can obliterate individuals.[23]

At the heart of Bull's problem is his assumption that, because international society is an anarchical society, it has no government. To equate statelessness with an absence of government makes it impossible to evaluate the remarkable character of anarchical order as a *political* process in which compliance to rules is secured through negotiation, arbitration and persuasion. Government (as we earlier noted) involves social coercion of an informal and diffuse kind, but its sanctions do not rest upon agencies exercising physical force. In other words, governmental constraints do not actually violate the *formal* freedom of individuals to decide for themselves, whereas the use of force certainly does.

Although Bull acknowledges the differences between anarchical order and statist order, he does not see one as an alternative to the other (at least in the modern world). Whatever happened in tribal societies, the ordered anarchy of international society is no more than an anarchy which operates *between* states. Statist and anarchical order simply complement one another: their comparative merits as methods of securing compliance to rules remains unexplored. Bull fails therefore to see that the three goals which he identifies with order – security, contract and property – can be promoted far more consistently in the anarchical than in the statist order. In stateless societies complementary and overlapping bodies self-consciously share power and have to tackle conflicting interests in a non-violent and consensual manner.

Of course this is not to deny (as Bull himself notes) that

international society differs radically from tribal anarchies. It now embraces the whole of humankind and manifestly lacks the cultural homogeneity and ethnic intimacy of these early societies.[24] But Bull misses the subversive potential of his own concepts when he reduces international society to a system of states. If (as he rightly says) international society is an anarchical *order*, then this can mean only that when states co-operate through common rules and institutions, they do so in a way which necessarily transcends their own sovereign statehood. Bull himself speaks at one point of the danger of a 'tyranny of existing concepts' which prevents theorists from enunciating new concepts of universal organisation. The point is well taken. For it is precisely this tyranny which frustrates the critical potential of his own concept of ordered anarchy as an alternative to the contradictory and paradoxical order secured by the state. It is revealing that when Bull contends (in a later argument) that without the state order is impossible, the word 'anarchy' is used only as a synonym for violence and chaos.[25]

Wanted: a post-liberal assessment of the 'new medievalism'

One of the alternatives which Bull explores to the contemporary states system is that of a 'new medievalism'. This he conceives as a 'a modern and secular counterpart' to the universal organization which existed in Western Christendom. Such a system would involve political communities sharing authority and loyalties with regional and world organizations on the one hand and with sub-state or sub-national institutions on the other.

The concept of a 'new medievalism' (as Bull expounds it) is problematic for two reasons. Firstly it is not clear whether these political communities are states. Bull sees the new medievalism as a structure of overlapping authorities and criss-crossing loyalties that holds people together in a universal society while avoiding the concentration of power inherent in the notion of world government as a state. At times he describes these authorities as states albeit of an apparently 'non-sovereign' variety.[26] However, what makes the argument even more misleading is the fact that Bull presents his concept of a new medievalism as an *alternative* to the existing states system. Yet the logic of his own argument suggests that inter-national society must be *more* than simply a system of states, and for this reason it can be said that a 'new medievalism' already exists, if only in partial and embryonic form. Indeed Bull himself underlines the reality of the new medievalism as an order moving beyond the state when he points to a number of developments which constitute (as he acknowledges) 'awkward facts' for the classical (i.e. state-centric) theory of world politics.[27]

The first of these 'awkward facts' arises from the dramatic expansion of international law in the twentieth century and particularly since the Second World War. International law now extends to states outside the European tradition, and it has come to embrace a whole range of matters relating to the economy, society, communications and the environment, which go well beyond traditional preoccupations with political and strategic affairs. The second of the 'awkward facts' challenging classical theories of world politics has been the growth of regional associations in Africa, Asia and of course in Europe. In Held's view the development of the European Union (for example) has meant that sovereignty is clearly divided and any conception of sovereignty which assumes that it is 'an indivisible, illimitable, exclusive and perpetual form of public power' is now defunct.[28] A third 'awkward fact' is constituted by the break-up of older states as seccesionist movements or what Bull calls 'disintegrative tendencies' become more marked, and here it is impossible to avoid nothing just how dramatically these tendencies have accelerated recently in former Communist Party states like Yugoslavia and the old Soviet Union.

The proliferation of transnational organizations, scientific, professional, political as well as economic, constitute a fourth area in which 'awkward facts' for classical theory have arisen. Bull speaks of a 'technological unification of the world' shrinking the globe, and this has clearly circumscribed the capacity of states to pursue nationally focused economic policies. International movements of money and capital, technology and scientific skills now compel all states to confront what Held calls 'the disjuncture' between their apparent sovereignty and the conditions of modern economies. A wide range of sub-national and transnational institutions challenge the classical model of international relations and, taken as a whole, these 'awkward facts' suggest that it is not only those who (as James once put it) have acquired 'too much of a taste for political philosophy' who have doubts about sovereignty. Today scepticism about classical theories is openly raised in debates around federalism and the European Union in a way which is surely unprecedented.[29]

But even if the concept of the new medievalism as an alternative to the states system is contestable, Bull raises a question which clearly deserves our consideration. Would a universal society of a 'new medievalist' kind necessarily give birth to a more orderly world? It is one thing to argue for the incoherence of the state, the abstract character of classical concepts and the growing importance of non-statist institutions. But is it not possible, as Bull fears, that the new medievalism may generate a 'ubiquitous violence and insecurity' which would be even worse than the medievalism of the past?[30] If Bull's new medievalism is to create a more orderly world and strengthen anarchy in a positive rather than a pejorative sense, then such a development has to be 'post-liberal' in character. This post-liberal argument is premissed on the recognition that, for all its conceptual problems, the growth of the modern states system in the seventeenth and eighteenth centuries represented an important historical advance.

Indeed it can be said that modern nation states display three features which are positive in character. In seeking to centralize and monopolize power, states render violence accepable only if it is publicly subjected to constitutional and legal procedures. The savagery and ruination brought about by the Thirty Years War in the seventeenth century represent precisely the kind of internecine strife which made Hobbes's vision of a war of all against all seem credible to his readers. Secondly, the modern nation state links violence to legitimacy in a manner which is unprecedently explicit. Force has to be authorized. Laws *ought* to be obeyed and this has come to mean that people must have the right to make them. Thirdly, liberal modernity enshrines formal equality as the juridical norm of the states system. Equal rights for all citizens; equal rights for all states. Just as the medieval world has no conceptual space for the liberal concept of the individual as a citizen, so it is unable to conceptualize a world of free and equal sovereign states. International society, as Bull points out, is based on the rejection of a hierarchical ordering of states in favour of equality 'in the sense of the like application of basic rights and duties of sovereignty to like entities'.[31]

Of course, as we have argued in Part II, these 'subversive' liberal concepts also conceal and mystify repressive hierarchies of an exploitative, patriarchal, colonial and generally oppressive kind. Bull himself acknowledges that, if the states system rejects the notion of a hierarchical order, some disregard for the norms of sovereignty, equality and independence 'is characteristic of all international relationships'. Abstract egalitarianism (Bull refers to the idea of the balance of power for example) conceals of necessity some very real hierarchies.[32] Nevertheless abstractly emancipatory norms are preferable to what might be described as 'concretely' authoritarian ones, and Bull is therefore right to warn against any concept of a world community in which liberators vanquish heretics. As the whole history of communism after 1917 demonstrates, the idea that the states system could simply be swept away reflects a millenarianism which inevitably generates forms of hegemony and empire lacking even the 'immanently critical' character of the old liberal system.

Indeed this is why (as Bull notes) the countries of the Third World often see state sovereignty as a bulwark against attempts by more powerful states to rob them of their economic resources and manipulate them through policies of 'neo-colonialism'.[33] It is scarcely surprising that, when old empires break up and national liberation movements succeed, new sovereign states are formed since the sovereign state is itself premissed upon egalitarian norms. However abstract these norms, they constitute indispensable ideological weapons with which to resist the 'imperialist' oppressor. A post-liberal assessment of the new medievalism must offer a critique of the states system which seeks not to reject liberal norms but to *transcend* them. If the new medievalism is to bring about a more orderly world, then it is essential that the abstract ideals of the liberal tradition should be progressively realized.

A post-Hobbesian defence of common interests

Bull's concept of international society has been criticized on the grounds that it cannot provide any non-prudential reasons for ethical action, and is tied to a notion of 'consensus' which is 'outstandingly unhelpful'. One writer has protested that it is unclear whether Bull believes that states *do* or merely *should* have common interests.[34] His concept of common interests suffers from the same ambivalence we noted earlier in his relationship between justice and order. The concept 'should' point beyond the state but Bull can see no way in which this is possible. To establish the post-statist character of common interests (in a way which coherently links 'fact' and 'value'), we need to return briefly to Hobbes.

Although Bull calls Hobbes a 'realist', in fact Hobbes's notion of natural right (as we have already commented) is both prescriptive as well as descriptive. Hobbes, as Macpherson rightly points out, does have a notion of obligation which he deduces from 'his materialist model of man and his market model of society'.[35] The 'fact' that we need to survive provides the basis for the 'value' we place on self-preservation. If we are to sustain the post-liberal case for a new medievalism, then we need to construct what I want to call a post-Hobbesian concept of common interests. At the heart of Hobbes's argument is the insistence that without order life threatens to become nasty, brutish and short. The *logic* of this argument (when deconstructed) suggests that we all have a common interest in avoiding the war of all against all.

However, since Hobbes's individuals are discrete and atomistic in character, there is no place for common interests in his theory as it stands. The (naturally) anti-social appetites and separatist identities of individuals make it impossible for them to become members of a real community. But suppose we strip Hobbes's individuals of their abstract character so that they become social beings whose identities are forged through relationships with others. It would then be possible to locate the existence of common interests based upon a common desire by all individuals to avoid a world in which life is nasty, brutish and short. Violence after all makes social relationships impossible. Of course (as Harris notes) the forging of a consensus around common interests involves painful choices,[36] but the Hobbesian argument provides an 'absolute' basis for these 'relativistic' calculations: without agreement, survival cannot be secured.

The concept of common interests is central to our distinction between government and the state. Where common interests exist, we can identify an arena in which people can resolve conflicts without the need to resort to sanctions based on physical force. Hence the existence of these common interests explains (as Bull stresses) why states are able to respect international law in the absence of an overarching sovereign. Two important implications flow from this argument. The first is that, where conflicts are such that a common interest cannot emerge, then the movement beyond the state falters. States are symptoms rather than causes of disorder (however much they may make a bad situation worse). The root of the problem therefore lies not with the state as such but with the absence of common interests sufficiently cohesive to enable people to settle their differences governmentally. To imagine that international law and global agencies could bring about an orderly world while *radical* conflicts of interest remain would be merely naive.

This leads to the second consequence of the post-Hobbesian argument. Given the fact that an anarchic order has to secure compliance to rules in a way which preserves the formal freedom of its members, it follows that entry into such an order must derive from the formal consent of its participants. This is why, as noted at the outset, states are indispensable to statelessness. The movement *beyond* the states system has to involve states themselves as willing accomplices in their own transcendence. This argument requires states to accept that the only way they can avoid extinction – a war of all against all – is to work through (and accept the discipline of) international social institutions. But isn't all this simply an exercise in logical fantasy? Can we really expect states to transcend themselves in this way? The point is that this process has *already* begun. To the extent that the international order is an anarchical society, it is an order which is able to impose international laws and moral imperatives that necessarily compromise the sovereign state. But is there any reason to believe that this fragile and embryonic development can be consolidated?

There are three areas in particular in which a post-Hobbesian concept of common interests has acquired a cogency and relevance which it lacked in the past. The first is one Bull himself notes: the question of nuclear weapons. If all states have nuclear weapons, then (in Hobbes's words which Bull cites) 'the weakest has strength enough to kill the strongest'.[37] The sovereign right to employ nuclear weapons in the prosecution of war is now almost universally regarded as absurd, and an international consensus is developing around the proposition that, if it is absurd to use nuclear weapons, it is also absurd to have them. The second area in which states can rationally 'defend' their sovereignty only by giving it up arises (though less cogently) in relation to war in general. Although non-nuclear wars still continue in a nuclear world, nevertheless (as Bull noted) armed conflicts now occur against 'a background presence of nuclear weapons'.[38] The two do not and cannot inhabit tightly compartmentalized worlds, and this fact accounts for the fear that unless long-standing regional conflicts (like those in southern Africa or the Middle East for example) are resolved, they might escalate in a nuclear direction. It is becoming part of an international consensus that regional conflicts cannot be allowed to fester simply because they are prosecuted by sovereign states and their challengers. Here we should also note the tidal waves of refugees currently sweeping across Europe in the post-cold-war period as a result of economic dislocation and ethnic strife. It is not hard to see the problems which these refugees can pose for wealthier countries which wish to preserve liberal political institutions.

To the question of nuclear and regional war can be added a third area in which common interests have become increasingly obvious: the protection of the environment. Bull had already noted in 1977 that along with, for example, strategic discussions in NATO and economic negotiations in the then EEC, ecological problems were being seen as 'a technical problem of maximising the interests of the human species rather than a problem of reconciling different interests'. This probably puts the point too sanguinely, for conflicting interests on environmental issues still persist (particularly in the context of resource scarcities). Nevertheless it remains true that the common interest which all states have in avoiding ecological catastrophe is becoming increasingly self-evident. As Camilleri and Falk comment, nowhere does the discourse of sovereignty appear more unreal than in our understanding of the ecological dynamics of the biosphere.[39]

Two further points need to be made about the post-Hobbesian argument as it applies to these three areas. The first is that in each case common interests have emerged as the result of social and technological change. The concept cannot therefore be regarded (in the way Bull regards it) as some kind of 'empirical equivalent' to static and ahistorical conceptions of natural law. The second point is that taken on their own the three areas identified above – nuclear war, regional conflicts and the environment – are simply a beginning. Unless they form a part of a political process which consolidates, deepens and expands areas in which common interests can be identified, the argument for a post-statist international society breaks down. The key to sustaining this momentum lies with the question of resources and power.

Bull himself had noted that no international consensus is possible which does not take account of the demands of the African, Asian and Latin American countries of the Third World. Not only must colonialism be eliminated, but there must be a movement away from a relationship of dependency and subordination of the poor upon the wealthy countries.[40] Otherwise a defensive retreat into state sovereignty will occur. The fear of nuclear war would promote not universal disarmament but general proliferation; attempts to negotiate solutions to regional conflicts are likely to be resisted; pressures from refugees would simply provoke an authoritarian response, while lack of resources would make it impossible for poorer countries to protect the environment. In zero sum conditions of scarcity and inequality, the 'shrinking of the globe' brought about by technological unification and a globalized economy will merely lead to claustrophobic outbursts of ethnic chauvinism and an intensification of nationalist rivalries. Under these circumstances even human rights doctrines appear as no more than legal instruments used by the strong to beat the weak. The point is that it is simply not possible for people to assert interests in common if they inhabit radically variant economic and social worlds.[41]

Just as states can currently perceive that nuclear war and ecological catastrophe would make the world unbearable for everyone, so the perception needs to grow that the radical disparities between north and south – crushing debt burdens, poverty, patriarchy, disease, repression and unfair trading practices – menace the whole of humankind. Yet Bull, as we have seen, is generally pessimistic about the prospects of a world beyond the state. At one point he argues that states would never accept that policies dealing with immigration, trade and fiscal matters, and civil and international conflict should be regulated according to the general interests of the world community. Indeed he concludes *The Anarchical Society* with the words: 'It is better to recognise that we are in darkness than to pretend that we can see the light.'[42]

But this pessimism arises from an assumption that a world community can be consolidated only through some kind of utopian abolition of the international 'society of states'. If Bull could not actually *see* the practical outlines of an alternative world organization, he felt *intuitively* that such an alternative (however abstractly conceived) lies buried within the contradictory logic of states themselves. His notion of an international society as both an anarchical order on the one hand and a system of states on the other classically exemplifies a subversive abstraction trapped by the conceptual tyranny which its logic transcends. Hence it is Bull himself who unwittingly demonstrates that the only way a state can *preserve* its independence and equality is to become more self-consciously integrated into a world order which goes beyond the statist institutions of classical liberalism.

SUMMARY

● Bull conceives of international society as an anarchic order. It would appear therefore that global political institutions have already begun to develop beyond the state.

● However, Bull also characterizes this international society as nothing more than than a society of states, and he sees government and the pursuit of order as the product of sovereign force. His uncritical view of the state is linked to an uncritical view of sovereignty.

● Bull correctly identifies international law as a body of 'anarchic' rules which are not imposed through force. But he fails to see that the 'new medieval' world is not an alternative to the contemporary system. This world is already coming about as a result of the expansion of international law and the growth of continental and transnational organizations.

- Nevertheless Bull's concept of common interests (when interpreted dynamically) does enable us to locate arenas in which supra-statist institutions can operate effectively. On the basis of his argument we can look towards a world in which states themselves increasingly accept the need for stateless government.

13

Democracy and the Movement Beyond the State

As I have noted elsewhere, democracy is generally regarded as the most contentious and controversial of all our political concepts.[1] Here I want to argue that its tantalizing ambiguities and frustrating elusiveness derive essentially from its relationship to the state. The debates and arguments which the concept generates turn on the question: why do we need the state? Theorists may not articulate the problem in these terms but this question constitutes the silent sub-text underpinning democratic discourse.

Hence we must insist that the argument for looking beyond the state is not some kind of exotic or 'extremist' import into an otherwise sane and sober political theory. It is a problem inherent in democracy as a concept tied (as Dahl recently put it) to a 'daring vision' which forever invites us to 'look beyond, and to break through' existing limits.[2] At the heart of these limits lies the state. Democracy can be coherently grasped only as a concept which resists the spatial and temporal constraints which the state imposes upon the political process. Its emphasis upon popular empowerment is at once local and regional, national and global, and democracy can be realized only when these dimensions complement each other.

In this final chapter, I shall seek to defend one very simple proposition. Those who speak the language of democracy are, whether they realize it or not, seeking to move society beyond the state. The problem, I shall argue, is that democracy is frequently analysed as though it is nothing more than a form of the state. This leads writers to suppress its anti-statist potential as a concept which makes the case for popular self-government.

Thus those who argue that democracy might manifest itself as a 'tyranny of the majority' assume that democracy can exist as a repressive hierarchy in which some rule at the expense of others, while the identification of democracy with the welfare state makes sense only in so far as the provision of welfare actually strengthens the capacity of individuals to govern their own lives. This, I shall argue, is the test. The case for respecting plural identities and encouraging participation will likewise contribute to democracy only when these measures facilitate government in place of the state, while the argument for a cosmopolitan democracy turns on the creation of international institutions which require a residual use of state force in order to cement the basis of a stateless global community.

Ten confusing models of 'capitalist democracy'

There has been a tendency particularly since the Second World War to argue (as Weldon puts it) that 'democracy', 'liberalism' and 'capitalism' are different words for the same thing.[3] As long as democracy is conceived in this way, it is impossible to identify its anti-statist character.

This is the problem with a recent work which identifies no fewer than ten models of what its author calls 'capitalist democracy'. These range from participatory, mediatory, paternalistic, manipulatory, hegemonic, regulatory, elitist through to compensatory, minimalist and conservatory.[4] All these models rest upon the assumption that liberalism, capitalism and democracy coincide, and hence a democracy is possible even where the conflict of interests in a divided society makes the state necessary. Thus J. S. Mill and Bryce are presented as advocates of a 'mediatory' model which emphasizes the importance of the leadership of an educated and propertied minority in order to *limit* the dangers of popular rule. Smith's 'paternalist' model of democracy assumes that most people are simply not competent to manage their own affairs, while his 'elitist' model of democracy makes its disdain for the demos even more apparent.

The advocates of Smith's model of a 'hegemonic' capitalist democracy (like Veblen and Hobson) argue that popular government is *undermined* by the divisive agents of liberal capitalism, and it is clear that the more 'mediatory', 'paternalistic', 'elitist' or 'hegemonic' the model, the less democratic it appears to be. Smith's 'compensatory' model raises the same problem in a different way, for here its proponents (like Crosland and Galbraith) argue for democratic policies which would move society beyond capitalism. It is true that some proponents of the 'minimalist' model do argue that capitalism alone can provide a secure basis for a democratic society. But Milton Friedman (as one of Smith's minimalist democrats) identifies democratic freedom with what Macpherson has persuasively argued is despotic coercion for those who have no choice but to work for others, while another of Smith's minimalists is Hayek, who makes no secret of his reservations about democracy.[5]

Smith's own preference is for a 'green' conservatory model but this model (as he himself makes clear) is likely to drive a wedge between liberal capitalism on the one hand and democracy on the other.[6] In presenting his models as models of 'capitalist democracy', Smith uncritically reflects the way in which democracy has been 'redefined' in the twentieth century so as to rob it of its egalitarian and anti-statist characteristics. By the 1950s (as Arblaster for example has pointed out) American political scientists were using arguments in *defence* of democracy which their liberal predecessors had hurled against the concept only two generations before.[7]

Tension and harmony in the problematic relationship

The argument that liberalism, capitalism and democracy are merely different words for the same thing would certainly have raised eyebrows in the past. When Madison complained that democrats sponsor wicked projects like the abolition of debt or the use of paper money, he was assuming (as the ancients did) that democracy was a government by the poor – a system which (in Rousseau's words) rests upon 'a large measure of equality in rank and fortune'. Indeed Rousseau's critique is particularly important here since he identifies democracy as 'a government without government': it is contrary to the natural order that the greater number should govern and the smaller number be governed. It is an argument premissed on the assumption that democracy itself is a (highly problematic) form of the state. It embodies conflicting interests which can be ordered only through 'collective force'.[8]

This assumption takes us to the heart of the liberal problem.

Radical conflicts of interest generated by property and the market in the possessive individualist society are unavoidable. Given the need for a state, what makes democracy the meanest and worst of all governments (as the seventeenth-century New England divine John Cotton put it) is that if everyone governs themselves, whom are they supposed to govern? It is the anti-statist character of democracy which accounts for its *tension* with liberalism, and hence democracy becomes hopelessly ambiguous when this anti-statism is 'redefined' or 'revised' away. On the other hand, if there is tension between democracy and liberalism, there is also harmony. What makes this relationship *problematic* is the fact that liberalism both opposes and yet contributes to democracy. But it is impossible to grasp this paradoxical point unless we focus attention on the state. For liberalism (as we have already argued) is a statist doctrine which rests upon anti-statist premises. Its elitist practices are continuously vulnerable to subversion from within.

This accounts for the otherwise puzzling fact that, even when liberals explicitly repudiated the concept of democracy, they were still taken by their opponents to be democrats. Take the case of the hapless King Charles in the seventeenth century who felt it necessary to reproach the rather conservative parliamentarians (who had taken him prisoner) for 'labouring to bring in democracy'. Clearly alarmed by the logic of their liberalism, he proceeded to deliver a homily on the state. 'I must tell you that . . . liberty and freedom consists in having of government.' A subject and a sovereign are 'clear different things': it is only democrats who confuse them! Liberalism (Charles is saying) leads inexorably to democracy and democracy subverts the state.[9] Indeed nowhere are the anti-statist implications of democracy more graphically demonstrated than in the conservative critique of Plato.

On the one hand Plato attacks a form of popular rule that seems to be umambiguously statist in character since (as we have noted elsewhere) Athenian democracy excluded women, slaves and foreigners. The material benefits which its enfranchised minority enjoyed derived from a imperialist relationship between Athens and its neighbours. Yet none of this prevents Plato from arguing that in a democracy natural hierarchies are turned upside down. Slaves enjoy the same freedom as their owners; the distinction between citizens and alien and stranger is erased and equality between the sexes promoted. Such is the extremism of democratic principles that in the end 'even the domestic animals are infected with anarchy'. It is a remarkable argument. It captures with extraordinary prescience the notion of democracy as a subversive and anti-statist concept and shows how (despite the statist character of the ancient democracies) the logic of democracy points to the empowerment of ever broadening sections of the population.[10]

It is ironic therefore that Dicey could argue in 1905 that democracy 'in its stricter and older sense' means 'not a state of society, but a form of government' under which 'sovereign power is possessed by the numerical majority of the male citizens'.[11] For, as we have seen, anti-statism is most evident in the older usages of democracy. It is when the term is reduced to a form of sovereign power that its critical character is emasculated. It then becomes impossible to understand that curious mixture of tension and harmony inherent in the problematic relation between liberalism and democracy.

Democracy and the tyranny thesis

We have already noted that the historic opposition to democracy derives from liberal support for property and the market, but this opposition raises a further problem which we must now tackle. For liberals themselves have frequently contended that it is precisely because they favour a limited state that they are against democracy. Democracy, far from constituting an antithesis to the state, generates statism in an absolutist and even totalitarian form.

I shall call this argument the 'tyranny thesis' since democracy (it is asserted) promotes a 'tyranny of the majority' which undermines the freedom of minorities and therefore freedom itself. This tyranny thesis is presented in a lively form by Crick, who draws upon the classic arguments of J. S. Mill and Tocqueville to argue that, while democracy as majority rule *may* stabilize free regimes, it need not. Crick endorses what Popper has called 'the paradox of freedom' – the proposition that democrats are obliged to accept a decision reached by the majority even when (here Popper echoes an argument of Plato's) the majority favour rule by a tyrant. Crick instances the German elections of 1933 while Goodwin has noted recently the case of the Islamic Liberation Front of Algeria which (had it been permitted to take office in 1991) would have instituted a non-democratic Islamic theocracy.[12] If Popper's paradox holds, then democracy can lead to tyranny and, in Crick's view, may itself be tyrannical in form.

Both Tocqueville and J. S. Mill have emphasized in their particular version of the tyranny thesis that the 'omnipotence' of the majority may take the form of a despotic public opinion. But it is clear (for reasons presented in my chapter on anarchism) that majorities cannot dominate minorities in a repressive fashion unless their opinions are reinforced by the state. Crick, it seems to me, implicitly concedes this point by identifying the tyranny of the majority with the notion of popular *sovereignty*, and (as he makes clear) this sovereignty is necessarily embodied in a state. It is however one thing to argue that sovereignty is oppressive (even when it takes an ostensibly popular form), quite another to identify a statist tyranny as a coherent expression of democracy as a concept. It is true that ancient Greek critiques do link democracy with popular *despotism*, and Crick cites Robespierre's 'democratic' defence of terror.[13] But Greek conservatives and French Jacobins saw democracy as a form of the state, and it is the same statist view which leads Crick to depict totalitarian communists as the advocates and practitioners of majority rule.

Whether the concept is expressed positively or negatively as class dictatorship or popular sovereignty, democracy is instantly rendered paradoxical when it is expressed through the monopolistic and absolutist institution of the state. The tyranny thesis presents a view of 'majority rule' which is logically vulnerable and empirically invalid. The problem was put clearly by Lukács when shortly after the Russian Revolution he speaks of the proletariat turning 'its dictatorship against itself '.[14] The formulation conveys an impossible paradox, for how they can a people be free when they are also oppressed?

Logically the tyranny thesis can be sustained only if it assumes a non-relational view of the individual. This non-relational view can take a 'positive' form when individuals are confronted with an abstract and authoritarian collectivity which 'frees' them against their own will. The kind of force envisaged by Lukács (or Rousseau for that matter) explicitly subordinates the will of some to others so that people cease to be subjects and become things. Since force prevents individuals from governing their own lives, it must constitute a negation of democracy. Dahl is therefore right to argue that, when individuals are forced to comply with laws, democracy is to that extent compromised. Although (as we shall see) he is pessimistic about the prospects of attaining a stateless democracy, he does challenge the logic of the 'positive' version of the tyranny thesis – that force is compatible with self-government.[15]

But there is a more widely held 'negative' version which argues that majority rule can be tyrannical not because a majority oppresses itself but because it oppresses *others*. But this version of the tyranny thesis also rests upon a non-relational view of the individual since it assumes that individuals can act violently towards others without degrading and subordinating themselves in the process. If the positive version ignores the separateness of individuals, the negative version ignores the mutuality of their relationships. Not only is freedom a relationship *between* individuals, but the whole point about the sovereign state (as we have already noted) is that its monopoly of legitimate force is intended to apply to society as a whole. Hence there is no way in which a majority can confine its tyrannical pressures to its opponents.

Empirically it is not difficult to see that, if minorities cannot freely express their views and promote their interests, then the question inevitably arises: how can the members of the majority say or do what *they* want without fear of being considered traitors or subversives? The 'Protestant state of the Protestant people' like the 'dictatorship of the proletariat' is a tyranny in which *no one* can be said to govern their own lives. Hence Dahl again is right to argue that the members of an association cannot govern themselves democratically if they strip a minority of its political rights. Thus, when Tocqueville argues that 'democratic despotism' arises from 'a people composed of individuals nearly alike and entirely equal', he unwittingly demonstrates the Hobbesian premises of the tyranny thesis.[16]

The tyranny thesis can be sustained only if we accept the abstract individualism of its assumptions: democracy is the Hobbesian Leviathan in majoritarian form. Why does the utilitarian concept of the greatest happiness of the greatest number appear so menacing to some liberals? Because each individual is assumed to be an egoistical 'utility maximizer' who seeks to dominate others. As Hodgson has argued in his critique of the New Right,[17] the fear of democracy stems from a possessive individualism which denies the existence of those common interests which (as we have seen in our previous chapter) have to be radically strengthened if the mechanisms of government are to replace those of the state.

Ultimately the tyranny thesis is an argument not against democracy but against the state. Indeed Crick himself makes this clear when he contends that the very concept of sovereignty contradicts his (pluralistic and conciliatory) view of politics. His argument ironically underlines the point central to this chapter: that democracy can exist in conditions of real pluralism and diversity only if it looks beyond the absolutist and monopolistic institutions of the state.[18]

Democracy and the welfare state

If the tyranny of the majority is an incoherent concept which dissolves when we challenge its liberal premisses, what of the argument that democracy necessarily gives rise to a 'welfare' state which tyrannically subverts liberal institutions? We have seen that the abstract anti-statism of the liberal tradition conceals dramatic inequalities of power beneath its benevolent protestations of rights. Inevitably therefore the extension of the franchise to those who are the victims rather than the beneficaries of the market generates powerful pressures for social reform.

The last quarter of the nineteenth century witnessed the rise of what Polanyi has called 'anti-liberal legislation' in regard to public health, factory conditions, municipal trading, public utilities and so on. This development fuelled the argument (recently revived by the New Right) that democracy, far from reducing the power of the state, promotes a welfare Leviathan which crushes individual initiative and independence. As De Jasay complains, functions which were once performed by the people themselves are taken over by the state. Democracy promotes wasteful public expenditure so that with the welfare state comes 'an ant-hill of bureaucracies, each acting in their own selfish interest'.[19]

It is certainly true that the New Liberals in the late nineteenth century argued the case both for social reforms and for increased powers to the state. The state in the work of Green becomes positively idealized as a universal bulwark against selfish interests, and Hobhouse supports a 'liberal socialism' which locates the place of the self-governing individual within the self-governing state. Yet what has this inflation of the state to do with democracy? As Hodgson has argued persuasively, once capitalism moves beyond the most primitive form of factory production, it requires the state to protect, regulate, subsidize, standardize and intervene. This was as much true of Victorian Britain as it was of Bismarck's Prussia, France of the Third Republic or the Habsburg Empire.[20] It is worth recalling that the New Liberals (as I have noted elsewhere) justified reform in the name of a common social interest rather than in terms of the 'democratic argument' and their notion of community assumed patriarchy, class divisions, political elitism and a point about which Hobhouse was particularly anxious – imperialism. If Tories like Disraeli could defend the extension of the suffrage on the grounds that 'elevating the condition of the people' meant upholding the Empire, then it is hardly surprising that the increased provision of welfare did not diminish but *intensified* the paternalistic power of the state.[21]

As Wolin has noted, the 'affinity' between 'democracy and empire' had been demonstrated already by the ancient Greeks. It would therefore be naive to assume that the development of a system of popular subsidies and allowances is itself democratic unless we assume a statist model of the kind which I have argued is logically incoherent and empirically untenable. Weber had already seen welfare provision as integral to the state's claim to exercise a monopoly of legitimate force, and the development of a welfare state in conditions of increasing concentrations of capitalist power involves marginalizing and neutralizing the poor. Wolin graphically demonstrates how a population dependent on welfare handouts constitutes a group of 'virtueless citizens' whose presence is both a creation of, and justification for, state power. Whether welfare functions are provided directly by central government or, as in the last decade, handed over to private concerns, the paternalist provision of welfare increases the power of the state by radically undermining the capacity of people to govern their own lives.[22]

Detailed, mystifying and ever changing rules about entitlement create proliferating instruments of statist power which leave the welfare-dependent sections of the population suspended between hope and despair – a dangling population integral to the functioning of the modern state. For all its anti-statist rhetoric, this is why authoritarianism has intensified under New Right administrations as the provision of welfare has become more selective, more arbitrary and more punitive. What we see (as Wolin has rightly argued) is not so much the dismantling of the welfare state as the intensification of its statist features.[23]

Pateman has recently commented that in the 1980s most Western welfare states were not only warfare states, but they were structured around the patriarchal assumption that women are basically unpaid domestic workers dependent upon men. The key to extending social rights and citizenship is employment in the 'outside' economy and ironically (as Pateman notes) women are simultaneously praised for their (unpaid) provision of welfare – care of the sick, the infirm, the elderly, the young – and excluded through tax systems and the eligibility for allowances from the welfare state's (masculinist) construct of an autonomous citizen.[24]

However it would be wrong to deny *any* link between the rise of the welfare state and the development of democracy. As feminist theorists in particular have stressed, the provision of welfare by the state is also a product of popular pressure to extend political rights into the social arena. Even if (as Pateman points out) the public provision of welfare means that women have become directly dependent on the state, this means that they no longer suffer the 'private' capriciousness of patriarchal husbands behind closed doors. The campaign for greater democracy can now take place on a public terrain.[25] Indeed it is this argument which leads Dahlerup, for example, to contend that the state itself should not be thought of as inherently patriarchal since welfare policies (like family allowances payable directly to women) provide resources for 'mobilization, protest and political influence'.[26] The same point could be made about the (relative) empowerment of the poor and dependent in general.

But the state which dispenses welfare still remains a (patriarchal and indeed class-biased) institution which claims a monopoly of legitimate force. The provision of resources to the vulnerable and dependent serves to emphasize the contradictory character of the state as it comes under democratic pressures to yield real power to its citizens. The rise of the welfare state therefore exemplifies the wider tensions within liberalism itself. This point underpins Pateman's argument for welfare policies which provide a guaranteed income for everyone. This would give people a real choice as to how and in what way they wished to 'work', and it would radically challenge conventional notions of employment, and traditional distinctions between paid and unpaid, full-time and part-time work. It would empower the citizenry as a whole, and (Pateman argues) challenge the basic structures of a capitalist economy and the radical conflicts of interest which it generates.[27]

But none of this is even conceptually possible unless we first take for granted the liberal assumption that men and women, rich and poor are all free and equal individuals. For all its limitations the welfare state bears out the argument central to this chapter. Without liberal theory, there can be no democratic practice, but at the same time there can be *no* democratic practice which does not challenge the hierarchies of the state.

Participation, identity and common interests

Offe has made the rather startling assertion that *if* we accept that the democratic state is a welfare state, this is not because but in spite of democracy. The production of public goods, he argues, depends upon some notion of commonalty of interest so that the better-off tax payers feel that those whom they are helping are part of the same society. What has brought the welfare state into crisis, he suggests, is that the old identities of nation, class, religion and culture are now disintegrating. Over the past decade this has led to attacks on the collective provision of welfare, as high and seemingly permanent unemployment has diminished fears among those with jobs that a 'surplus population' can threaten their livelihoods. Under conditions of growing fragmentation and individualization, democracy itself seems to work against the provision of welfare since in a democracy (Offe tells us) there is 'by definition' no ultimate authority able to order the production of public goods by the fiat of its sovereign power.[28]

The problem with Offe's argument however is that it rests on the assumption that democracy can exist within a possessive individualist society in which the rich not longer feel 'responsible' for the poor. Once we challenge the statist character of this democracy, his argument becomes problematic. Walzer has suggested that, the more dissociated individuals are, the stronger the state is likely to be[29] and, the stronger the state, the less individuals can be said to govern their own lives. The attacks on welfare arise not as a consequence of democracy but as a result of its diminution. The fact is that democracy cannot be promoted through individuals simply protecting narrowly conceived self-interests, and this point is borne out by the enormous literature which has been generated around the question of participation.

Given that democrats believe people to be capable of running their own lives, they must address themselves to all social institutions which exercise power and not simply to the formal law-making bodies which exist at national and local level. If the internal governments (as Dahl calls them) of economic enterprises are despotic, then this represents a serious limitation on the democratic character of society. To assess this democratic character, we must consider (as Bobbio rightly insists) not merely the number of people with a right to vote but also the number of places in addition to the 'traditional area of politics' in which this vote is exercised.[30] Putting democracy into a wider social context means reconceptualizing the nature of voting. In classical liberal theory the vote is seen as having a purely 'protective' function in which individuals express interests which have been fixed in advance. For the vulnerable, the poor and the dependent, the problem is that interests need to be *developed* rather than protected. Special efforts (along with deliberate resource provision) are necessary to establish, as in the feminist practice of 'consciousness raising', an identity that *had not existed before*. In this sense democracy requires participation – the development of capacities and identities (and in this sense 'interests') hitherto silenced by oppression and disadvantage.

Offe's argument that attacks on welfare arise out of a 'democratic' individualism ignores the link between democracy, participation and empowerment. But this link is also ignored if participation is *counterposed* to voting, and face-to-face meetings in which people decide issues directly are considered more democratic than the election of representatives who act on their behalf. A democratic concept of autonomy (as Beetham has argued) requires the right of all individuals to take part in decision-making as equals, but this must mean that in a society with millions of citizens – most of whom have neither the time nor the expertise to be full-time legislators – representation is the only way to maximize democratic autonomy.[31] Even in the most direct democracy some individuals must be mandated to act on behalf of others, so that the real challenge facing democrats is one of establishing voting as a more 'participatory' process. Representatives should be more accountable, assemblies more representative, voters more readily mobilized and the political impact of economic inequalities reduced – through the exercise (for example) of popular control over pension funds and employee control over company profits. The point is that an agenda for democratization requires concepts of representation and participation which mutually reinforce one another.[32]

If democracy is undermined by abstract individualism, it is also vitiated by abstract notions of participation which (as Phillips has argued) necessarily generate elitism, parochialism and intolerance. But this is not an argument (as democratic elitists like Sartori suppose) against participation: it is is an argument against *all* forms of decision-making which are exclusive, unaccountable and involve the continuing subordination of the vulnerable and the weak.[33] Participation becomes statist and thus undemocratic when it is tied to notions of citizenship which implicitly or explicitly exclude women, the poor and the marginal. It is for this reason that Young argues that Barber's participatory democracy runs the risk of promoting a stifling community in which the very existence of division signifies (as Barber puts it) that 'mutualism has failed'. Inevitably the voices of the disadvantaged and the oppressed are silenced when a universal identity is projected in this way.[34]

Against this 'democratic communitarianism' (as she calls it), Young postulates a form of group representation in which public funding would enable oppressed and disadvantaged groups to veto decisions on matters which directly affect their concerns. All citizens would participate in general decision-making forums but, in addition, groups (like women, gays, blacks, the old, working-class people, the mentally and physically disabled, etc.) would be separately constituted so as to communicate with others in a way which makes their particularity and difference explicit.[35] But this raises the question as to whether democratic participation would actually be strengthened by an explicit recognition of different groups. There is certainly a strong case for legislative assemblies (and other public forums) becoming more representative of the population at large, and Phillips argues that the use of gender quotas in the Nordic countries, for example, has dramatically increased the number of women who are elected to parliaments and local councils. The problem arises however when hitherto excluded groups are to be given institutionalized recognition, for this (Phillips suggests) might create the danger of a group 'closure' as oppressive as any abstract and thus exclusionary universal norm.[36]

Her critique of Young raises sharply the relationship between statism, identity and common interests. Young's problem, it seems, is this. In arguing for group representation, she inverts rather than transcends the abstract universality which she rightly criticizes. In other words, she attacks the abstract face of statism only to embrace its 'concrete' underbelly, for in the modern world it is the state which imprisons identities in particularistic frameworks even as it presents its monoplistic claims in universalizing terms. It is true that Young argues that group identities do not derive from fixed 'natural' attributes but are multiple and overlapping so that 'every group has group differences cutting across it.'[37] But if (as Young rightly suggests) group identities are essentially relational in character, how can a group be given veto powers when its membership is pluralistic, interpenetrating and fluid?

Thus a poor black woman worker (for example) could find herself having to argue conflicting cases in four separate groups unless she privileged one of her identities over others in precisely the way that Young wants to avoid. Young insists that that it is the ideal of community itself which projects unity over difference by presuming that subjects can understand one another in just the same way that they understand themselves.[38] But why do we have to assume that community can take only an abstract, oppressive and (I have suggested) statist form? If individuals are conceived in relational terms, then this presupposes both sameness *and* difference. It is true (as Young argues) that no one can understand another as they understand themselves. But it is also true that no one can understand themselves unless they are *also* able (to a greater or lesser degree) to understand others. A relational identity assumes that irreducibly different beings are continually 'changing places', and Phillips is right therefore to argue that difference presupposes rather than excludes the 'aspiration' or the 'impulse' to universality.[39]

Soper has recently warned against identifying greed and egoism as simply self-expression. This egoism might take the form of the self-interested voter (as in Offe's argument) or the kind of closed group which Young's proposals might create. Merely to challenge the political collective as a false form of humanism can mean (Soper suggests) that we unwittingly grant legitimacy to the tribalist, racist, nationalist and sexist divisiveness which has become painfully evident in the post-cold-war period. The key to this question is the state, for democracy can be understood only as a process which breaks with all temptations to a 'discursive neo-fascism' (as Soper calls it)[40] if it is rooted in common interests developed through the participation of individuals able to acknowledge their differences. The disintegration of old collectivities will strengthen democracy only if new and more comprehensive collectivities replace them. Otherwise (as is painfully evident today) this disintegration merely strengthens the state. A relational view of common interests requires us to break both with an abstract individualism which conceives conflicts of interests in zero sum terms and with an abstract communitarianism which denies that differences exist at all.[41]

If the concept of community suppresses difference or the notion of difference problematizes community, then we are stuck with the state. A democratic conception of common interests must accept that conflict, though inevitable, can be resolved governmentally (even if this involves broadly defined coercion) rather than through force. Without this relational view of identities, it is impossible to postulate a coherent notion of democracy which looks beyond the state.

The post-statist logic of cosmopolitan democracy

In my view the concept of a 'democratic state' is paradoxical since it suggests that universal political rights can co-exist with an institution claiming a monopoly of legitimate force. But this paradox is frequently (but not always) ignored since the idea of establishing a stateless society in the future appears impossibly utopian. H. G. Wells recalls that when the supreme ruler of the moon was told that governments existed on earth in which 'everyone rules', he immediately ordered that cooling sprays should be applied to his brows.[42]

This extra-terrestrial scepticism is shared by a number of writers who are critical of 'actually existing' liberal democracies but who regard democracy nevertheless as a form of the state. While Dahl (for example) is concerned about the problem which physical force poses for consent, the notion of a 'democratic state' does not unduly worry him since he finds it impossible to imagine a democracy without one. Keane, though also critical of liberalism, complains that anti-statist doctrines ignore the likelihod of conflict in the post-capitalist order and fail to specify the political and legal mechanisms for dealing with it. Held for his part warns that any idea that either the state could replace society, or society the state, should be 'treated with caution'.[43] What none of these theorists takes into account however is the fact that one can reject anarchist notions of spontaneity and *still* distinguish between government and the state. Once physical force is disentangled from the kind of coercive pressures which are inherent in relationships in general, a much more nuanced and focused view of the state is possible.

Dahl concedes that stateless societies have existed in the past but he argues that the modern world is too densely populated and interdependent to make a return to the 'infancy of the species' plausible.[44] But the fact is that, precisely because the world *is* now modern and interdependent, the problem of government is a global one, and both Dahl and Held note the way in which democracy has changed its institutional and geographical focus over time. Until the late eighteenth century democracy was identified with the polis of the city state. In the centuries which followed, the principle of representation has made it possible to project democracy in national terms but today this focus appears archaic. It is true that even those who argue the case for a 'market socialism' have assumed that democracy is naturally located within the nation state but, as Dahl (and Held) rightly insist, we now need to think of democracy in global terms.[45]

It is this point above all which should cause us to question the permanence of the state. Dahl argues that, although we are witnessing a 'third transformation' in the scope of democracy, the prospects for transnational political structures are likely to remain weak in the foreseeable future. Held on the other hand is more positive. He seeks to construct the model of a cosmopolitan democracy and, as he does so, it becomes evident that despite his scepticism, this international polity can be democratic only if it has a post-statist character. In order to demonstrate this point, I need to consider his case in a little detail.[46]

Held contends (as indeed Dahl does) that people within states are increasingly affected in life-threatening ways by activities which occur outside their national borders. Whether we think (for example) of the movement of interest rates, the pattern of investment, the spread of AIDS or damage to the environment, it is clear (as he puts it) that 'the very process of governance can escape the reach of the nation-state'. Moreover, he insists (again rightly) that what thwarts the formation of democratic institutions at the international level is the 'deep structure' of the sovereign state. The postwar period has seen the development of a UN Charter Model which has made some inroads into the theory and practice of sovereignty, but which has not displaced what Held calls the Westphalian logic of the states system.[47] The five permanent members of the Security Council still have a veto power; states are rarely if ever compelled to comply with the Charter's obligation to settle disputes peacefully, and the possibility of mobilizing collective coercion against illegitimate state action has never materialized. Even if the model were extended by enhancing the UN's jurisdiction, making its Assembly more influential and the Security Council more representative, that would still represent only a movement towards a very partial or 'thin' form of democracy. Massive disparities of power and resources would remain, leaving us with 'a state-centred and sovereignty-centred model of international politics'. The crucial question which Held's argument raises therefore is this. Can the international order be democratized without questioning the centrality and the role of the state?[48]

Held argues that sovereign states are being challenged from above by processes of economic, military, political and legal interdependence, and from below as local groups, movements and nationalisms seek greater representativeness and accountability. The model of a cosmopolitan democracy requires the formation of regional parliaments capable of generating international law; referendums cutting across nations and nation states; a cluster of international rights (economic, social and civil as well as political) recognized by national parliaments and enforceable by international courts, and an authoritative international assembly initially representing the nations which are democratic. Although Held describes this model as a democratic network of civil societies and *states*, the logic of his argument is profoundly anti-or post-statist in character.[49]

In the first place Held makes it clear that in his cosmopolitan democracy state sovereignty would be explicitly eroded. International legal principles would delimit the scope and form of action of public and private organizations by laying down egalitarian standards which no civic association or political regime could legitimately violate. But secondly (and just as dramatically) 'the principle of non-coercive relations', as Held puts it, would govern the settlement of disputes. It is true that he envisages the use of force as a weapon of last resort in the face of tyrannical attacks to eradicate democratic international law.[50] But this in itself does not contradict the post-statist logic of a cosmopolitan democracy. For the use of force (as I have already argued) is inevitable where a peaceful resolution of differences is impossible. Such force is always problematic in terms of its legitimacy but it *can* contribute to the consolidation of democracy if (and only if) it is a self-annulling process which makes the further use of force increasingly unnecessary.

Held, it seems to me, takes this point when he argues that the settlement of disputes requires non-coercive (or what I prefer to call non-violent) relations 'in principle'. Force, he suggests, is a weapon of last resort to be provided by the existing states themselves. It is true that he does see the secondment of a growing proportion of the state's coercive capability to regional and global institutions as 'permanent' in character, but the crucial point of his argument is this. The use of this force is *residual* and not central to the processes of international governance. The aim of this 'permanent secondment' is the 'demilitarization and the transcendence of the war system', and hence it is clear that the international polity cannot be called a 'transnational state' (to use a problematic phrase of Dahl's).[51]

To the extent that the cosmpolitian democracy succeeded in drawing more nation states into its 'networks', it would be able to tackle radical disparities of wealth and resources within the international system, compel states to settle their internal differences peacefully, and resolve international differences in a non-violent manner. Democratization must imply the gradual transformation of constituent states into national *governments* which both acknowledge an increasing dispersal of power within their societies and accept the existence of cosmopolitan government at the global level. However 'permanent' Held believes the secondment of state force to be, the point remains that statist methods of resolving disputes are no longer central to the pursuit of order. Held himself makes this clear when he stresses that 'the creation of a new international democratic culture and spirit' is necessarily 'set off' from 'the partisan claims of the nation-state'.[52]

Moreover he reinforces the post-statist logic of his argument by insisting that the development of a cosmopolitan democracy would require a critical assessment of 'a number of conceptual polarities frequently found in political discourse' – between (for example) globalism and cultural diversity, participatory and representative democracy, governance from above and the extension of grassroots associations from below. These and related polarities and dualisms (which Held seeks to transcend) derive their abstract and polarizing logic from the absolutism and divisiveness of the state.

Clearly these developments could take decades to materialize, but Held is right to argue that they involve what he calls a utopianism which is 'embedded' in the world as it is.[53] For this is an argument which reinforces a central premiss of my own critique. Just as liberalism provides a necessary platform for democracy, so the state is indispensable to statelessness. A cosmopolitan democracy can consolidate itself as a post-statist order only as states themselves recognize that the only way in which they can secure order and justice is to yield up power to regional, local and global bodies. What makes the 'seconded' force of states self-dissolving is the fact that it has to be employed only to underpin resource distributions and participatory schemes which entrench and extend common interests. States therefore have a key role to play in converting their sovereign power into local, national, regional and global government. The logic of democracy itself demands it.

SUMMARY

- The almost universal support for democracy in the postwar period is significant since democracy is a concept which postulates popular self-government and therefore looks beyond the state.

- However, the concept is often taken simply as a form of the state. Hence it is argued that democracy can express itself as a 'tyranny of the majority'. But a system is democratic only to the extent that it enables *all* individuals to control their lives. Thus the welfare state (with which democracy is also identified) is democratic only in so far as it strengthens individual autonomy.

- The debate over democracy and participation, like the analysis of democracy in terms of pluralistic identity, must turn on the question of displacing statist force by governmental co-operation. Where 'abstract' forms of participation and pluralism lead to division, they simply strengthen the state.

- Democracy must be seen as a governmental process which exists at the global as well as at regional, national and local levels. International (like domestic) political institutions will still require the use of force where differences cannot be resolved governmentally. But this force can be justified only if creates space for policies which make the state itself increasingly redundant.

Notes

Chapter 1 Overview

1 One writer has described the nation state as the 'dominant formation of our time': to suggest its demise 'may seem presumptuous if not actually alarming'. D. Beetham, 'The future of the nation state', in G. McLellan, D. Held and S. Hall (eds), *The Idea of the Modern State* (Open University Press, Milton Keynes and Philadelphia, 1984), pp. 208–22, esp. p. 208. Indeed a recent work argues that today we are no longer concerned with the origin and justification of the state, but much more inclined to ask whether a planned economy is consistent with individual liberty or if private property is compatible with social justice, than to worry about whether 'there should be some state as opposed to none'. L. Green, *The Authority of the State* (Clarendon, Oxford, 1990), p. 2; p. 4.

2 R. Miliband, *The State in Capitalist Society* (Quartet, London, 1973), p. 3.

3 As indexed by officially published statistics, military expenditures amounted to $159 billion in 1966, $200 billion in 1973 and by 1985 stood at some $600 billion. World military expenditure is greater than the Gross National Product of the whole of the African continent, South Africa included. Even in the field of the most sophisticated weapons system, some Third World countries possess equipment as advanced as that of the American military. Although only six countries are known to have exploded a nuclear device, many more have separable plutonium sufficient to build nuclear weaponry. Virtually every state across the globe now possesses armed strength far in excess of that of any traditional empire. A. Giddens, *The Nation-State and Violence* (Polity, Cambridge, 1985), pp. 246–53; pp. 326–7.

4 F. Fukuyama, *The End of History and the Last Man* (Penguin, Harmondsworth, 1992), pp. xi–xii.

5 Fukuyama, *The End of History*, pp. 201–2. For a recent (and highly perceptive) critique, see J. McCarney, 'The end of history?', in K. Hudson (ed.), *Questions of Ideology* (South Bank University, London, 1993), pp. 1–19, esp. p. 13.

6 A. Vincent, *Theories of the State* (Blackwell, Oxford, 1987), p. 3.

Chapter 2 Can the State be Defined?

1 G. Sabine, 'The state', in *Encyclopedia of the Social Sciences* (Macmillan, New York, 1934), p. 328. This comment is also cited in G. Almond, 'The return to the state', *American Political Science Review*, 82 (1988), pp. 854–74, esp. p. 856.

2 Cited by K. Dyson, *The State Tradition in Western Europe* (Martin Robertson, Oxford, 1981), p. 205. I take the point put to me by Andrew Vincent that Müller's argument for indefinability is very different from those made by the theorists I consider in this chapter.

3 D. Easton, *The Political System*, 2nd edn (Alfred Knopf, New York, 1971), pp. 106–15.

4 M. Mann, 'The pre-industrial state', *Political Studies*, 28 (1980), pp. 297–304, esp. p. 296. See also R. Miliband, *The State in Capitalist Society*, p. 4; N. Barry, *An Introduction to Modern Political Theory* (Macmillan, London, 1981), pp. 46–7.

5 D. Easton, 'The political system besieged by the state', *Political Theory*, 9 (1981), pp. 303–25, esp. p. 303.

6 Easton, 'The political system besieged by the state', pp. 305–6.

7 Ibid., p. 308.

8 Ibid., pp. 307–16.

9 F. Watkins, 'The state', in *International Encyclopedia of the Social Sciences* (Macmillan, New York, 1968), p. 156.

10 R. Pringle and S. Watson, ' "Women's interests" and the post-structuralist state', in M. Barrett and A. Phillips (eds), *Destabilizing Theory* (Polity, Cambridge, 1992), pp. 53–73, esp. p. 63.

11 I am grateful to Andrew Mason for raising this objection. The reference to the Sphinx can be found in T. Carlyle, *Past and Present* (Dent, London, 1960), p. 7.

12 Thus Foucault argues, for example, that there is no reason to suppose that the state constitutes the centre, apex or focus for the exercise of power: 'maybe, after all, the State is no more than a composite reality and a mythical abstraction whose importance is a lot more limited than many of us think'. M. Foucault, 'On governmentality', *Ideology and Consciousness*, 6 (1979), pp. 5–21, esp. p. 20. See also R. Pringle and S. Watson, 'Fathers, brothers, mates', in S. Watson (ed.), *Playing the State* (Verso, London, 1990), pp. 229–43, esp. p. 233.

13 A. Bentley, *The Process of Government* (Harvard University Press, Cambridge, Mass., 1967), p. 263; p. 300.

14 T. Weldon, *The Vocabulary of Politics* (Penguin, Harmondsworth, 1953), pp. 47–9.

15 Easton, *The Political System*, p. 112.

16 Ibid., p. 109.

17 Ibid., p. 113.
18 Ibid., p. 119; p. 115.
19 Ibid., p. 113.
20 D. Easton, 'Political anthropology', in B. Siegel (ed.), *Biennial Review of Anthropology* (Stanford University, Cal., 1959), pp. 210–62, esp. p. 226.
21 D. Easton, *A Framework for Political Analysis* (Prentice-Hall, Englewood Cliffs, N.J., 1965), pp. 32–3; Easton, 'Political anthropology', p. 219; D. Easton, 'Political system', in V. Bogdanor (ed.), *Blackwell's Encyclopedia of Political Science* (Blackwell, Oxford, 1987/91), p. 479.
22 Easton, 'Political system', p. 480; Easton, *Framework for Political Analysis*, p. 33; p. 44.
23 D. Easton, *The Analysis of Political Structure* (Routledge, London and New York, 1990), p. 259.
24 Easton, 'Political system', p. 478; Easton, 'Political science' in *International Encyclopedia of the Social Sciences*, p. 283.
25 Easton, *Analysis of Political Structure*, p. 202; Easton, 'Political science', p. 285.
26 Easton, *Analysis of Political Structure*, p. 10; p. 92; p. 299 fn.
27 J. Hoffman, *State, Power and Democracy* (Wheatsheaf, Brighton, 1988), pp. 25–8.
28 Easton, *The Political System*, pp. 136–7.
29 Ibid., p. 141; p. 135.
30 Easton, *Framework for Political Analysis*, p. 83; P. Converse, 'Review of D. Easton's *Systems Analysis of Political Life*', *American Political Science Review*, 59 (1965), pp. 1061–2.
31 R. Dahl, 'The science of politics, new and old', *World Politics*, 7 (1954–5), pp. 479–89, esp. p. 483.
32 Easton, 'Political science', p. 478; Easton, *Analysis of Political Structure*, p. 3.
33 R. Dahl, *Modern Political Analysis*, 4th edn (Prentice-Hall, Englewood Cliffs, N.J., New 1984), pp. 16–17.
34 G. Almond and G. Powell, *Comparative Politics* (Little, Brown, Boston, 1966), p. 17.
35 Easton, *Analysis of Political Structure*, p. 299n. The work which did more than any other to revive interest in the state was perhaps P. Evans, D. Rueschemeyer and T. Skocpol (eds), *Bringing the State Back In* (Cambridge University Press, Cambridge, London and New York, 1985).
36 Almond, 'Return to the state', p. 862.
37 T. Lowi, in 'The return to the state: critiques', *American Political Science Review*, 82 (1988), pp. 875–901, esp. p. 885.
38 S. Fabbrini, in 'Return to the state: critiques', *American Political Science Review*, 82 (1988), pp. 875–901, esp. p. 898.
39 Lowi, 'Return to the state: critiques', p. 888.

Chapter 3 Force, State and Government

1 J. Nettl, 'The state as a conceptual variable', *World Politics*, 20 (1967–8), pp. 559–92, esp. p. 559. Nettl of course also argues (p. 564) that states exist (as both domestic and external entities) only in some societies and not in others.

2 See also Dyson's arguments in *The State Tradition in Western Europe*, p. 3; p. 8.

3 Dahl, *Modern Political Analysis*, p. 17.

4 Almond and Powell, *Comparative Politics*, pp. 17–18.

5 Easton, 'Political anthropology', pp. 218–19.

6 Watkins, 'The state', p. 153; also cited in Almond, 'Return to the state', p. 855. See Evans, Rueschemeyer and Skocpol, *Bringing the State Back In* at pp. 6–7 for example. Indeed Mann argues that Skocpol in her 'excellent' *States and Social Revolutions* draws upon Marx and Weber in 'about equal quantities'. M. Mann, *States, War and Capitalism* (Basil Blackwell, Oxford, 1988), p. 3. As for Mann himself, 'my provisional working definition' of the state (he tells us in the first volume of his *magnum opus*) 'is derived from Weber.' M. Mann, *The Sources of Social Power*, vol. 1 (Cambridge University Press, Cambridge, 1986), p. 37.

7 J. Hall and G. Ikenberry, *The State* (Open University Press, Milton Keynes, 1989), pp. 1–2; p. 101 n. 2.

8 For a sample of otherwise very different theorists, see Miliband, *State in Capitalist Society*, pp. 46–7; M. Taylor, *Community, Anarchy and Liberty* (Cambridge University Press, Cambridge, 1982), p. 4; A. De Jasay, *The State* (Oxford, Blackwell, 1985), pp. 67–8; M. Laver, *Invitation to Politics* (Blackwell, Oxford, 1983), p. 8; R. Nozick, *Anarchy, State and Utopia*, (Blackwell, Oxford, 1974), p. 23; B. Crick, *In Defence of Politics*, 2nd edn (Penguin, Harmondsworth, 1982), pp. 29–30.

9 H. Gerth and C. Wright Mills (eds), *From Max Weber* (Routledge, London, 1991), p. 78.

10 Gerth and Mills (eds), *From Max Weber*, p. 7. See also R. Barker, *Political Legitimacy and the State* (Clarendon, Oxford, 1990), p. 46, and P. Dunleavy and B. O'Leary, *Theories of the State* (Macmillan, London and Basingstoke, 1987), pp. 3–4.

11 Cited by G. Poggi, *The Development of the Modern State* (Hutchinson, London, 1978), p. 100.

12 Gerth and Mills (eds), *From Max Weber*, p. 78.

13 A point crisply raised by Green, *Authority of the State*, p. 75.

14 Here I agree with Easton, *Analysis of Political Structure*, p. 284.

15 T. H. Green, *Lectures on the Principles of Political Obligation* (Longmans, London, 1941), p. 217. James Meadowcroft has pointed out to me that the celebrated dictum – 'will, not force, is the basis of the state' – was a subtitle added by Nettleship when he edited Green's lectures for publication. Nevertheless, as Nicholson observes, the comment 'is very much in the

spirit of Green'. P. Nicholson, *The Political Philosophy of the British Idealists* (Cambridge University Press, Cambridge, 1990), p. 226.

16 Gerth and Mills (eds), *From Max Weber*, p. 78; p. 121; p. 134.

17 Easton, *Analysis of Political Structure*, p. 284.

18 Easton, 'Political anthropology', p. 218.

19 See, for example, A. Leftwich, *Redefining Politics* (Methuen, London and New York, 1983) p. 28; D. Held, 'The development of the modern state', in S. Hall and B. Gieben (eds), *Formations of Modernity* (Polity, Cambridge, 1992), pp. 72-122, esp. p. 72.

20 Easton, 'Political anthropology', p. 217. Balandier argues that political anthopologists have played a crucial role in 'breaking the spell' between political theory and the state. G. Balandier, *Political Anthropology* (Allen Lane, Penguin, London, 1970), p. 195.

21 Gerth and Mills (eds), *From Max Weber*, p. 78.

22 A. Radcliffe-Brown, 'Preface', in M. Fortes and E. Evans-Prichard, *African Political Systems* (Oxford University Press, London, 1940), pp. xi-xxiii, esp. xiv and xxiii. These comments are also critically cited in L. Mair, *Primitive Government* (Penguin, Harmondsworth, 1962), p. 17.

23 G. Poggi, *The State* (Polity, Cambridge, 1990), p. 7.

24 Mair, *Primitive Government*, pp. 14-15. This point is also emphasized by I. Schapera, *Government and Politics in Tribal Societies* (Watts, London, 1956), pp. 11-16.

25 P. Clastres, *Society Against the State* (Urizen, New York, 1977), p. 131; p. 175.

26 S. Roberts, *Order and Dispute* (Penguin, Harmondsworth, 1979), p. 97.

27 Roberts, *Order and Dispute*, p. 20; p. 136; p. 27.

28 Easton, 'Political anthropology', p. 217. P. Nicholson argues that in stateless societies force was used to secure compliance to rules but here the enforcement was diffuse rather than concentrated, and it was left to anyone and everyone to enforce the rules. See his 'Politics and force', in A. Leftwich (ed.), *What is Politics?* (Blackwell, Oxford, 1984), pp. 33-45, esp. p. 42-3. The problem here, as Easton's argument itself makes clear, is that the more 'diffuse' the force, the more problematic the use of the term certainly in its physical sense.

29 Mair, *Primitive Government*, p. 12. Schapera notes in his *Government and Politics in Tribal Societies*, p. 192; p. 218 that, among the Bantu-speaking tribes in South Africa like the Zulu, Swazi and Tswana, power had become more concentrated and (in my view) more 'state-like'. Among those whom he calls the Bergdama and the Bushmen, violations of accepted norms are dealt with largely or even solely by self-help, and the authorities have no special means of force at their disposal.

30 Roberts, *Order and Dispute*, pp. 117-119; Clastres, *Society Against the State*, p. 21.

31 Roberts, *Order and Dispute*, p. 88; Clastres, *Society Against the State*, p. 175.

32 Schapera, *Government and Politics in Tribal Societies*, p. 218.

33 Laver, *Invitation to Politics*, p. 8; Dahl, *Modern Political Analysis*, p. 10.
34 Miliband, *State in Capitalist Society*, pp. 46–7. See also H. Laski, *The State in Theory and Practice* (Allen Unwin, London, 1935), p. 23.
35 See, for example, B. Parekh, 'When will the state wither away?', *Alternatives*, 15 (1990), pp. 247–62, esp. p. 251. Also Vincent, *Theories of the State*, pp. 29–30.
36 Miliband, *State in Capitalist Society*, p. 47.
37 Dahl, *Modern Political Analysis*, pp. 9–10; p. 16.
38 Roberts, *Order and Dispute*, p. 12; Laver's argument is set out in *Invitation to Politics* in his chapter 3 (pp. 47–66), tantalizingly entitled 'When we don't need governments'.
39 Foucault, 'On governmentality', p. 13; pp. 19–20.
40 L. Hobhouse, *Liberalism* (Oxford University Press, Oxford, 1964), p. 81.

Chapter 4 When Does the State Become the State?

1 Nettl, 'The state as a conceptual variable', p. 561. For a detailed rebuttal of this position, see J. Meadowcroft, 'The state, "statelessness" and British political argument', PSA paper, Leicester, April 1993.
2 M. Weber, *The Theory of Social and Economic Organisation* (Macmillan, New York and London, 1964), pp. 155–6.
3 Poggi, *The Development of the Modern State*, p. 153; Poggi, *The State*, p. 25. See also B. Parekh, 'When will the state wither away?', pp. 247–62, esp. p. 258.
4 Gerth and Mills (eds), *From Max Weber*, p. 252.
5 Ibid., pp. 81–2.
6 Giddens, *Nation-State and Violence*, p. 18.
7 Dunleavy and O'Leary, *Theories of the State*, p. 2; p. 6. See also Parekh, 'When will the state wither away?', p. 258; Vincent, *Theories of the State*, pp. 11–16.
8 Dunleavy and O'Leary, *Theories of the State*, p. 2.
9 See here Vincent, *Theories of the State*, p. 13; p. 15; S. Hall, 'The state in question', in McLennan, Held and Hall (eds), *The Idea of the Modern State*, pp. 1–28, esp. p. 3; Q. Skinner, 'The state', in T. Ball, J. Farr and R. Hanson (eds), *Political Innovation and Conceptual Change* (Cambridge University Press, Cambridge, 1989), p. 115.
10 Skinner, 'The state', p. 90; Vincent, *Theories of the State*, pp. 17–18.
11 Poggi, *The Development of the Modern State*, p. 26; p. 31; see also F. Watkins, *The State as a Concept of Political Science* (Harper, New York and London, 1934), p. 17.
12 See here A. D'Entreves, *The Notion of the State* (Clarendon, Oxford, 1967), p. 85.
13 See the discussion in Giddens, *Nation-State and Violence*, pp. 49–50; also S. Hall and J. Anderson, *The Evolution of the Modern State* (Open University Press, Milton Keynes, 1986), p. 27.

14 Giddens, *Nation-State and Violence*, p. 40; p. 57; Held, 'The development of the modern state', p. 79.

15 Hall and Anderson, *Evolution of the Modern State*, p. 35.

16 Hall and Ikenberry, *The State*, pp. 22–3.

17 D'Entreves, *Notion of the State*, p. 34; Watkins, *The State as a Concept of Political Science*, p. 42.

18 See the comments by Poggi, *The State*, p. 5 and Parekh, 'When will the state wither away?', p. 249.

19 Giddens, *Nation-State and Violence*, p. 20.

20 Roberts, *Order and Dispute*, p. 32. Mann also embraces a broad view which enables him to contrast modern with 'archaic' states. He still characterizes the feudal polity as a *state* albeit as a form of the state which is low in both what he calls despotic and infrastructural power. Mann, *States, War and Capitalism*, p. 7; pp. 33–72.

21 B. Parekh, *Hannah Arendt and the Search for a New Political Philosophy* (Macmillan, Basingstoke, 1981), pp. 7–10. See also Watkins, *The State as a Concept of Political Science*, p. 7.

22 D'Entreves, *Notion of the State*, p. 23; p. 47.

23 Hall and Ikenberry, *The State*, p. 78.

24 Hall and Ikenberry, *The State*, p. 13; p. 23. Indeed Giddens notes that the relatively high degree of autonomy of peasant communities in traditional states means that the main sanction which the dominant class must invoke in the case of non-compliance is the direct use of force. This violence is even more blatant, direct and explicit than the 'disciplinary' forms of surveillance which characterize the internal affairs of modern states. See his *Nation-State and Violence*, pp. 70–1; p. 187. Mann emphasizes the distinction between the 'despotic' and 'infrastructural' power in the state in his *States, War and Capitalism*, pp. 5–9. See also his recent *The Sources of State Power*, vol. 2 (Cambridge University Press, Cambridge, 1993), p. 59–60.

25 A. Southall, 'Stateless societies', in *International Encyclopedia of the Social Sciences*, pp. 166–7.

26 P. Crone, 'The tribe and the state', in J. Hall (ed.), *States and History* (Blackwell, Oxford, 1986), pp. 48–77, esp. p. 65.

27 Hoffman, *State, Power and Democracy*, pp. 28–32.

28 Hall and Ikenberry, *The State*, p. 18. See also here Mann, *The Sources of Social Power*, vol. 1, pp. 67–9.

29 De Jasay, *The State*, p. 3.

30 Parekh, 'When will the state wither away?', pp. 248–9.

31 Held, 'The development of the modern state', p. 73; Hall, 'The state in question', p. 2.

32 Hall, 'The state in question', p. 2; Held, 'The development of the modern state', p. 73.

33 D'Entreves, *Notion of the State*, pp. 71–2; p. 80.

34 Giddens, *Nation-State and Violence*, p. 57.

35 Balandier, *Political Anthropology*, p. 149.

36 D'Entreves, *Notion of the State*, p. 23; M. Forsyth, 'State', in D. Miller et al. (eds), *The Blackwell Encyclopedia of Political Thought* (Blackwell, Oxford, 1987), pp. 503–6, esp. p. 506.
37 Giddens, *Nation-State and Violence*, p. 20; p. 120.
38 Nicholson, 'Politics and force', p. 40. This argument does, it seems, undermine Nicholson's own thesis that even the politics of stateless societies is based on force. Watkins defends a broad view of the state in terms of a concentration of power which 'is capable of almost infinite variation in the matter of degree'. Watkins, *The State as a Concept of Political Science*, pp. 45–6.
39 D'Entreves, *Notion of the State*, p. 85; Giddens, *Nation-State and Violence*, p. 81.Mann notes that Christianity carried a 'radical, profound, but simple and true message to the world' in the way it facilitated the birth of a notion of 'the collective existence of humanity' in a universal organization. Mann, *The Sources of Social Power*, vol. 1, p. 326.
40 Giddens, *Nation-State and Violence*, p. 94.
41 Poggi, *Development of the Modern State*, p. 13; p. 23. An observation made all the more interesting when we recall Poggi's commitment to the limitation thesis.
42 Poggi, *The State*, p. 20; see also Giddens, *Nation-State and Violence*, p. 94.

Chapter 5 The State as Contradiction

1 Giddens, *Nation-State and Violence*, p. 120.
2 Hall and Ikenberry, *The State*, p. 20.
3 Taylor, *Community, Anarchy and Liberty*, p. 5; Nozick, *Anarchy, State and Utopia*, p. 23.
4 Giddens, *Nation-State and Violence*, pp. 120–1.
5 Parekh, 'When will the state wither away?', p. 260.
6 Hall and Ikenberry, *The State*, p. 2.
7 Parekh, 'When will the state wither away?', p. 250.
8 Vincent, *Theories of the State*, p. 19; p. 29.
9 Parekh, 'When will the state wither away?', p. 249.
10 Giddens, *Nation-State and Violence*, pp. 220–1.
11 Parekh, 'When will the state wither away?', p. 260.
12 Vincent, *Theories of the State*, p. 29; Poggi, *Development of the Modern State*, p. 93.
13 Beetham, 'The future of the nation state', p. 217.
14 J. J. Rousseau, *Social Contract and Discourses*, rev. edn (Dent, London, 1973), p. 99; also Hoffman, *State, Power and Democracy*, p. 35.
15 See for example the arguments of R. Barker, *Political Legitimacy and the State*, p. 46; Dunleavy and O'Leary, *Theories of the State*, pp. 3–4; pp. 254–5, and Green, *Authority of the State*, p. 69.
16 We see this problem clearly when (curiously named) structural Marxists like Louis Althusser (and at times Nicos Poulantzas) identify the state as

essentially a factor of cohesion in society, and therefore define as ideological *state* apparatuses, religious, educational, trade union and even family institutions. See N. Poulantzas, *Political Power and Social Classes* (New Left Books, London, 1973), and L. Althusser, *Lenin and Philosophy and Other Essays* (New Left Books, London, 1971).

17 Vincent, *Theories of the State*, pp. 220–1.
18 Barker, *Political Legitimacy and the State*, pp. 149–50.
19 Hall and Ikenberry, *The State*, p. 2; Watkins; *The State as a Concept of Political Science*, p. 42. It is worth noting that while Mann favours a definition of the state which contains 'a predominant institutional element', he also emphasizes that his definition contains a 'functional' element: 'the essence of the state's functions is a monopoly of binding rule-making'. Mann, *States, War and Capitalism*, p. 4. See also Mann, *Sources of Social Power*, vol. 2, p. 44; p. 88.
20 Vincent, *Theories of the State*, p. 221.
21 Poggi, *The Development of the Modern State*, p. 96; Poggi, *The State*, p. 78.
22 D'Entreves, *Notion of the State*, p. 2.
23 Dyson, *State Tradition in Western Europe*, p. 7; p. 37; Nettl, 'The state as a conceptual variable', p. 566. We would certainly accept Mann's argument that the state is autonomous and distinctive since, as he puts it, 'only the state is inherently centralized over a delimited territory over which it has authoritative power'. Mann, *States, War and Capitalism*, p. 16. The point is that, although the state is autonomous, its autonomy is highly problematic.
24 Crick, *In Defence of Politics*, p. 28.
25 Poggi, *The Development of the Modern State*, p. 96.
26 Giddens, *Nation-State and Violence*, p. 91; p. 282. See also Poggi, *The Development of the Modern State*, p. 90.
27 Barker, *Political Legitimacy and the State*, p. 9; Watkins, *The State as a Concept of Political Science*, p. 56.
28 Parekh, 'When will the state wither away?', p. 250. In a world where states seek to tackle the AIDS crisis by advising people to alter their sexual mores, it is questionable as to whether even the 'most intimate private realm' is excepted from the state's sovereign concerns.
29 Vincent, *Theories of the State*, p. 26; p. 31.
30 Parekh, 'When will the state wither away?', p. 250.

Chapter 6 The Problem of Legitimacy

1 Hoffman, *State, Power and Democracy*, pp. 73–4.
2 Laski, *State in Theory and Practice*, p. 15.
3 Barker, *Political Legitimacy and the State*, p. 23; p. 35; p. 40.
4 Dunleavy and O'Leary, *Theories of the Modern State*, p. 3.
5 De Jasay, *The State*, p. 67.

6 Barker, *Political Legitimacy and the State*, p. 57.
7 Ibid.
8 Ibid., p. 166.
9 D. Beetham, *The Legitimation of Power* (Macmillan, Basingstoke, 1991), p. 8 For a recent debate over Beetham's book, see R. O'Kane, 'Against legitimacy' and D. Beetham, 'In defence of legitimacy', *Political Studies*, 41 (1993), pp. 471–91.
10 Beetham, *Legitimation of Power*, p. 12; p. 25.
11 Rousseau, *Social Contract*, p. 52.
12 Barker, *Political Legitimacy and the State*, pp. 114–15; p. 109.
13 Ibid., p. 116; p. 113; p. 132.
14 Ibid., p. 152; p. 32.
15 Cited in ibid., p. 58.
16 Beetham, *Legitimation of Power*, pp. 32–3.
17 Ibid., pp. 16–17; p. 19.
18 Ibid., p. 31.
19 Ibid., p. 89.
20 Ibid., p. 31. Stress in the original.
21 Ibid., p. 35.
22 Arendt acknowledges the role of force within the legitimate power relationship when she argues that even when we consider 'the most despotic domination we know of' – the rule of masters over slaves – power does not rest on the superior means of coercion as such, but on a superior organisation of power. Cited by S. Lukes, *Power* (Macmillan, London, 1974), p. 30.
23 Beetham, *Legitimation of Power*, p. 28.
24 Ibid., p. 40.
25 Ibid., p. 87; p. 13.
26 Ibid., p. 87; pp. 29–30.
27 Ibid., p. 87.
28 Dahl, *Modern Political Analysis*, p. 37.
29 Ibid., p. 46.
30 Beetham, *Legitimation of Power*, p. 27; p. 31; p. 87.
31 Hoffman, *State, Power and Democracy*, pp. 121–2.
32 Beetham, *Legitimation of Power*, pp. 138–9.
33 Rousseau argues in the *Social Contract*, p. 49, that 'those who think themselves the masters of others are indeed greater slaves than they'. It is an argument which captures well the mutually degrading character of repression.
34 Rousseau, *Social Contract*, p. 53.

Chapter 7 Liberalism

1 J. Dunn, *Western Political Theory in the Face of the Future* (Cambridge University Press, Cambridge, 1979), p. 29; Gray describes liberals as

'definitely modern in character'. See J. Gray, *Liberalism* (Open University Press, Milton Keynes, 1986), p. x.

2 D. Smith, 'Liberalism', in *International Encyclopedia of the Social Sciences*, p. 276.

3 F. Watkins, 'The state', p. 152.

4 Aristotle, *The Politics* (Penguin, Harmondsworth, 1962), p. 28.

5 The position of Strauss as cited by a sceptical Gray, *Liberalism*, p. 8. See also D. Held, 'Central perspectives on the modern state' in McLennan, Held and Hall (eds), *The Idea of the Modern State*, pp. 29–79, esp. p. 32, where he argues that Hobbes's theory is at once profoundly liberal and illiberal in character.

6 J. Locke, *Two Treatises of Civil Government* (Dent, London, 1924), p. 118.

7 D. Ritchie, *Natural Rights* (Macmillan & Swan Sonnenschein, New York and London, 1895), p. 25.

8 E. Meiksins Wood and N. Wood, *Class Ideology and Ancient Political Theory* (Blackwell, Oxford, 1978), p. 89; p. 94.

9 B. Haddock, 'Saint Augustine: *The City of God*', in M. Forsyth and M. Keens-Soper (eds), *A Guide to the Political Classics: Plato to Rousseau* (Oxford University Press, Oxford, 1988), pp. 69–95, esp. p. 89.

10 See Gray, *Liberalism*, p. 2; E. Barker, *Greek Political Theory*, 2nd edn (Methuen, London, 1925), p. 62.

11 Barker, *Greek Political Theory*, p. 68.

12 L. Strauss, *Natural Right and History* (University of Chicago Press, Chicago, 1953), pp. 114–15.

13 M. Finley, 'Greek political thought', in *The Blackwell Encyclopedia of Political Thought*, pp. 181–3. Finley argues that not even utopian thought in this period was egalitarian. It is interesting that although Ritchie emphasizes (in my view exaggerates) the continuity between Sophistic ideas and those of liberalism, he himself notes the general irreverence of the Sophists towards constitutions and government of any kind. Ritchie, *Natural Rights*, p. 27.

14 J. Zvesper, 'Liberalism', in *Blackwell Encyclopedia of Political Thought*, pp. 285–9, esp. p. 295. Also P. Riley, 'Social contract', *Blackwell Encyclopedia of Political Thought*, pp. 478–80, esp. p. 479.

15 C. Pateman, *The Problem of Political Obligation* (Polity, Cambridge, 1985), p. 2; p. 12.

16 Pateman, *The Problem of Political Obligation*, p. 167.

17 D. Easton, 'Walter Bagehot and liberal realism', *American Political Science Review*, 43 (1949), pp. 17–37, esp. pp. 17–18.

18 Ritchie, *Natural Rights*, p. 153.

19 Pateman, *The Problem of Political Obligation*, p. 37.

20 Ibid., pp. 52–3.

21 Ibid., pp. 54–5.

22 Ibid., p. 65.

23 Ibid., p. 63.

24 Ibid., pp. 65–6.

25 Ibid., p. 72.
26 Hoffman, *State, Power and Democracy*, pp. 159–60.
27 D. Hume, *Moral and Political Philosophy* (Hafner, New York, 1970), p. 358. This is quoted also in Pateman, *The Problem of Political Obligation*, p. 33.
28 D. Miller, 'David Hume', in *Blackwell Encyclopedia of Political Thought*, pp. 226–8.
29 Easton, 'Walter Bagehot and liberal realism', pp. 19–20.
30 Gray, *Liberalism*, p. x; p. 19; p. 24.
31 See the arguments in B. Fine, *Democracy and the Rule of Law*, (Pluto, London, 1984), p. 46, and C. B. Macpherson, 'The economic penetration of political theory', *Journal of the History of Ideas*, 39 (1978), pp. 101–18, esp. p. 108.
32 Pateman, *Principles of Political Obligation*, p. 168.
33 Hobhouse, *Liberalism*, pp. 37–41.
34 Gray, *Liberalism*, p. 30.
35 R. Bellamy, *Liberalism and Modern Society* (Polity, Cambridge, 1992), p. 26.
36 Ibid., p. 32; p. 39; p. 56.
37 Ibid., p. 100, p. 139.
38 Ibid., p. 149; p. 165; p. 209.
39 See the interesting entry by E. Cassirer, 'Kant', in *Encyclopedia of the Social Sciences*, pp. 538–43, esp. p. 540.
40 I. Harris, *Kant: Moral Philosophy and Politics* (Department of Politics, University of Leicester, 1992), p. 14; p. 18.
41 Bellamy, *Liberalism and Modern Society*, p. 161.
42 Pateman, *Principles of Political Obligation*, pp. 114–15.
43 Ibid., p. 118; p. 127. For a concise exposition of Rawls, see (for example) S. Gorovitz, 'John Rawls: a theory of justice', in A. de Crespigny and K. Minogue (eds), *Contemporary Political Philosophers* (Methuen, London, 1976), pp. 272–89.
44 M. Forsyth, 'Hayek's bizarre liberalism: a critique', *Political Studies*, 36 (1988), pp. 235–50, esp. p. 250. This point is also made by J. Sheamur, 'Hayek', in *Blackwell Encyclopedia of Political Thought*, pp. 194–6. For Gray's point, see his *Liberalism*, p. 37. On Hayek's authoritarianism, see Hoffman, *State, Power and Democracy*, p. 197.
45 Pateman, *Principles of Political Obligation*, p. 150.
46 Ibid., p. 156.
47 Ibid., p. 160.
48 Rousseau, *Social Contract and Discourses*, p. 54.
49 Rousseau, *Social Contract*, p. 97.
50 A. Levine, *The End of the State* (Verso, London, 1987), pp. 33–6.
51 Pateman, *Principles of Political Obligation*, p. 157. Rousseau's argument that only those who use the term 'citizen' exclusively understand the real meaning of the term is quintessentially liberal in character. See his *Social Contract*, p. 61.

Chapter 8 Anarchism

1 This view is shared by D. Miller, *Anarchism* (Dent, London, 1984), p. 3. For treatment of the forerunners of anarchism, see for example P. Marshall, *Demanding the Impossible* (Fontana, London, 1993), Part Two.

2 J. Joll, 'Anarchism – a living tradition', *Government and Opposition*, 5 (1970), pp. 541–54, esp. p. 554. This comment is also cited by A. Arblaster, 'The relevance of anarchism', in *Socialist Register 1971* (Merlin, London, 1971), pp. 157–84, esp. p. 184. See also A. Heywood, *Political Ideologies* (Macmillan, Basingstoke, 1992), p. 196. There is a perceptive analysis of anarchism in B. Goodwin, *Using Political Ideas*, 3rd edn. (John Wiley, Chichester, 1992), Chapter 6. This account draws heavily upon Miller, *Anarchism*, pp. 18–22, and Marshall, *Demanding the Impossible*, pp. 204–10.

4 Pateman, *Principle of Political Obligation*, p. 138. See also A. Carter, *The Political Theory of Anarchism* (Routledge Kegan Paul, London, 1971), p. 17.

5 Pateman, *Principle of Political Obligation*, pp. 138–9; Marshall, *Demanding the Impossible*, p. 40; p. 207.

6 On Godwin's relations to Rousseau, see G. Crowder, *Classical Anarchism* (Clarendon, Oxford, 1991), p. 40.

7 Pateman, *Principle of Political Obligation*, p. 140.

8 See Marshall, *Demanding the Impossible*, pp. 224–8; Miller, *Anarchism*, p. 23. Thomas argues that Stirner's egoism if realized would destroy all societies once and for all. However he does note the ways in which Stirner differentiated his opposition to society from his opposition to the state, but these points do not affect our argument. See P. Thomas, *Karl Marx and the Anarchists* (Routledge & Kegan Paul, London, 1980), p. 129; p. 133.

9 Thomas, *Karl Marx and the Anarchists*, p. 155. See Miller, *Anarchism*, p. 25.

10 Cited by R. Dahl, *Democracy and its Critics* (Yale University Press, New Haven, 1989), p. 348.

11 Dahl, *Democracy and its Critics*, p. 348. See also Pateman, *Principles of Political Obligation*, p. 137. This point is rather missed by the argument that Wolff merely swings from an unconditional to a conditional view of authority and therefore simply subscribes to the widely accepted justification for constitutional government. See H. Frankfurt, 'The anarchism of Robert Paul Wolff ', *Political Theory*, 1 (1973), pp. 405–14, esp. p. 414.

12 G. Wall, 'Philosophical anarchism revisited', in J. R. Pennock and J. Chapman (eds), *Anarchism* (New York University Press, New York, 1978), pp. 273–93, esp. pp. 283–6.

13 M. Rothbard, *For a New Liberty* (Collier Macmillan, London, 1978), p. 15. Rothbard vigorously denies that he is an 'atomist' but argues that society, as he sees it, is not 'a living entity, but simply a label for an interacting set of individuals' (p. 37).

14 Miller, *Anarchism*, pp. 33–4.
15 Cited by Marshall, *Demanding the Impossible*, p. 561.
16 Miller, *Anarchism*, pp. 36–7.
17 M. Rothbard, 'Society without a state' in Pennock and Chapman (eds), *Anarchism*, pp. 191–207, esp. pp. 197–204.
18 Ibid., p. 193.
19 For a brief summary of Nozick's position here see N. Barry, *Introduction to Modern Political Theory* (Macmillan, Basingstoke, 1981), p. 79, and for a more extended acount R. P. Wolff, 'Robert Nozick's derivation of the minimal state', in J. Paul (ed.), *Reading Nozick* (Blackwell, Oxford, 1981), pp. 77–104.
20 J. Paul, 'The withering of the minimal state', in Paul (ed.), *Reading Nozick*, pp. 68–76, esp. pp. 70–3.
21 Hoffman, *State, Power and Democracy*, pp. 58–9.
22 Rothbard, 'Society without a state', p. 205. Rothbard also argues that one of the reasons why bandit rule is unlikely is because historically it has been very difficult for a state to supplant a stateless society. But the point is that states *have* arisen despite the market attractions of a Lockean state of nature, and to say that this is through conquest rather than by internal evolution begs the question as to how conquering states themselves come about.
23 C. Stone, 'Some reflections on arbitrating our way to anarchy', in Pennock and Chapman (eds), *Anarchism*, pp. 208–14, esp. p. 210.
24 Marshall, *Demanding the Impossible*, p. 565.
25 Ibid., p. 291.
26 Ibid., p. 13.
27 Ibid., p. 14.
28 Ibid., pp. 358–9; Miller, *Anarchism*, p. 54; p. 75.
29 Miller, *Anarchism*, p. 54; p. 70; Marshall, *Demanding the Impossible*, p. 290.
30 Marshall, *Demanding the Impossible*, p. 12; p. 16.
31 Taylor, *Community, Anarchy and Liberty*, p. 14; pp. 24–5; Hoffman, *State, Power and Democracy*, pp. 121–8.
32 Marshall, *Demanding the Impossible*, p. 649.
33 Arblaster, 'The relevance of anarchism', p. 182.
34 A. Carter, 'Anarchism and violence', in Pennock and Chapman (eds), *Anarchism*, pp. 320–40, esp. p. 324.
35 Marshall, *Demanding the Impossible*, p. 630.
36 Miller, *Anarchism*, p. 63.
37 Rothbard, 'Society without a state', p. 205.
38 Hoffman, *State, Power and Democracy*, pp. 62–3.
39 Marshall, *Demanding the Impossible*, p. 625.
40 Miller, *Anarchism*, pp. 97–8.
41 Marshall, *Demanding the Impossible*, p. 631. Miller, *Anarchism*, p. 95.
42 Miller, *Anarchism*, pp. 106–7.
43 The words of Walter which Arblaster cites in his 'Relevance of anarchism', p. 166.

44 See Miller, *Anarchism*, pp. 98–9; Marshall, *Demanding the Impossible*, p. 632.
45 Tolstoy asks whether there is any difference between killing a revolutionary and killing a policeman and replies that there is as much difference 'between cat-shit and dog-shit . . . I don't like the smell of either'. Cited by Marshall, *Demanding the Impossible*, p. 377. See also Carter, 'Anarchism and violence', p. 327.
46 Marshall, *Demanding the Impossible*, p. 633.
47 Carter, 'Anarchism and violence', p. 337; p. 334. Marshall cites Cafiero's comment that 'our action must be permanent rebellion, by word, by writing, by dagger, by gun, by dynamite, *sometimes even by ballot*' (stress added), *Demanding the Impossible*, p. 632. The implication, as Carter suggests, is that bullets are fine while ballots are only weapons of last resort!
48 Marshall, *Demanding the Impossible*, p. 650; Miller, *Anarchism*, p. 51.

Chapter 9 Marxism

1 For references, see D. Tarschys, *Beyond the State: The Future Polity in Classical and Soviet Marxism* (Laromedelsforlagen, Uddevalla, Sweden, 1971), p. 79; J. Hoffman, *The Gramscian Challenge* (Blackwell, Oxford, 1984), pp. 42–5. For Marx and Engels's general position, see H. Draper, 'The death of the state in Marx and Engels', in *Socialist Register 1970* (Merlin, London, 1970), pp. 282–307.
2 J. Hoffman, 'The state: has the "withering away" thesis finally withered away?', *Journal of Communist Studies*, 8 (1992), pp. 84–106.
3 Bernstein, as one of the classic exponents of 'revisionist' socialism, declares that 'the so-called coercive associations, the state and the communities, will retain their great tasks in any future I can foresee'. Cited by P. Gay, *The Dilemma of Democratic Socialism* (Collier, New York, 1962), p. 246.
4 J. Femia, 'Gramsci: Marxism's saviour or false prophet?', *Political Studies*, 37 (1989), pp. 282–9, esp. p. 283.
5 J. Femia, *Marxism and Democracy* (Oxford University Press, Oxford, 1993), p. 143.
6 A. Callinicos, *The Revenge of History* (Polity, Cambridge, 1991), p. 17. The same point is made by H. Gwala, 'Let us look at history in the round', *The African Communist*, 123 (1990), pp. 39–48, esp. p. 40.
7 L. Kolakowski, *Main Currents of Marxism*, vol. 2 (Clarendon, Oxford, 1978), p. 42.
8 Femia, *Marxism and Democracy*, p. 144.
9 See J. Hoffman, *Has Marxism a Future?* (Department of Politics, University of Leicester, 1991), pp. 2–4.
10 Femia, *Marxism and Democracy*, p. 146.
11 Cited by Femia, *Marxism and Democracy*, p. 147.

12 For references and further argument, see Hoffman, *Gramscian Challenge*, p. 22.
13 Ibid., p. 25. Also Hoffman, 'The state: the "withering away" thesis', p. 86.
14 D. McLellan, *Karl Marx: Selected Writings* (Oxford University Press,Oxford, 1977), p. 35; p. 56. For the later position, see for example Engels to Bernstein, 24 March 1884 in *Marx Engels: Selected Correspondence* (Progress, Moscow, 1975), p. 350. For further references, M. Levin, 'Marxism and democratic theory', in G. Duncan (ed.), *Democratic Theory and Practice* (Cambridge University Press, Cambridge, 1983), pp. 79–95, esp. p. 80.
15 See the two volumes of R. Hunt, *The Political Ideas of Marx and Engels* (Macmillan, London, 1974 and 1984).
16 Carter, 'Anarchism and violence', p. 323.
17 For relevant excerpts, see *Marx Engels Lenin: Anarchism and Anarcho-Syndicalism* (Progress, Moscow, 1972), p. 168; p. 101; p. 151.
18 Femia, *Marxism and Democracy*, p. 152. It is true that Femia sees this socialist model as one with (limited) state power, but it has been argued that despotism is even *less* likely in the kind of communist society envisaged by Marx. See Hunt, *Political Ideas of Marx and Engels*, vol. 2, p. 144. M. Levin, *Marx, Engels and Liberal Democracy* (Macmillan, Basingstoke, 1989), p. 123.
19 Femia, *Marxism and Democracy*, pp. 157–62; also p. 174.
20 McLellan, *Selected Writings*, p. 47.
21 Ibid., pp. 54–5; p. 47.
22 Ibid., p. 88.
23 Ibid., p. 156.
24 Ibid., p. 183; Thomas, *Karl Marx and the Anarchists*, pp. 163–8.
25 Hoffman, 'The state: the "withering away" thesis', p. 87.
26 Femia, *Marxism and Democracy*, p. 165. The passage about the proletariat's aims is also criticized for its elitist implication by Levin, 'Marxism and democratic theory', p. 83. For a spirited rebuttal of this argument, see (for example) D. Lovell, *From Marx to Lenin* (Cambridge University Press, Cambridge, 1984), p. 65; Hunt, *Political Ideas of Marx and Engels*, vol. 1, p. 165
27 Hoffman, 'The state: the "withering away" thesis', pp. 87–8.
28 Hoffman, *The Gramscian Challenge*, p. 168.
29 Cited by Levin, *Marx, Engels and Liberal Democracy*, p. 69.
30 Hunt, *Political Ideas of Marx and Engels* vol. 1, pp. 176–91. J. Hoffman, 'Karl Marx and Friedrich Engels: *The Communist Manifesto*', in M. Forsyth, M. Keens-Soper and J. Hoffman (eds), *The Political Classics: Hamilton to Mill* (Oxford University Press, Oxford, 1993), pp. 168–203, esp. .p. 199.
31 N. Harding, *Lenin's Political Thought*, vol. 2 (Macmillan, Basingstoke, 1981), p. 86. For a rebuttal, Hoffman, *Gramscian Challenge*, pp. 170–3.
32 Hoffman, 'The state: the "withering away" thesis', p. 91.
33 S. Avineri, *The Social and Political Thought of Karl Marx* (Cambridge

University Press, Cambridge, 1970), p. 210; Hunt, *Political Ideas of Marx and Engels*, vol. 2, p. 144.
34 A. Polan, *Lenin and the End of Politics* (Methuen, London, 1984), p. 70. Miller raises similar objections to anarchist criticisms of the rule of law, *Anarchism*, p. 176.
35 R. Luxemburg, *Selected Political Writings* (Jonathan Cape, London, 1972), p. 250.
36 For an argument that Lenin had earlier taken a more positive view of democratic rights under capitalism, see F. Claudin, *Eurocommunism and Socialism* (New Left, London, 1977), p. 77.
37 V. Lenin, *Collected Works*, vol. 25 (Progress, Moscow, 1965), p. 424. Polan, *Lenin and the End of Politics*, p. 57.
38 Tarschys, *Beyond the State*, p. 137; p. 144. Hoffman, 'The state: the "withering away" thesis', pp. 94–5.
39 Polan, *Lenin and the End of Politics*, p. 57.
40 Hoffman, 'The state: the "withering away" thesis', p. 95.
41 Ibid., p. 96.
42 Tarschys, *Beyond the State*, pp. 193–220; Hoffman, 'The state: the "withering away" thesis', p. 98.
43 Hoffman, 'The state: the "withering away" thesis', p. 99.
44 R. Sakwa, 'The new conception of democracy under perestroika', in D. McLellan and S. Sayers (eds), *Socialism and Democracy* (Macmillan, Basingstoke, 1991), pp. 136–63, esp. p. 149.
45 N. Geras, 'Democracy and the ends of Marxism', in G. Parry and M. Moran (eds), *Democracy and Democratization* (Routledge, London, 1994), pp. 69–87, esp. pp. 75–6.
46 Ibid., p. 79.
47 Ibid., p. 80.
48 McLellan, *Selected Writings*, p. 222; Geras, 'Democracy and the ends of Marxism', pp. 80–1.
49 Cited by S. Lukes, *Marxism and Morality* (Oxford University, 1987), p. 119.
50 Lukes, *Marxism and Morality*, pp. 5–7; Hunt, *Political Ideas of Marx and Engels*, vol. 2, p. 187.
51 Geras, 'Democracy and the Ends of Marxism', p. 83.
52 See Engels's 'Letters on historical materialism', in R. Tucker (ed.), *The Marx–Engels Reader*, 2nd edn (Norton, London, 1978), pp. 760–8.
53 V. Lenin, *The Three Sources and Three Components of Marxism* (Progress, Moscow, 1969), p. 5.
54 Cited by Lukes, *Marxism and Morality*, p. 122.

Chapter 10 Feminism

1 C. MacKinnon, *Towards a Feminist Theory of the State* (Harvard University Press, Cambridge, Mass., 1989), p. 157; p. 170.

2 Allen, 'Does feminism need a theory of "the state?" ' in S. Watson (ed.), *Playing the State* (Verso, London, 1990), pp. 21–37, esp. p. 27; p. 21.

3 Z. Eisenstein, *The Radical Future of Liberal Feminism* (Longman, London, 1981), p. 4.

4 D. Coole, *Women in Political Theory* (Harvester-Wheatsheaf, Hemel Hempstead, 1988), pp. 44–5.

5 S. Okin, 'Philosopher queens and private wives: Plato on women and the family', in M. Shanley and C. Pateman (eds), *Feminist Interpretations of Political Theory*, (Polity, Cambridge, 1991), pp. 11–31, esp. pp. 20–1; pp. 24–7; Coole, *Women in Political Theory*, pp. 32–4; pp. 58–70.

6 See Coole, *Women in Political Theory*, pp. 76–7; C. Pateman, ' "God hath ordained Man a helper": Hobbes, patriarchy and conjugal right', in Shanley and Pateman (eds), *Feminist Interpretations of Political Theory*, pp. 53–73, esp. p. 60.

7 C. Pateman, 'Hobbes, patriarchy and conjugal right', p. 60. See also C. Pateman, *The Sexual Contract* (Polity, Cambridge, 1988), p. 44. Pateman argues that (as far as Hobbes is concerned) in the logical beginning, all political right is maternal right, while in the historical beginning, masculine right holds sway. See her 'Hobbes, patriarchy and conjugal right', p. 66. But this conflict between logic and history makes no sense in terms of Hobbes's methodology, and it is a further reason why his analysis of sexual relations explodes the conceptual foundations of his own argument. Hence my support for Coole, *Women in Political Theory*, p. 83, who argues (in opposition to Pateman) that Hobbes's view of women rests upon naturalistic assumptions. See also D. Coole, 'Patriarchy and contract: reading Pateman', *Politics*, 10 (1990), pp. 25–9 and Pateman's reply, pp. 30–2.

8 Coole, *Women in Political Theory*, pp. 107–10; M. Butler, 'Early liberal roots of feminism: John Locke and the attack on patriarchy', in Shanley and Pateman (eds), *Feminist Interpretations of Political Theory*, pp. 74–94, esp. p. 91. Butler also notes Locke's tentative support for divorce and his view that women can develop their capacity to reason through education. See Coole, *Women in Political Theory*, p. 99.

9 Eisenstein, *Radical Future of Liberal Feminism*, p. 65; p. 68; Coole, *Women in Political Theory*, p. 117.

10 Coole, *Women in Political Theory*, pp. 120–3. This account largely derives from Coole, *Women in Political Theory*, pp. 124–30; M. Gatens, ' "The oppressed state of my sex": Wollstonecraft on reason, feeling and equality', in Shanley and Pateman (eds), *Feminist Interpretations and Political Theory*, pp. 112–28, esp., pp. 117–24; V. Bryson, *Feminist Political Theory* (Macmillan, Basingstoke, 1992), pp. 22–7.

11 Bryson, *Feminist Political Theory*, p. 27.

12 Coole, *Women in Political Theory*, p. 144. Bryson, *Feminist Political Theory*, pp. 55–63.

13 Bryson, *Feminist Political Theory*, p. 60; p. 64. Coole, *Women in Political Theory*, pp. 144–6; M. Shanley, 'Marital slavery and friendship: John Stuart

Mill's *The Subjection of Women*, in Shanley and Pateman (eds), *Feminist Interpretations and Political Theory*, pp. 164–80, esp. p. 168; p. 175.

14 K. Sacks, 'Engels revisited: women, the organization of production and private property', in M. Rosaldo and L. Lamphere (eds), *Women, Culture and Society*, (Stanford University Press, Stanford, Cal., 1974), pp. 207–22, esp. p. 207; Coole, *Women in Political Theory*, p. 192.

15 Bryson, *Feminist Political Theory*, pp. 68–72; Sacks, 'Engels revisited', pp. 207–11. Coole, *Women in Political Theory*, p. 198.

16 Coole, *Women in Political Theory*, p. 200; Bryson, *Feminist Political Theory*, pp. 94–5.

17 McLellan, *Selected Writings*, pp. 166–7; C. Di Stefano, 'Masculine Marx', in Shanley and Pateman (eds), *Feminist Interpretations and Political Theory*, pp. 146–63, esp. p. 153.

18 I. Balbus, *Marxism and Domination* (Princeton University Press, Princeton, 1982), pp. 268–72; Di Stefano, 'Masculine Marx', p. 154.

19 Di Stefano, 'Masculine Marx', p. 155 where she quotes also O'Brien's extremely interesting comparison between the mother and the architect.

20 Engels eloquently notes the way in which production can unintentionally damage the environment, commenting that 'we by no means rule over nature like a conqueror over a foreign people'. See F. Engels, *The Dialectics of Nature* (Progress, Moscow, 1964), p. 183.

21 Di Stefano, 'Masculine Marx', p. 152; p. 157. Di Stefano cites Chodorow's argument that the division of labour in child-rearing results in people being treated as things. This is of course is precisely Marx's own critique of the fetishism of commodity production. See also S. Benhabib and D. Cornell, 'Introduction', in S. Benhabib and D. Cornell (eds), *Feminism as Critique* (Polity, Cambridge, 1987), pp. 1–15, esp. p. 2.

22 Cited H. Moore, *Feminism and Anthropology* (Polity, Cambridge, 1988), p. 46.

23 J. Bamberger, 'The myth of matriarchy: why men rule in primitive society', in Rosaldo and Lamphere (eds), *Women, Culture and Society*, pp. 262–80, esp. p. 280; G. Lerner, *The Creation of Patriarchy* (Oxford University Press, New York, 1986), p. 31.

24 Lerner, *Creation of Patriarchy*, pp. 41–2.

25 R. Connell, *Gender and Power* (Polity, Cambridge, 1987), pp. 82–3; pp. 139–40.

26 Ibid., p. 80; Lerner, *Creation of Patriarchy*, p. 42.

27 Balbus, *Marxism and Domination*, p. 341.

28 Lerner, *Creation of Patriarchy*, pp. 44–5; p. 29. For a critique of Chodorow, see N. Fraser and L. Nicholson, 'Social criticism without philosophy', in L. Nicholson (ed.), *Feminism/Postmodernism* (Routledge, London, 1990), pp. 19–38, esp. p. 29–31.

29 Balbus, *Marxism and Domination*, p. 331.

30 Lerner, *Creation of Patriarchy*, p. 89; p. 76; p. 101; p. 106; p. 212.

31 Ibid., p. 75. Also p. 88; p. 47; p. 212; p. 99.

32 In her comparative study of the position of women among four tribes at

different stages of development, Sacks argues that the Mbuti people of Zaire with their subsistence economy based on communal net hunting and the gathering of vegetable food are the most egalitarian of the societies she looks at. Among the other tribes however– the Lovedu, Pondo and Ganda – the greater the development of production for exchange and involvement in war and raiding, the more women are excluded from government and control over property. Sacks, 'Engels revisited', pp. 213–19. See also Lerner, *Creation of Patriarchy*, p. 47; Bamberger, 'The myth of matriarchy', p. 266.

33 Connell, *Gender and Power*, pp. 12–14; pp. 126–8.
34 Lerner, *Creation of Patriarchy*, pp. 79–80.
35 MacKinnon, *Towards a Feminist Theory of the State*, pp. 139–40; pp.174–6.
36 Ibid., p. 141; C. Pateman, *The Disorder of Women* (Polity, Cambridge, 1989), p. 82.
37 MacKinnon, *Towards a Feminist Theory of the State*, pp. 161–2.
38 Lerner, *Creation of Patriarchy*, p. 217.
39 Ibid., p. 47; p. 42.
40 Ibid., p. 217.
41 MacKinnon, *Towards a Feminist Theory of the State*, pp. 177–8. Pateman, *Disorder of Women*, p. 12.
42 Allen, 'Does feminism need a theory of "the state"?', p. 22.
43 Eisenstein, *Radical Future of Liberal Feminism*, pp. 22–3.
44 Pateman, *Disorder of Women*, p. 34; Crick, *In Defence of Politics*, p. 18.
45 D. Dahlerup, 'Confusing concepts – confusing reality: a theoretical discussion of the patriarchal state', in A. Showstack Sassoon (ed.), *Women and the State* (Hutchinson, London, 1987), pp. 93–127, esp. p. 101.
46 MacKinnon, *Towards a Feminist Theory of the State*, pp. 120–1.
47 Pateman, *Disorder of Women*, p. 133.
48 MacKinnon, *Towards a Feminist Theory of the State*, p. 169.
49 Allen, 'Does feminism need a theory of "the state"?', p. 27.
50 MacKinnon, *Towards a Feminist Theory of the State*, p. 161.
51 Pateman, *Disorder of Women*, p. 136.
52 Ibid.

Chapter 11 Postmodernism

1 K. Marx, *Capital*, vol. 1 (Lawrence & Wishart, London, 1970), p. 20.
2 Fraser and Nicholson, 'Social criticism without philosophy', p. 19. The editors of an. influential anthology of postmodernist writings argue that the dialogue with postmodernism has begun to enrich and reinvigorate many elements of social theory and cultural practice. See R. Boyne and A. Rattansi, 'The theory and politics of postmodernism: by way of an introduction', in R. Boyne and A. Rattansi (eds), *Postmodernism and Society* (Macmillan, Basingstoke, 1990), pp. 1–45, esp. p. 30.

3 Foucault, 'On governmentality', p. 20. See also M. Philp, 'Foucault', in *Blackwell Encyclopedia of Political Thought*, pp. 158–60.

4 C. Jencks, 'The post-modern agenda', in C. Jencks (ed.), *The Post-Modern Reader* (St Martins, London and New York, 1992), pp. 10–39, esp. p. 34.

5 This draws upon Coole's 'feminist' list in *Women in Political Theory*, p. 1. For a postmodernist account of dualism which is particularly influenced by Derrida, see D. Gregory, 'Foreword', in J. Der Derian and M. Schapiro (eds), *International/Intertextual Relation* (Lexington, Mass., 1989), pp. xiii–xxi.

6 Gregory, 'Foreword', p. xvi.

7 R. Ashley, 'Living on border lines: man, poststructuralism and war', in Der Derian and Schapiro (eds), *International/Intertextual Relation*, pp. 259–321, esp. p. 263. See also Fraser and Nicholson, 'Social criticism without philosophy', p. 22.

8 Ashley, 'Living on border lines', p. 268.

9 The phrase (which we have cited before) is Parekh's in his 'When will the state wither away?', p. 290.

10 Ashley 'Living on border lines', p. 268; p. 286; p. 295; p. 300. Elsewhere Ashley refers to the state as 'immunised from reasoned criticism because it must be taken as the principle of reasoning discourse in itself '. R. Ashley, 'Untying the sovereign state: a double reading of the anarchy problematique', *Millenium*, 17 (1988), pp. 227–62, esp. p. 231.

11 I. Young, 'The ideal of community and the politics of difference', in Nicholson (ed.), *Feminism/Postmodernism*, pp. 300–23, esp. p. 302.

12 Fraser and Nicholson, 'Social criticism without philosophy', pp. 22–3.

13 Cited by Poggi, *Development of the Modern State*, p. 100. Here it is hard to resist quoting Hegel's superlatively logocentric comment that 'Truth is the Unity of the universally and subjective Will; and the Universal is to be found in the State, in its laws, its universal and rational arrangements'. G. Hegel, *The Philosophy of History* (Dover, New York, 1956), p. 39.

14 Ashley, 'Living on border lines', p. 319.

15 W. Connolly, 'Identity and difference in global politics', in Der Derian and Schapiro (eds), *International/Intertextual Relation*, pp. 325–42, esp. p. 339.

16 Ashley, 'Living on border lines', p. 283.

17 Ibid., p. 269.

18 Fraser and Nicholson, 'Social criticism without philosophy', p. 20. Just how contentious this argument is can be seen from other articles in the Fraser and Nicholson volume. Note also S. Lovibond, 'Feminism and postmodernism', *New Left Review*, 178 (1989), pp. 5–28, as well as M. Zalewski, 'The debauching of feminist theory: the penetration of the postmodern', *Politics*, 11 (1991), pp. 30–6.

19 Fraser and Nicholson, 'Social criticism without philosophy', p. 34.

20 Ashley, 'Living on border lines', p. 268; p. 303.

21 Cited by Fraser and Nicholson, 'Social criticism without philosophy', p. 28.

22 Ashley, 'Living on border lines', p. 279.

23 Ibid., p. 320; pp. 280-2.
24 M. Ryan, 'Postmodern politics', *Theory, Culture and Society*, 5 (1988), pp. 559-76, esp. 567; S. Crook, 'The end of radical social theory: radicalism, modernism and postmodernism', in Boyne and Rattansi (eds), *Postmodernism and Society*, pp. 46-75, esp. pp. 57-8; Fraser and Nicholson, 'Social criticism without philosophy', p. 25. For a similar criticism of Lyotard, see S. White, *Political Theory and Postmodernism* (Cambridge University Press, Cambridge, 1991), p. 136.
25 Ashley, 'Living on border lines', p. 278.
26 S. Harding, 'Feminism, science and the anti-Enlightenment critiques', in Fraser and Nicholson (eds), *Feminism/Postmodernism*, pp. 83-106, esp. p. 100.
27 A. Yeatman, 'A feminist theory of social differentiation', in Fraser and Nicholson (eds), *Feminism/Postmodernism*, pp. 281-99, esp. pp. 292-3.
28 Connolly, 'Identity and difference in global politics', p. 336. See F. Dallmayr's review of Connolly's *Political Theory and Modernity* in *Political Theory*, 18 (1990), pp. 162-9, esp. p. 168. For a powerful critique of Nietzsche, see also Lovibond, 'Feminism and postmodernism', pp. 15-19.
29 Ryan, 'Postmodern politics', pp. 563-4; White, *Political Theory and Postmodernism*, p. 133.
30 S. Benhabib, 'Epistemologies of postmodernism: a rejoinder to Jean-François Lyotard', in Fraser and Nicholson (eds), *Feminism/Postmodernism*, pp. 107-30, esp. p. 124; White, *Political Theory and Postmodernism*, p. 93. For reference to Rorty's 'astonishing fatalism' and 'self-defeating solipcism', see N. Rennger, 'No time like the present: postmodernism and political theory', *Political Studies*, 40 (1992), pp. 561-70, esp. p. 569.
31 Ashley, 'Living on border lines', p. 310; p. 299; White, *Political Theory and Postmodernism*, p. 32.
32 One writer, while noting the 'fascinating interweaving and intersecting of poststructuralism and postmodernism', has argued that post-structuralism is a French phenomenon which provides less a theory of postmodernity than a theory of modernism at its stage of exhaustion. A. Huyssen, 'Mapping the postmodern', in Fraser and Nicholson (eds), *Feminism/Postmodernism*, pp. 234-77, esp. pp. 257-8. I will assume however for purposes of the argument here as (as Ashley seems to) that the two 'isms' can be broadly assimilated. Ryan also comments that 'postmodernism is to art what poststructuralism is to philosophy and social theory' ('Postmodern politics', p. 560), while Bryson incorporates 'a plethora of overlapping schools of thought under the general heading of postmodernism' (Bryson, *Feminist Political Theory*, p. 225).
33 Ashley, 'Living on border lines', p. 284.
34 Ibid., p. 292; see also Connolly, 'Identity and difference in global politics', p. 338.
35 Ashley, 'Living on border lines', p. 292; p. 269.
36 Ibid., p. 260.
37 Ibid., p. 283; p. 308. This is the major argument of his 'Untying the sovereign state', p. 252.

38 Young, 'The ideal of community and the politics of difference', p. 317; Fraser and Nicholson, 'Social criticism without philosophy', p. 23; White, *Political Theory and Postmodernism*, p. 27; p. 61; p. 99; p. 137.

Chapter 12 International Society

1 R. Berki, 'On Marxian thought and the problem of international relations', *World Politics*, 24 (1971), pp. 80–105, esp. p. 98. See also J. Hoffman, *Hedley Bull's Conception of International Society and the Future of the State* (Department of Politics, University of Leicester, 1992), pp. 1–2.

2 Hoffman, *State, Power and Democracy*, p. 56.

3 S. Hoffman, 'International society', in J. Miller and R. Vincent (eds), *Order and Violence: Hedley Bull and International Relations* (Clarendon, Oxford, 1990), pp. 20–37, esp. p. 22; I. Harris, 'Order and justice in "the anarchical society"', *International Affairs*, 69 (1993), pp. 725–41, esp. p. 726.

4 Bull, *The Anarchical Society* (Macmillan, Basingstake, 1947), pp. 9–10; p. 13; p. 27.

5 H. Bull, 'The emergence of a universal international society', in H. Bull and A. Watson (eds), *The Expansion of International Society* (Clarendon, Oxford, 1984), pp. 117–26, esp. p. 126. See also M. Wight, *Power Politics* (Penguin, Harmondsworth, 1970), pp. 96–7.

6 H. Bull, 'Martin Wight and the theory of international relations', *British Journal of International Relations*, 2 (1975), pp. 101–16, esp. p. 112. R. Jones, 'The English school of international relations: a case for closure', *Review of International Studies*, 7 (1981), pp. 1–13, esp. p. 6.

7 Bull, *The Anarchical Society*, p. 87; p. 90, p. 92.

8 Ibid., p. 22; p. 275.

9 Ibid., p. 318; p. 275.

10 Ibid., p. 8; p. 24.

11 Harris, 'Order and justice', pp. 728–32. See also H. Bull, *Justice in International Relations* (University of Waterloo, Ontario, 1983), p. 18, and N. Wheeler, 'Hedley Bull's pessimism and the future of international society', Paper for the European Consortium for Political Research, Limerick, March–April 1992, p. 11.

12 This follows the argument of Harris, 'Order and justice', pp. 736–9. But see also M. Forsyth, 'Thomas Hobbes and the external relations of states', *British Journal of International Studies*, 5 (1979), pp. 196–209, esp. p. 209.

13 Bull, *The Anarchical Society*, pp. 8–9. See also M. Wight, *Systems of States* (Leicester University Press, Leicester, 1977), p. 135.

14 Bull, *The Anarchical Society*, p. 37.

15 R. Keohane, 'International relations theory: contributions of a feminist standpoint', in R. Grant and K. Newland (eds), *Gender and International Relations* (Open University Press, Milton Keynes, 1991), pp. 41–50, esp. p. 43; R. Grant, 'The sources of bias in international relations theory' in

Grant and Newland (eds), *Gender and International Relations*, pp. 8–26, esp. p. 18.

16 Bull, *The Anarchical Society*, p. 37. For contemporary restatements of the theory of sovereignty, see J. Camilleri and J. Falk, *The End of Sovereignty?* (Edward Elgar, Aldershot, 1992), pp. 36–7. See also Hinsley's comments cited by D. Held, *Political Theory and the Modern State* (Polity, Cambridge, 1989), p. 237; H. Hart, *The Concept of Law* (Clarendon, Oxford, 1961), p. 217. For a recent discussion which is highly critical of sovereignty, see M. Hoffman, 'Agency, identity and intervention', in I. Forbes and M. Hoffman (eds), *Political Theory, International Relations and the Ethics of Intervention* (Macmillan, Basingstoke, 1993), pp. 194–211, esp. pp. 200–3.

17 Bull, *The Anarchical Society*, p. 8. For an elaboration of this distinction, see H. Bull, 'The state's positive role in world affairs', *Daedalus*, 108 (1981), pp. 111–23, esp. p. 118. Here Bull argues that a state's claim to external sovereignty is not a right to be asserted against the international order, but is conferred by it as 'the foundation of the whole edifice'.

18 G. Almond, 'Review article: the international–national connection', *British Journal of Political Science*, 19 (1989), pp. 237–59, esp. p. 240; p. 257.

19 Bull, *The Anarchical Society*, p. 152. Hence a recent work refers rightly to the 'absolutist tendencies inherent in the concept'. See Camilleri and Falk, *The End of Sovereignty?*, p. 31.

20 Camilleri and Falk, *The End of Sovereignty?*, p. 37; Bull, *The Anarchical Society*, p. 57; p. 77. Watkins warns that, if we seek to eliminate the fiction of absolute sovereignty, then we undermine the state itself. Watkins, *The State as a Concept of Political Science*, p. 59.

21 Bull, *The Anarchical Society*, p. 5; p. 55. Not only is it hard to see how the use of violence can secure individuals against 'bodily harm', but keeping promises and the stability of possessions are not really compatible with statist concentrations of power. As one champion of the state ruefully notes, the state 'makes laws for those who are unequal in status to itself'. M. Forsyth, *Unions of States* (Leicester University Press, Leicester, 1981), p. 14.

22 Bull, *The Anarchical Society*, p. 62; p. 132.

23 Ibid., pp. 47–50. See also H. Bull, 'Hobbes and the international anarchy', *Social Research*, 48 (1981), pp. 717–38, esp. p. 733.

24 Bull, *The Anarchical Society*, pp. 64–5; p. 267.

25 Ibid., p. 267; Bull, 'The state's positive role in world affairs', p. 112; p. 117; p. 122.

26 Bull, *The Anarchical Society*, pp. 254–5; also Bull, 'The state's positive role in world affairs', p. 112.

27 Bull, *The Anarchical Society*, p. 274.

28 Ibid., pp. 146–7; pp. 264–6; Held, *Political Theory and the Modern State*, p. 234.

29 Bull, *The Anarchical Society*, p. 275; Held, *Political Theory and the Modern State*, p. 230; Camilleri and Falk, *The End of Sovereignty?*, p. 7. A. James,

'Theorizing about sovereignty', in W. Olson (ed.), *The Theory and Practice of International Relations*, 8th edn (Prentice-Hall, Englewood Cliffs, New Jersey, 1991), pp. 120–3, esp. p. 121.

30 Bull, *The Anarchical Society*, p. 255; This point is also vigorously pressed in Bull, 'The state's positive role in world affairs', p. 115.

31 Bull, *The Anarchical Society*, p. 228.

32 Ibid., p. 214.

33 Ibid., p. 292. In 1981 Bull also argues that the USSR and the other socialist countries see in the state a 'bulwark of security against imperialist aggressor'. But the collapse of the 'existing socialist world' surely casts doubt on Bull's argument that this constituted yet another source of the state's permanence and centrality in international society. Bull, 'The state's positive role in world affairs', p. 120.

34 N. Rennger, 'A city which sustains all things? Communitarianism and the foundations of international society', Paper for the European Consortium for Political Research, Limerick, April 1992, pp. 19–20; Harris, 'Order and justice', p. 733; G. Berridge, *International Politics* (Wheatsheaf, Brighton, 1987), p. 144.

35 C. B. Macpherson, *The Political Theory of Possessive Individualism*, (Oxford University Press, Oxford, 1962), p. 265; see also p. 75.

36 A compromise he suggests is a condition in which two people both agree to do what each believes to be wrong. Harris, 'Order and justice', p. 733.

37 Bull, *The Anarchical Society*, p. 50.

38 Ibid., p. 190.

39 Ibid., p. 177; Camilleri and Falk, *The End of Sovereignty?*, p. 171.

40 Bull, *The Anarchical Society*, p. 300.

41 This is most memorably put argued in Rousseau, *The Social Contract*, p. 68.

42 Bull, *The Anarchical Society*, p. 320; see also p. 87. Vincent stresses the importance of Bull's 'tantalizingly brief' passage at the beginning of *The Anarchical Society* in which he argues that world order is morally prior to the order of states. See R. Vincent, 'Order and international politics', in Miller and Vincent (eds), *Order and Violence*, pp. 38–64, esp. p. 43. For a sharp critique of the passage, see M. Forsyth, 'The classical theory of international relations', *Political Studies*, 26 (1978), pp. 411–16, esp. p. 416.

Chapter 13 Democracy and the Movement Beyond the State

1 Hoffman, *State, Power and Democracy*, pp. 131–3.

2 R. Dahl, *Democracy and Its Critics* (Yale, University Press, New Haven, 1989), p. 312.

3 Weldon, *Vocabulary of Politics*, p. 86.

4 D. Smith, *Capitalist Democracy on Trial* (Routledge, New York and London, 1990), pp. 191–2. For a critical review of Smith, see J. Hoffman,

'Capitalist democracies and democratic states: oxymorons or coherent concepts?', *Political Studies*, 39 (1991), pp. 342–9, esp. p. 344.

5 Smith, *Capitalist Democracy on Trial*, p. 164; p. 162; C. B. Macpherson, *Democratic Theory* (Clarendon, Oxford, 1973), p. 146; Hayek, *The Constitution of Liberty* (Routledge & Kegan Paul, London, 1956), p. 106. For a recent critique of Hayek's views of democracy, see C. Pierson, 'Democracy, markets and capital: are there necessary limits to democracy?', in D. Held (ed.), *Prospects for Democracy* (Blackwell, Oxford, 1992) and also *Political Studies*, special issue, 40 (1992), pp. 83–98, esp. pp. 83–5.

6 Smith, *Capitalist Democracy on Trial*, p. 9.

7 For references and further argument, see J. Hoffman, 'Liberals versus socialists: who are the true democrats?', in D. McLellan and S. Sayers (eds), *Socialism and Democracy* (Macmillan, Basingstoke, 1991), pp. 32–45, esp. p. 33.

8 Hoffman, 'Who are the true democrats?', pp. 32–3; Hoffman, *State, Power and Democracy*, p. 136; Rousseau, *Social Contract*, pp. 112–14; p. 60.

9 Hoffman, *State, Power and Democracy*, pp. 154–5.

10 Plato, *The Republic* (Penguin, Harmondsworth, 1955), p. 366. Hoffman, *State, Power and Democracy*, pp. 144–8. For a classic analysis of the emancipatory logic of democracy, see A. de Tocqueville, *Democracy in America*, vol. 1 (Fontana, London and Glasgow, 1966), p. 8.

11 Cited by M. Levin, *The Spectre of Democracy* (Macmillan, Basingstoke, 1992), p. 208.

12 Crick, *In Defence of Politics*, pp. 58–9; Goodwin, *Using Political Ideas*, pp. 238–9.

13 Crick, *In Defence of Politics*, pp. 60–1; See also Aristotle, *The Politics* (Penguin, Harmondsworth, 1967), p. 117; Plato, *The Republic*, p. 228.

14 Cited by I. Meszaros, 'Political power and dissent in post-revolutionary societies', in Il Manifesto (ed.), *Power and Opposition in Post-revolutionary Societies* (Ink Links, London, 1979), pp. 105–29, esp. p. 116.

15 Dahl, *Democracy and Its Critics*, p. 37; p. 90 and p. 51.

16 Ibid., p. 171. Dahl, it seems to me, is moving towards what I have called a 'relational' view of the individual when he argues that 'a person's interests may be, and usually are, broader than merely one's *private* or *self-regarding* interests' (p. 73).

17 G. Hodgson, *The Democratic Economy* (Penguin, Harmondsworth, 1984), pp. 36–7.

18 Crick, *In Defence of Politics*, p. 61.

19 Polanyi is cited by Hodgson, *The Democratic Economy*, p. 84. De Jasay, *The State*, p. 210; p. 247; p. 259. See also Hodgson, *The Democratic Economy*, p. 35.

20 Hodgson, *The Democratic Economy*, p. 84.

21 Hoffman, *State, Power and Democracy*, p. 181.

22 S. Wolin, 'Democracy and the welfare state: the political and theoretical connections between Staatsräson and Wohlfahrtsstaaträson', *Political Theory*, 15 (1987), pp. 467–500, esp. pp. 468–75.

23 Wolin, 'Democracy and the welfare state', pp. 477–9.
24 Pateman, *The Disorder of Women*, p. 179; pp. 186–7.
25 Ibid., p. 200.
26 Dahlerup, 'A theoretical discussion of the patriarchal state', pp. 120–1.
27 Pateman, *The Disorder of Women*, pp. 202–3.
28 C. Offe, 'Democracy against the welfare state? Structural conditions for neoconservative political opportunities', *Political Theory*, 15 (1987), pp. 501–37, esp. pp. 524–7.
29 M. Walzer, 'The communitarian critique of liberalism', *Political Theory*, 18 (1990), pp. 6–23, esp. p. 17.
30 Dahl, *Democracy and Its Critics*, p. 327; N. Bobbio, *Democracy and Dictatorship* (Polity, Cambridge, 1989), p. 157.
31 D. Beetham, 'Liberal democracy and the limits of democratization', in D. Held (ed.), *Prospects for Democracy*, pp. 40–53, esp. p. 48.
32 Beetham, 'Liberal democracy and the limits of democratization', pp. 48–9.
33 A. Phillips, 'Must feminists give up on liberal democracy?', in Held (ed.), *Prospects for Democracy*, pp. 68–82, esp. p. 74; A. Phillips, *Engendering Democracy* (Polity, Cambridge, 1991), pp. 130–6.
34 I. Young, 'Polity and group difference: a critique of the ideal of universal citizenship', *Ethics*, 99 (1989), pp. 250–74, esp. pp. 255–6.
35 Young, 'Polity and group difference', pp. 263–4.
36 A. Phillips, 'Democracy and difference: some problems for feminist theory', *Political Quarterly*, 63 (1992), pp. 79–90, esp. p. 85. This also seems to be the problem with Burnheim's argument that the traditional mode of representation by geographical areas ought to be abandoned in favour of the representation of interests. See J. Burnheim, 'Democracy, nation states and the world system', in D. Held and C. Pollitt (eds), *New Forms of Democracy* (Sage, London, 1986), pp. 218–39, esp. p. 227.
37 Young, 'Polity and group difference', p. 260.
38 Young, 'The ideal of community and the politics of difference', p. 302.
39 A. Phillips, 'Universal pretensions in political thought', in Barrett and Phillips (eds), *Destabilizing Theory*, pp. 10–30, esp. p. 26.
40 K. Soper, 'Postmodernism and its discontents', *Feminist Review*, 39 (1991), pp. 97–108, esp. pp. 107–8.
41 Thus Waltzer comments saliently that the 'communitarian correction of liberalism' can either strengthen the old inequalities of traditional ways of life or can counteract the new inequalities of the liberal market and the bureaucratic state. Walzer, 'The communitarian critique of liberalism', p. 23.
42 See J. Burnheim, *Is Democracy Possible?* (Polity, Cambridge, 1985), p. 19. Wells is cited by M. Cornforth, *The Open Philosophy and the Open Society* (Lawrence & Wishart, London, 1977), p. 244.
43 Dahl, *Democracy and Its Critics*, p. 37. For a critique of Dahl, see Hoffman, 'Capitalist democracies and democratic states', pp. 346–8. J. Keane, *Democracy and Civil Society* (Verso, London, 1988), p. xiii; p. 27. D. Held, 'Democracy: from city-states to a cosmopolitan order?', in Held (ed.), *Prospects for Democracy*, pp. 10–39, esp. p. 19.

44 Dahl, *Democracy and Its Critics*, p. 46.
45 Pierson, 'Democracy, markets and capital', p. 96; Dahl, *Democracy and Its Critics*, p. 194.
46 Dahl, *Democracy and Its Critics*, p. 320. See also D. Held, 'Democracy, the nation-state and the global system', in D. Held (ed.), *Political Theory Today* (Polity, Cambridge, 1991), pp. 197–235.
47 Held, 'Democracy: from city-states to a cosmopolitan order?', pp. 21–2.
48 Ibid., pp. 30–1.
49 Ibid., p. 34.
50 Ibid., p. 36.
51 Dahl, *Democracy and Its Critics*, p. 348.
52 Held, 'Democracy: from city-states to a cosmopolitan order?' p. 37.
53 Ibid., p. 38.

Index